Movies Ate My Brain

ROBERT FONTAINE

PENUMBRA PRESS
www.penumbrapress.ca

 Copyright 2006 © Robert Fontaine
and Penumbra Press

Published by PENUMBRA PRESS
Copy-editing by Douglas Campbell
Design by Mag Carson
Cover design after a concept by David Fontaine

No part of this publication may be reproduced, stored in a retrieval system or transmitted, in any form or by any means, without the prior written consent of the publisher or a licence from The Canadian Copyright Licensing Agency (Access Copyright). For an Access Copyright licence, call toll free to 1-800-893-5777 or visit www.accesscopyright.ca

LIBRARY AND ARCHIVES CANADA CATALOGUING IN PUBLICATION
Fontaine, Robert, 1958-
  Movies ate my brain / Robert Fontaine.
ISBN 1-894131-94-0
1. Motion pictures--Reviews. I. Title.
PN1995.F59 2006   791.43'75   C2006-901207-5

Canadä

Penumbra Press gratefully acknowledges the financial support of the Government of Canada through the Book Publishing Industry Development Program (BPIDP) for our publishing activities. We also acknowledge the Government of Ontario through the Ontario Media Development Corporation's Ontario Book Initiative.

For Sylvie and David

Contents

Acknowledgements
Introduction

1	The Adventures of Rocky & Bullwinkle	21
2	Armageddon	29
3	The Beach	31
4	The Big Lebowski	36
5	The Bone Collector	41
6	Boogie Nights	45
7	Capote	52
8	Casino	58
9	Cellular	62
10	Chicken Run	68
11	Childstar	73
12	City of God	78
13	Confessions of a Dangerous Mind	83
14	The Day After Tomorrow	88
15	Dogtown and Z-Boys	94
16	Downfall	99
17	Eyes Wide Shut	104
18	Fahrenheit 9/11	110
19	Far from Heaven	116
20	The Fog	122
21	The Game	127
22	Godzilla	132
23	Grace of My Heart	137
24	The Hitchhiker's Guide to the Galaxy	143

25	House of Wax	149
26	I Am Sam	154
27	Jurassic Park III	159
28	Kinsey	162
29	The Lord of the Rings: The Return of the King	170
30	Lost in Space	175
31	Lost in Translation	180
32	Mission to Mars	186
33	Mulholland Drive	190
34	Open Range	197
35	Open Water	202
36	Pollock	207
37	Psycho	212
38	The Rock	217
39	Seducing Doctor Lewis	221
40	Shaun of the Dead	226
41	The Snow Walker	231
42	Star Trek IX: Insurrection	237
43	Star Wars: Episode III – Revenge of the Sith	242
44	The Sum of All Fears	249
45	Sweet and Lowdown	253
46	Swimming Pool	259
47	3,000 Miles to Graceland	265
48	Vampires	269
49	Vertical Limit	274
50	The X-Files	279

Appendix

Acknowledgements

I would like to thank the following people for helping in various ways to make this book a reality:

Robert McMillan at the University of Ottawa for his guidance and wisdom; Jennifer Fry for her intelligence and unwavering support through the years; Ken Rockburn for the many times he made me sound better than I was; Brent Bambury for his wit and sense of fun; Wendy Robbins for always lending a sympathetic ear; Barbara Brown for her cheerful encouragement; Dan Turner for his friendly, insightful critiques; Pierre Millette for going above and beyond the call on many occasions; George Regan for his valuable feedback and moral support; Bruno Riel, Karin Hinzer, Christine Hinzer, Charles Gordon, Randall Ware, Tom McSorley, Bruce White, Jay Stone, Noel Taylor, Luc Monast, Anne Michaud, and Brian Gorman for many stimulating conversations; Linda Russell, my producer at CBC Radio, for her intelligence and exceptional dedication to "getting it right"; John Flood at Penumbra Press for believing in the project; my editor Douglas Campbell for making the creation of this book an enjoyable and rewarding experience by his insight, patience, and erudition; my mother for passing on her love of movies and her determination; Ginette and Serge for always being there; my wife Sylvie and my son David for their love and unconditional support through all the ups and downs; and a very special thank you to all the loyal *All in a Day* listeners who have welcomed me into their homes, offices, and automobiles over the years.

— R.F.

Introduction

This book could have been called "The Movies Rearranged My Neurons." Movies have had a profound effect on my thinking ever since I was taken to see *Bambi* as a five-year-old child, and was scared out of my wits by the death of Bambi's mom. Up until that time, it had never occurred to me that children — even animal ones — could be orphaned. Yet there she was, up on the big screen in Technicolor, shot dead by hunters. It was more than I could take. My older sister, Ginette, had to remove me from the theatre as I screamed, "It's not possible! How can she die? She can't be dead! I want to go home!" I seem to recall now — I'm having a flashback, folks! — that Bambi's mom dies during a blizzard. No wonder I hate winter ...

When I have the (always enjoyable) opportunity of chatting with CBC Radio listeners or with film or journalism students, often the first question I am asked is "What's the deal with the Boston Red Sox?" Unfortunately, I have no "deal" with the Red Sox, although I wish I did. I also wish they had kept Bill Mueller and Dave Roberts and Pokey Reese and Orlando Cabrera and Derek Lowe, but there it is. Some teams just can't deal with success. After I have explained that my family began spending summer vacations in New England in 1991, around the time my son David was born, and that we just naturally joined Red Sox Nation, the next question is often "How did you become a movie critic?"

That's a tougher one.

Human beings are natural critics. I'm sure that fifteen thousand years ago, when our ancestors were drawing bison and deer in the caves of Lascaux, some smart aleck bozo was heard to comment, "Those aren't nearly as good as the ones Grok did last week!"

Criticism was born.

I think that to some degree all moviegoers are critics. People generally know what they like and don't like, and most of us enjoy voicing our opinions to our friends about whether or not such and such a movie was "stupid," or "really exciting," or "crushed under the weight of its vacuous, cliché-heavy script."

The first movie critic I was ever in contact with — my critical mentor, if you will — was my father. Dad enjoyed B-movies — more specifically, westerns and science-fiction films — and he would occasionally take me to a Saturday matinee in Ottawa, just across the river from our home in Hull. By this time I had recovered sufficiently from the *Bambi* incident, and I enjoyed going to the movies immensely. I have particularly fond memories of seeing *Dracula, Prince Of Darkness*, starring the charismatic Christopher Lee, when I was about eight years old. One particularly gruesome scene remains with me to this day: after placing Dracula's ashes in the bottom of an open crypt, one of Dracula's servants knocks a man unconscious, suspends the unlucky visitor upside down over it, and then slashes his throat. The blood gushes noisily and messily onto the ashes, and Dracula's body is magically re-formed from the mysterious wisps of smoke that arise when the fresh blood mixes with the ashes. Both Dad and I were mesmerized by this scene, and I remember my father looking at me and commenting, "Wowie! They're not fooling around! This is amazing!"

I understood immediately that "they" were the producers of the movie, and that "they" had somehow pulled off a fantastic feat, giving us a scene both magical and disgusting — a scene that somehow truly captured the essence and horror of Dracula. I think that the reason his comment was a revelation to me was that it was the first time I had thought (I mean *really* thought) about the fact that what I was watching up on the big screen was the result of careful, intelligent craftsmanship — an image created by someone in order to generate a specific response from the audience.

My world (and my neurons) would never be the same again.

From that point on I had to take into account the fact that movies are carefully manipulated works, that consequently there are different ways of presenting a story, and that some ways are more effective than others.

I had become a movie critic, sort of.

I don't mean to imply that this revelation came to me immediately, and all at once, when my father commented on the scene. It was, of course, a gradual process — I am not now, nor have I ever been, a genius. But over the course of the next year or so I began to look at movies in a slightly different way. I began for the first time to notice that similar subjects could be presented in different ways, and I began to make comparisons. I began to ask myself such questions as "Why are Hammer horror movies unlike Universal horror movies?" "Why is Bela Lugosi's Dracula unlike Christopher Lee's Dracula?" "Why is a movie scarier in colour than it is in black and white? Or is it?" My reflections were still pretty primitive, and my understanding of techniques such as editing was non-existent, but I knew that different studios ("movie companies," I called them) and directors and actors had different approaches to storytelling.

The next profoundly significant event of my young movie-going life happened in 1968, when I was ten, and Dad took me to see the new science-fiction movie that everyone was talking about, *2001: A Space Odyssey*.

That was the one that truly re-arranged my neurons.

I spent just about the entire two and a half hours — I remember that there was an intermission — in a state of wonderment and dizziness that bordered at times on vertigo. I was truly, totally amazed at what I was seeing.

The film, which was in Super Panavision, was a marvel of precision. Everything seemed so precise, so clinical, so perfectly scientific, so *plausible*. It was the realism of it all that most impressed me. I thought it particularly fascinating that Kubrick chose not to have any sound in the outer space scenes; there is, of course, no sound in space, because there is no air to propagate the sound waves. Also, being a ten-year-old, I thought the zero-gravity toilet was a nice touch. And at a time when we were all excited about the upcoming moon landing — Apollo 11 was still several months away — this movie made the idea of working and living in space seem … inevitable. The pace of the film — leisurely, almost slow — made the unfolding events seem somehow more realistic, even when there wasn't much going on in the plot. It seemed as if this living, breathing future world would some day inevitably exist.

The talking computer, the HAL 9000, was also a source of great amusement and wonder. Personal computers were at that time still years away — in fact the whole concept of computers was quite new — and here was one that displayed human emotions and attitudes. For weeks afterwards I thought about HAL, and new ideas surfaced in my brain: "Would we one day interact with computers as part of our daily lives? Would they think like people? Would they have personalities? Would they perhaps be a danger to us?" Kubrick's cautionary tale about giving our machines too much decision-making power and about the dehumanizing effects of technology left an indelible impression on me.

2001: A Space Odyssey also contains one of my favourite cinematic moments. It occurs near the beginning, when one of our ape-like ancestors discovers that bones can be used as weapons, a discovery that will lead to the development of rudimentary tools, and, eventually, technology. Holding a large bone in his hand, the ape strikes repeatedly at the pile of bones from which he has picked his weapon, and then sends the bone flying up into the air — in slow motion. As it rises and then slowly descends, we cut to ... a white, gleaming, cylindrical spaceship falling gracefully into Earth orbit. This is a magnificent moment of pure cinema. By connecting the shots in this way, Kubrick spans four million years of human evolution in a few seconds. I have watched the scene many times since, and it never fails to take my breath away.

And then, of course, there was the way-out, psychedelic, mind-blowing ending.

Wow, man, the *colours*!

But what did it mean? Why did we see a fetus — which seemed to my eyes to be the size of a planet — floating out in space after the hero had seen himself as a dying old man? I was in a daze. By the end of my first viewing of *2001*, my way of seeing the world — my understanding of what was meant by up and down, huge and small, beginning and ending — had been turned inside out.

When we walked out into the late-afternoon sun, Dad looked at me and asked me what I thought the ending meant. Fearful of saying something silly, I frowned. Looking as thoughtful and as serious as possible, I weighed the question for a minute and answered, "I don't know, I need to see it again. I think it's about starting over. Like it never ends, but we learn something — like reincarnation." He seemed not too displeased with my answer, and I quickly changed the subject, asking him, "Will I ever see 2001?" He assured me that I would. My mind was reeling. How old would I be? I made some mental calculations. "Forty-three," I thought. I would be forty-three, older than Dad was right now. It seemed unreal, impossible.

As I write this, I am forty-seven, and 2001 has come and gone. And so has Dad.

Tempus fugit.

* * *

Artie Shaw (1910–2004), a particularly wise and erudite gentleman as well as a great musician, once said, "Time is the most precious commodity. Time is all you've got."

How right he was.

If you were on your deathbed, preparing to breathe your last, what would you give to recoup the hours you wasted watching bad movies? Would you sell your soul in order to get back the three and a half hours you lost watching Michael Bay's *Pearl Harbor*?

I'll bet you would.

Since 1993, when I began reviewing movies for *All in a Day*, CBC Ottawa's daily drive-home program, I have seen approximately *nine hundred* movies. I actually don't know exactly how many I've seen, and to tell you the truth I don't really care to know, because the whole idea of watching that many movies gives me the creeps. But the point is that they weren't all masterpieces worthy of my (or anyone else's) time. In fact, let's be honest, a lot of them stank.

It has been my privilege over the years to warn CBC listeners away from these stinkers. Of course, many of you disregarded my advice and went to see them anyway, but I tried — Lord knows I tried! — to warn you. And I also tried to entertain you while I was warning you. And many of you *were* entertained, while others simply turned off your radios in frustration and annoyance at my digressions and non sequiturs.

C'est la vie.

The other side of the coin is that I also try to point listeners toward films that I feel are worthy of their time — sometimes rather obscure films that would perhaps be overlooked if I didn't make some positive noises about them. This is also a pleasure and a privilege. But the fact of the matter is that most of the movies I review are neither very good nor very bad; they are mediocre, just so-so.

Those movies are not the subject of this book.

The movies reviewed, discussed, deconstructed, and ruminated upon in this book represent some of the very best I have seen since 1993 — and some of the very worst. They are the ones that stand out in my mind, the ones that most inspired me. They were all originally reviewed on radio, and I have used my original radio scripts as the jumping-off point for the texts included in *Movies Ate My Brain*. But writing for radio and writing for a reader are very different processes. The literary format has forced me to transform, and to considerably expand, my original comments, and it has allowed me to dig deeper into my impressions of the films. I had not seen some of these films in several years, and in many cases I felt that it was necessary to watch them again. To my surprise, the thoughts and impressions that were triggered by viewing them again were sometimes quite different from my original observations — not radically different in the sense that I suddenly had an epiphany and realized that *Armageddon* was actually a masterpiece (it is not; it still stinks), but different in the sense that ideas that had not occurred to me at the time of the original reviews began to manifest themselves.

That is one of the things I love about movies: the truly memorable ones, good or bad, are a bit like the people who watch them — they seem to change in subtle ways over time. When I watch a favourite movie today — *2001: A Space Odyssey*, for example — it is a different experience than it was when I first saw it in 1968. It has changed because I have changed. Yet it remains the same. If we think of movies as both window and mirror — window into another world, real or imagined, and mirror of society and also of self — then I think we begin to understand with what subtlety and complexity they really are able to re-arrange our neurons, both collectively and individually.

Far out, eh?

* * *

For those who have wondered over the years whether there is actually any method to my madness, let me say that when I evaluate a film, I ask myself three fundamental questions:

(1) What story is the film trying to tell? Is it an interesting story? Is it believable or unbelievable? Is it a fable, a parable, a fantasy? Is it well told — that is, is the script literate, intelligent, effective? Are the characters in the story engaging? Does the story have socio-political resonance? Is it a morality tale, a cautionary tale, a "true" story, or pure escapism? Is it perhaps propaganda?

(2) What cinematic means has the director used to tell the story, and how successfully have they been used? How do all of the techniques of film-making — cinematography, editing, lighting, camera angles, set design, musical score, casting, special effects — conspire to tell the story? Does the director appear to have a solid grasp of these techniques?

(3) How does the film connect with the social environment that spawned it?

This third point is probably the most challenging for the critic. Several years ago, when I was just beginning to review films for CBC Radio, my producer Hal Doran took me aside one day. Having been particularly unimpressed with my latest review, he said to me, "We don't pay you to give us a plot synopsis. We pay you to make connections."

After thinking about this for a few days I decided that he didn't mean that the plot was unimportant, but rather that he didn't want me to dwell on it too much. He was saying that I should not hesitate to communicate my impressions of the film, and to relate the film to other aspects of popular culture, and even to my own life.

Since that time, I have tried to connect every film I review to the social milieu in which it was created, and also to explore how it may or may not resonate with my own personal experiences. Sometimes the connections I make are tenuous at best, and sometimes they are unashamedly silly or intentionally preposterous. But I do approach each movie as a small part of a complex and colourful cultural mosaic, and I endeavour to see how each movie "fits" — how it floats or swims or sinks in the cultural soup in which we are adrift.

Criticism, no matter how well informed, remains a highly subjective form of expression. It is not rocket science. Indeed it is not a science of any kind, but rather — in my mind at least — a form of artistic expression. The reviews contained in this book represent my opinions and mine alone. And whether you agree with me, disagree, or think that I am ready for a rubber room, you must keep in mind that although I am a movie critic, I am above all a movie-*lover*. Movies have inspired me — sometimes to flights of total silliness, sometimes to meditations on the very meaning of existence — for just about as long as I can remember. And my favourite movies contain moments of magic. As Artie Shaw said, time is our most precious commodity, but time spent on this earth without a bit of magic is empty indeed.

— R.F.

1

The Adventures of Rocky & Bullwinkle

The beloved television program *Rocky and His Friends* had its debut on network television in 1959. That makes Rocket J. Squirrel almost *exactly* my own age. I haven't seen Rocky for a while, but I hope that his fur isn't thinning as much as my hair is. I used to be pretty fast, too — well maybe not as fast as old Rock — but these days I have slowed down considerably, and sometimes I feel about as sharp mentally as Bullwinkle J. Moose. But at least I'm not as thoroughly confused as Captain "Wrongway" Peachfuzz.

Not yet, anyway.

You may wonder about the middle initial "J" in Rocky and Bullwinkle's names. This is an in-joke tribute to creator Jay Ward. Matt Groening's Bartholomew J. Simpson (Bart), Homer J. Simpson, and Abraham J. Simpson (Grandpa) also sport the middle initial J in tribute to Jay Ward's cartoons.

Some of my best memories of television in the early to mid-sixties are connected to *Rocky and His Friends*. This was a show that helped me, as a six-year-old, to better define myself as a separate entity from my parents — more specifically, from my father. Quite simply put, I thought that this show was hilarious, although at the time I didn't "get" many of the references to politics and popular culture, but my dad thought that it was just about the stupidest show he had ever seen. For the very first time in my life I realized, with shock and dismay, not only that my father did not know everything, but that in the case of *Rocky and His Friends* Dad was terribly, completely wrong. This shook up my childish vision of a world in which adults actually knew the difference between good and bad, but it also made me feel that I was a part of a select group — comprised almost exclusively of kids — that had the good taste and critical judgment to fully appreciate the absurdist universe of R&B.

And you thought "R&B" meant Rhythm and Blues ...

Forty years later (!), many of the names and catchphrases that the show popularized have worked their way into popular speech. When you derisively call someone a "Bullwinkle" or a "Fearless Leader," most people know what you're talking about, and phrases like "This time for sure!" and "And now here's something we hope you'll really like!" have become part of the vernacular.

While I'm on the subject of fondly remembered kids' shows, was there ever a program more interesting, more educational, more musical, more life-affirming, more *attractive* than *The Friendly Giant*, which premiered on CBC television in 1958? American-born actor Bob Homme was a great entertainer and educator, and he received a richly deserved honour when he was made a Member of the Order of Canada in the late 1990s. He passed away in 2000, and I think that there should be a statue erected in his honour on Parliament Hill. As far as I'm concerned, Bob Homme was a more shining example for Canadian kids, and a more influential force for universal good, than any Canadian politician presently immortalized in bronze in Ottawa, except for Lester B. Pearson.

Rocky and His Friends ran from 1959 to 1964. Back then, in the Jurassic days of mass communication, television sets were square boxes with metal rabbit ears on top, and all programs were in black and white. The appeal of the show — as far as my six-year-old critic's brain could tell — came from its absolute, uncompromising silliness. Looking at it now, I realize of course that it was to a large extent a parody of the Cold War, but back then I thought it was just wonderfully silly. It was filled with awful puns and sometimes very bad jokes, but it was also one of the few shows that made me laugh out loud.

The Adventures of Rocky & Bullwinkle is the latest attempt in a dubious series of experiments started about ten years ago, consisting of revivals for the big screen of once-popular television programs from the boomer generation. The results have often been dismal. *The Avengers*, *Lost in Space*, and *My Favourite Martian* immediately spring to mind as particularly excruciating examples.

The biggest challenge facing the producers of *R&B* "the movie" was how to take a cartoon show that is a veritable pop culture icon of the sixties and transform it into something relevant to pop culture in 2000.

Is this possible? Is it even a good idea to try? Should anyone be shot for even suggesting it? Is this only another cynical attempt to cash in on the public's vulnerabilities by desecrating the graves of long-gone childhood heroes? Do Rocky and Bullwinkle really live again, or are they undead zombies, animated only by the greed of evil, corporate money-changers? Should this movie have perhaps been called *Night of the Living Moose*?

Q: Why has this movie really been made, and what does it mean for the future of animation? What does it mean for the future of the entire human race, for that matter?

A: I suggest that the most important reason this movie exists is that digital technology *allows* it to exist. The medium is the message, remember? The technology now makes it possible for Rocky and Bullwinkle to enter the "real" world and interact with real actors.

Having cartoon characters interact with live actors is nothing new. Frenchman Émile Cohl, who is credited with making the very first animated film, *Fantasmagorie*, in 1907, mixed live action with animation in his 1909 film *Clair de lune espagnol*. Gene Kelly danced along with cartoon character Jerry the mouse in the MGM musical *Anchors Aweigh* in 1945. Up until that time, nothing as ambitious had ever been attempted, and the scene, which took months to create and which was animated by William Hanna and Joseph Barbera, cost approximately $100,000, an enormous amount of money in the days when the average cost of going to the movies was thirty-five cents.

One of the most celebrated scenes mixing live actors with animated characters occurs in *Mary Poppins* (1964). It's a delightful scene, one that still preserves its charm today. But the process made a quantum leap in 1988 with the release of *Who Framed Roger Rabbit*? For the first time, an entire film was devoted to the interaction of live actors and 'toons. For the first time also, the technology allowed animated characters to manipulate real objects, as in the scene where animated penguin waiters in a bar carry real trays, from which they serve real drinks.

In 2000 the technology is much more sophisticated and powerful than it was even a few years ago. So, the boomer generation is now applying its computer expertise to erasing the line between the real and the unreal, between fantasy and reality.

It's all about cartoon immortality.

The boomers have decided that their childhood icons will live again, not only in cartoon form, but also in the world of live action, taking their rightful places among the living. This is crucially important for a generation of people that profoundly identifies with its cultural cartoon icons. In 2000, it seems that all you need is a wave of the digital magic wand, and presto! our animated heroes can live on — and become *more real than ever before*. Digital technology allows the boomer generation to realize two cherished dreams: to bring into their now adult world to comfort them the beloved cartoon icons they lost when they grew up, and, secondly, to satisfy the desperate need to rekindle the magic of a time when, as children, they could escape to a world populated by their best cartoon buddies, good guys who always prevailed in the end over the evildoers.

This movie is partly a nostalgia-driven trip into the fantasyland of eternal youth, and partly a reflection of the growing power of technology as an end unto itself: if we *can* do it, we *must* do it. Just the fact that we are *able* to create a world in which Rocky and Bullwinkle are made "real" is much more important than whatever plot or story is actually being told on the screen. This movie, quintessentially, is about medium as message.

At this point, dear reader, perhaps your vision is blurring, and you are rolling your eyes and mumbling, "Lighten up, oh long-winded master of the absurd over-analysis, it's only a cartoon, and the real reason it's happening is that everybody loves Rocky and Bullwinkle, period." If that's true, then riddle me this: if the prime motivation behind this movie is simply to bring back R and B, why not just make a full-length animated feature? The answer is that the boomers are no longer content, technologically speaking, with having Rocky and the gang existing as cartoons in their cartoon world, they want them to be out here, now, for real, with us.

There are only certain animated characters who are so well loved that they have won the honour of being made what I call "honorary people." By being invited into the real world via the magic of computer animation, Rocky and Bullwinkle are taking their places alongside such luminaries as Bugs Bunny and Daffy Duck, who received the same honorific treatment in *Space Jam*.

The plot of *The Adventures of Rocky & Bullwinkle* is really about turning the technology inside out. On the one hand, the movie celebrates the fact that we can bring these characters to life, but on the other, it is a cautionary tale, a warning about the dangers of unleashing our imaginary bad guys on the world. Fearless Leader and Boris and Natasha escape from their cartoon universe into the real world with a plot to "zombify" the entire population of America by broadcasting mind-numbingly bad television programs (!). From high atop his headquarters in New York, Fearless Leader controls RBTV (Really Bad Television), which broadcasts shows that are turning everyone into vegetables. The unsuspecting people who watch these shows become glassy-eyed; their minds become numb, unable to resist any suggestion.

Kind of like what happens when you watch the Home Renovation Channel for eight hours, right?

Once everyone is "zombified," Fearless Leader plans to go on national television and convince the now docile masses to make him President. Rocky and Bullwinkle are recruited by the FBI to work with special agent Karen Sympathy (Piper Perabo) to stop this nefarious scheme. *Rocky & Bullwinkle* quickly turns into a road movie, with our heroes trying to make it to New York in time to pull the plug on the villains from Pottsylvania.

I won't criticize the film for its lack of emphasis on character development, because let's face it, how much character development can you have when one of the heroes has antlers and can't remember what he had for breakfast? This is a character after all who likes nothing better than to curl up in front of a fire with a pile of good books. As he says, "They burn so nice and slow."

All of this discussion about computer-generated characters makes it easy to forget that there are also flesh and blood people involved. June Foray — who did the voices of Rocky and Natasha in the original cartoon series — does a splendid job voicing Rocky. Foray has had a long career doing cartoon voices. One of her best performances is certainly as the cackling witch Hazel in the hilarious Bugs Bunny spoof of Hansel and Gretel.

Jason Alexander does a good job as Boris Badenov; ditto René Russo as Natasha. It's not easy to portray a cartoon character. The actor has to walk the razor-thin line between being suitably cartoonish and tumbling into caricature. And if you don't get the mannerisms and attitude just right, things can become very embarrassing very quickly. Believe it or not, when portraying a cartoon, it is possible to be too ... animated. An example of someone who does a good job — not great — as a cartoon personality is John Goodman as Fred Flintstone. An example of someone who turns in a stupifyingly bad performance is Robin Williams as Popeye.

Ben Affleck as Capt. Rafe McCawley in *Pearl Harbor* doesn't count, because he's not actually portraying a cartoon character — at least I don't *think* he is.

Robert De Niro as Fearless Leader is essentially a waste of a great talent. He does have a few good lines — his "Are you talking to me?" parody of *Taxi Driver* is pretty funny — but he really doesn't get enough screen time to leave a lasting impression.

The Adventures of Rocky & Bullwinkle tries to straddle the fence by pleasing the boomers who remember the TV show while amusing the new kids who are discovering R and B for the first time. The result is a movie that pleases no one completely.

Technically, the movie is brilliant, but all of its bells and whistles can't overcome its plodding script. If I were Rocky and Bullwinkle's agent, I would recommend that they retire to lovely Frostbite Falls and not entertain any more offers unless there is serious talk of a new cartoon television series.

2

Armageddon

Michael Bay seems to believe that pure cinematic excitement can be generated by numerous loud bangs, and by having characters yell at each other as loudly as is humanly possible while he jiggles the camera around and makes your eyeballs flutter and your brain rattle around in your head. Another exciting technique used by Bay is editing so jumpy and fast and incoherent that you have no idea what's going on. When he is satisfied that the audience has been whipped into a foaming, frothing frenzy of confusion, he tops it off by showing Bruce Willis in extreme close-up yelling, "This is our last drill bit!"

Wow!

In *Armageddon*, an asteroid roughly the size of the Royal Bank's profit margin is hurtling through space on a collision course with Earth. Hoping to save the day — and everything else — NASA recruits expert oil driller Harry Stamper (Willis) and his motley devil-may-care we-spit-in-the-face-of-death-and-asteroids crew. The crew includes "Rockhound" (Steve Buscemi, the only truly effective actor in this disaster, used almost exclusively for comedy relief) and A.J. Frost (Ben Affleck — as effective as he usually is, which is to say not very). The plan is simple: the crew will undergo a twelve-day astronaut crash course (!), and then be flown up in the space shuttle to intercept the asteroid. The shuttle will then land on the asteroid (!!), allowing Bruce and the boys to drill deep into its surface to insert a thermonuclear device and blow it to smitheroons before it hits Earth.

Piece of cake.

Liv Tyler plays Stamper's daughter Grace. She is in love with Frost. While the mission is on, Grace, back on Earth, spends the entire movie looking desperately worried, her stunning eyes filled with glycerine tears. Billy Bob Thornton portrays Mission Control administrator Dan Truman. Billy Bob gets to frown a lot in this one. His big moment comes when he gets to announce — while frowning — that the remote detonator isn't working, and that someone (read: Willis's character) is going to have to detonate the device manually, thereby giving his life to save humanity, so that future generations can marvel at how anyone could have spent so much time and money making such a monumentally obnoxious movie.

3

The Beach

Allow me to reminisce a bit for a moment. When I was a young man just starting out in the big world, and looking not a whole lot older than Leonardo DiCaprio, I was living on my own in an apartment for the first time, and my dinners consisted of stuff in cans and stuff left over and *still* in the can. Back then, Tupperware was way beyond my knowledge or budget, so I just left everything in the can. Director Danny Boyle's movie *The Beach* is not unlike the contents of my refrigerator all those years ago: a colourful but unappealing mishmash that tastes as if it has been left too long in the can. Novelist Alex Garland and screenwriter John Hodge should apologize, I think, to the writers of *Apocalypse Now* and *The Deerhunter* and *Jaws* and *Lord of the Flies*, as well as to the authors of a bunch of other movies I can't think of right now. The plot of *The Beach* "borrows" not too cleverly from all of those movies, and maybe even from *Gidget Goes Hawaiian*, God help us, if you can imagine Gidget on pot.

No, don't imagine that.

I have been critical of Leonardo DiCaprio in the past. It's not that I don't think he has talent, but rather that he looks so young and is sometimes terribly miscast. He is very good at portraying a young, bubbly, excitable character, as he did in *Titanic*. In that waterlogged epic he was believable. I could believe Mr DiCaprio also in a remake of *Leave It to Beaver.* In *The Beach*, however, he's in over his head. He is acting without a life jacket. I simply do not find him believable when he is portraying a darker, more menacing figure. When, near the end of *The Beach*, his character was transformed into a darker, more menacing figure, it actually made me laugh. I wanted to tell him to go brush his teeth.

Leonardo is Richard, the narrator of the story. Unsure about what to do with his life, Richard has arrived in Thailand looking for adventure. To show the audience how tough Richard really can be behind those Rodeo Drive, Hollywood High good looks, the script has him drink a shot of "snake blood," which is being hawked by a seedy-looking hustler in an outdoor market. He knocks it back and looks the hawker straight in the eye like a tough guy.

Well, big deal!

I'd like to see Richard after a shot of my aunt Rosie's dandelion wine. One shot of that brew and you felt like you were swimming in Jello.

Anyway, while bumming around in Thailand, Richard meets up with a nutcase named Daffy, portrayed by Robert Carlyle, of *The Full Monty* fame. At first, Daffy speaks with an almost opaque Scottish accent. When they get together in Daffy's seedy hotel room, he turns Richard on with some "movie marijuana." For those of you unfamiliar with movie marijuana, I'll explain that MM makes characters who smoke it immediately and incredibly zonked, yet still able to deliver most of their lines with precision and clarity. In this case, the MM also clears up Carlyle's accent; he becomes easier and easier to decipher with every toke. After several tokes, Daffy hands Richard a map that he says will lead our hero to an island paradise, a kind of Neverland for dope smokers, where high-grade marijuana plants grow to dizzying heights and a magnificent beach is hidden away from the world and the weather is always perfect and you can do what you want all day long and you never have to deal with anything unpleasant or messy like installing snow tires or scooping up dog poop or even hearing Céline Dion sing the love theme from *Titanic*, ever again.

Sounds attractive, doesn't it?

Enter a young French couple, Étienne and his beautiful girlfriend Françoise. They are Richard's neighbours in the roach motel. Faster than you can say Doobie Brothers, our hero has persuaded them to join his quest to find the island paradise. Eight hundred miles and five minutes of screen time later they have hired a power boat to drop them on a small island that is within a few miles of the mythical island of pot. "All we have to do now," Richard explains to his two companions, "is swim a couple of miles in shark-infested waters to get there." What could be easier?

Before I nod off, let me explain an important pot — excuse me — *plot* twist: the night before the big swim, Richard meets some other dope-smoking Americans and has such a good time with them that he winds up giving them a copy of the map.

The voice-over narration spoken by DiCaprio's character becomes an unintentionally funny parody of Martin Sheen's narration in *Apocalypse Now*. Remember? "Never get out of the boat, absolutely goddamn right, unless you're going all the way ..."

Or unless the boat is the *Titanic*.

So our trio of dope seekers manages to swim to the island, where they discover giant fields of marijuana at one end and a hippie-type commune at the other. They are at first greeted with hostility by the hippies, but they manage to reassure the stoned inhabitants that there are only three of them and that nobody else has a map (oops!).

The political situation in the commune is interesting. It is a matriarchy, headed by an intense forty-something earth mother named Sal (Tilda Swinton). On the surface, everything seems to be like, really cool man. But is everything as hippydip as it seems? Our trio soon introduce trouble to paradise. Richard makes a move for Étienne's girlfriend Françoise, and Sal's boyfriend Bugs (hey, that's his name, talk to the writer) has a jealousy fit over Sal's interest in Richard. Several joints later, Richard goes for a swim and is almost eaten by a shark.

Are you still with me, man?

Later, Sal picks Richard to join her on an expedition to the mainland to purchase rice and various necessities the commune needs, such as batteries and make-up remover.

Make-up remover?

Anyway, guess who they bump into on the mainland?

Yup. The Americans who have a copy of the map.

Sal is considerably less than amused to learn that Richard has blabbed about the island. Not one to miss an opportunity, she coerces Richard into having sex by threatening to tell the commune that he is a blabbermouth. Never mind that the whole commune is going to go up in smoke and machine-gun fire when the ornery pot farmers find out that somebody is distributing maps.

Oh, and I almost forgot (sorry, short-term memory): some of the Swedish members of the commune are attacked by a shark. Gravely wounded, one of them winds up taking forever to die and making a great deal of noise — in Swedish — while doing it. This frightens all of the sensitive dopers so much that they decide to move the noisily dying man to a tent several miles away from the commune so that no one has to listen to him expire. This is certainly proof positive that smoking tons of dope does wonders for your compassion. No one objects to this inhumane treatment of the dying man except for the Frenchman Étienne. Our hero Richard doesn't object, because, as we shall soon realize, he seems to have all of the moral fibre of an avocado. Indeed, every time Richard is faced with a moral decision, he lights up a joint, inhales deeply, and looks contemplatively into the camera.

This is riveting stuff.

Other great moments include Richard playing with a Game Boy. Depending on your point of view, this scene can be interpreted as either blatant product placement or unequivocal proof that even if you are on an island paradise with your girlfriend and all the dope you can smoke, things can still get pretty boring.

Later, the script serves up a scene that echoes the Russian roulette scene in *The Deerhunter*, minus the suspense. Who in the audience would believe for a nanosecond that DiCaprio's character is going to be killed off?

Gimme a break.

As if the producers wanted the hordes of teenaged girls — who must make up fully seventy percent of the potential audience for *The Beach* and who paid to see it only because Leonardo is in it — to tell all of their teenaged girlfriends that Leonardo is killed at Russian roulette three-quarters of the way into the movie. After the first weekend, the bad word of mouth would assure a quick death at the box office.

I was in fact so concerned about Richard's possible demise during the Russian roulette scene that I cracked under the pressure and went to the snack counter for another overpriced bag of cherry flavoured Nibs. When I returned to my seat, he was still alive and kicking.

Phew.

That was close.

4

The Big Lebowski

Some critics felt that the violence in the Coen brothers' *Fargo* was gratuitous. I disagree. It was perfectly in tune with the story elements and contributed effectively, but not excessively, to the dramatic impact of the plot. Still, I am happy to report that no one gets shoved into the wood chipper in *The Big Lebowski*. The worst that happens is that the hero gets his head shoved into a toilet — certainly not a fun experience, but hardly comparable.

Bowlers (not the hats, but the people who enjoy throwing strikes and spares) will be hooked on this movie from the first frame, because there is a whole lot of bowling going on here. L.A. definitely seems to be the place to be if you're seriously into bowling. We're not talking about bowling a few frames with the kiddies on the weekend, we're talking about *serious* bowling, bowling as a way of life. We're talking about hanging at the bowling alley, chilling out while contemplating the meaning of life as applied to strikes and spares and Miller High Life, and about the deep satisfaction and inner peace that comes from the sound of ebonite bowling balls rolling smoothly down shiny, polished hardwood lanes. It's amusing to note, however, that in spite of the pervasive use of bowling as a leitmotiv in this movie, the hero is never actually shown bowling.

In the ten-pin absurdist universe of *The Big Lebowski*, there are kingpins who rule the lanes and unlucky souls who wind up in the gutter. And watching every existential frame unfold amid the clatter of human hearts being knocked down only to be set up for one more fall, contemplating life, overseeing the whole silly mess, is the Dude. From the privileged vantage point of his bar stool, sipping a white russian with Zen-like calm, the Dude takes it all in, taking her easy for all of us poor cowboys who are still trying, with mouths as dry as week-old cow pie, to lasso ourselves a little piece of heaven.

Jeff Bridges is Jeff "Dude" Lebowski. His friends just call him "the Dude" or "his Dudeness." The Dude is interested in three things: white russians (the drink), grass (the drug), and bowling. The unemployed Dude is enjoying a pretty cool (if pointless) life, when one day out of the blue two thugs break into his apartment, dunk his head ignominiously in the toilet, pee on his favourite Persian rug, and threaten worse things if he doesn't take care of his wife Bunny's debts. Bunny, it seems, owes money to some local pornographers, and the Dude is being held responsible. Only thing is, the Dude isn't married — doesn't even know anyone named Bunny — and he has not the faintest glimmer of what's going on. It seems that the idiotic thugs have him mixed up with another Jeff Lebowski, the *Big* Lebowski, a self-made millionaire who is married to a much younger ex-porno queen named Bunny.

Because no man is an island, the Dude can't be expected to face these trials and tribulations all by himself, so he recruits Walter (John Goodman), his best bowling buddy, a deranged Vietnam vet who takes bowling to previously unexplored heights of intensity. In a hilarious scene, Walter pulls a gun on a rival bowler during league play, because the guy has stepped over the foul line and refuses to acknowledge it. Walter points a gun at him and says, "This ain't Vietnam, buddy, this is bowling. There are *rules* here …"

After the Dude describes his unpleasant encounter with the intruders, Walter convinces him that he should confront the millionaire Lebowski and demand that the stained carpet be replaced. Our Dude makes his way to the millionaire's estate, meets with his rich, wheelchair-bound namesake, and tells him — joint in hand, as always — in no uncertain terms that "this aggression will not stand, man!" The Big Lebowski tells him, confidentially, that his wife Bunny has been kidnapped and is being held for ransom. Our stoned hero is easily snookered by his rich namesake into acting as a go-between with the kidnappers. Hired to make the ransom drop, the Dude brings Walter along.

Serious mistake.

The character of Walter — a part written specifically for John Goodman — reminds me a bit of legendary baseball manager Leo Durocher, a man of whom it was once said that he "possessed an almost infinite capacity to make a bad situation worse." If Walter is involved, you can be sure that the initial objective will soon be forgotten, erased by intense paranoia and total stupidity. Needless to say, the ransom drop is spectacularly botched: a bag of Walter's dirty underwear is handed over instead of the money.

It's not so much that this script is engorged with red herrings, it's more that the entire plot is a red herring. The Coens' script isn't content just to veer off the proverbial beaten track; it enthusiastically, joyfully, drives right off he proverbial cliff at full throttle.

The script has the Dude tailed by a totally inept private investigator and pursued by dangerous pornographers, and also by a group of neo-Nazi nihilists who barge in on him while he's in his bathtub. Armed with an attack marmot on a leash (!), they threaten to remove his "Johnson" if he doesn't co-operate. Later, in another surreal development, the Dude meets a performance artist (Julianne Moore) who may or may not be in league with the kidnappers. This rapidly becomes an extremely moot point, because the alleged kidnapping may not be anything of the sort: that is, Bunny may really just be visiting friends in Palm Springs (!?).

Confusing? Yes.

Entertaining? Absolutely.

When the Dude is drugged by the nasty pornographer, he experiences a bad trip for the ages, imagining himself plunged into an alternate universe, a prisoner in a surreal X-rated movie called *Gutter Balls*. While the Dude's hallucination isn't really X-rated, it certainly *is* a bad trip. Imagine going up to the counter to rent some bowling shoes and finding Saddam Hussein glaring down at you from a ten foot-high podium. The Dude's trip unfolds to the sound of "Just Dropped In (To See What Condition My Condition Was In)," an almost forgotten gem of commercially savvy pseudo-psychedelia recorded in 1968 by Kenny Rogers and the First Edition, and now forever salvaged from pop music oblivion by the fearless Coens.

Did I mention that all of this inspired nonsense is supposed to be taking place during the Gulf War? That certainly explains the reference to Saddam, although none of this is actually relevant to the plot. That being said, who's to say what is truly relevant in the theatre of the absurd that is the Coen universe? If you smoke enough weed, or deeply inhale the toxic emanations from those bowling shoes, the pieces may start to fall perfectly into place and you may be on your way to an epiphany of sorts. But probably not.

An important reason why this movie works is that the dialogue is wonderfully strange — filled with glorious non sequiturs. There are a lot of inspired physical gags also, expertly executed by Jeff Bridges. The scene in which the

Dude drops a tiny roach he has been trying to smoke into his lap while driving his car is priceless. All in all, Bridges gives a perfectly realized performance.

John Goodman is terrific also as Walter the gun nut. Steve Buscemi is perfect as the long-suffering Donny ("Shut the fuck up, Donny!"), the odd man out in the bowling triumvirate. John Turturro is memorable as the Hispanic glitter-glam psycho-bowler "Jesus" Quintana. "You don't mess with the Jesus," he says to our dumbstruck heroes, taunting them about the league finals. He then looks down the alley, and licks (!) his bowling ball before throwing a strike. It is a wonderfully weird moment.

Julianne Moore is lively as the self-described vaginal artist (!) who almost becomes the Dude's love interest, and Sam Elliot is perfect as the cowboy narrator of the story.

The Big Lebowski is a brilliant absurdist comedy, one of the great American films of the nineties (really!). Exuding a contagious joie de vivre, *The Big Lebowski* mows down the crassness, moral vacuity, and solipsism of West Coast popular culture with scattershot abandon.

In 2077, long after the sky has fallen, when Alien archaeologists pore over the tattered and twisted vestiges of America, they will perhaps discover a copy of this movie and plunk it into an old DVD player. Between fits of laughter, they will probably shake their antennae in disbelief that a culture could produce a work of art so brilliantly inane, so mockingly absurd, so wonderfully silly, and so profoundly *human*, but still not possess the wisdom to save itself from itself.

5

The Bone Collector

A few years ago Philip Noyce directed a thriller called *Dead Calm*. As far as pretty darn good thrillers go, it was pretty darn good. This time around, he chooses to adapt a totally forgettable novel by Jeffery Deaver.

Strike one.

Deaver also collaborates on the screenplay, adapting his own novel with the help of Jeremy Iacone. Previously, Iacone has penned the screenplay for a perfectly mediocre action flick called *One Tough Cop*.

Strike two.

Noyce casts Angelina Jolie as an NYPD beat cop (!).

Strike three (Take a seat!).

Jolie, who is the daughter of Jon Voight, began her career as a model, and also appeared in a number of music videos. I was surprised to learn that she had honed her acting skills at the very prestigious Lee Strasberg Institute. After watching her performance, I believe she needs more honing. In fairness to Ms. Jolie, however, perhaps the real problem is that she is miscast. No one is going to believe for a nanosecond that she is a cop, or that she could even have passed the physical. She is, quite simply, too thin. In fact, she looks exactly like those too-thin models we see in music videos (isn't *that* weird?).

If this casting gaffe were the only problem, the director might still be able to save his leaky script, but this is only the tip of the iceberg.

So much for mixed nautical metaphors.

Denzel Washington plays a brilliant New York detective named Lincoln Rhyme (!), who was paralysed from the neck down in an accident. He now lives as a semi-recluse with only his live-in nurse Thelma (Queen Latifah) for company.

We immediately feel enormous sympathy for this guy.

However, although he is supposed to have been bedridden for four years when the movie opens, he looks incredibly fit and powerful. In fact, he looks as if he could jump right out of bed and punch out the screenwriters who cooked up this trash.

Early in the proceedings, our bedridden hero asks a close friend to help him commit suicide. Given the character's vivacious nature, I was a bit surprised at this request — until I began to reflect on the fact that he often has only Queen Latifah to talk to. But then, suddenly, magically (i.e., five minutes later), our hero forgets all about killing himself and begins to get deeply engrossed in a serial murder investigation being discussed in his presence. Making the most of this Kodak Moment, the director gives us a big close-up of nurse Thelma beaming as she realizes that her boss now has *a reason to live*.

This is indeed good news for our hero, but the audience may not be so lucky.

Ms. Jolie (sporting a permanent pout) plays Amelia Donaghey, a young, brilliant, but psychologically scarred New York cop who must become Lincoln's arms and legs as they work against the clock to track down a slippery serial killer who is terrorizing the Big Apple.

Eschewing any semblance of realistic character development, the writers quickly present a noisy verbal confrontation that pits our quadriplegic hero against our pretty model cop. During this big rhubarb, we are treated to the "You think because you're paralysed that you can tell people what to do" speech, which is, I believe, explained in more detail on page three of *The Complete Hacker's Guide to Writing Powerful Confrontational Scenes Between Mismatched Partners While Desperately Trying to Find Ways to Make Your Female Lead Appear to Be a Tough Cop even though She Looks Exactly like a Thin Model in a Music Video*.

In another highly improbable (and totally unconvincing) plot development, Amelia's boss gives her hell for trying to protect the integrity of a murder scene. This is so weird and ridiculous that we immediately understand that it's only happening because the screenwriters hope the audience will suspect that her boss is the serial killer.

Duh!

Then, a little later, the writers strike again by having a detective snoop around Amelia's apartment. The explanation given by the character is that "he's checking to see if she's okay."

Duh-duh!

What is really going on here is that the writers want to

(1) make us think that maybe this snooping detective is the serial killer (unfortunately, this is completely lamebrained, because we have already seen the detective in other locations at the same time as the serial killer is committing a crime), and

(2) allow the detective to discover some old photographs taken during her former life as a model, before her policeman father's untimely death (we are told that her

father's death motivated her to give up modelling and become a cop).

The only reason for this entire scene, with the snooping detective and the "discovery" of the modelling photos, is that the writers were profoundly disturbed by the fact that Ms. Jolie is physically wrong for this role. In desperation, they contrived this nonsense in order to explain why she doesn't look or behave remotely like a real cop.

So, what have we got? A thin cop-model with a permanent pout, a brilliant detective paralysed from the neck down, and two screenwriters who seem to be paralysed from the neck up.

Bad combination.

I'll spare you any more details. If you are still conscious by the time this whole mess plays itself out, you may be forgiven for wondering how in heck it happens that every time we see the mystery killer's eyes in close-up they are blue, but when his identity is finally revealed the man's eyes are clearly brown. Is this just a continuity mistake (albeit a huge one) or intentional trickery? Did our ingenious writers hope to confuse us even further? Was the killer prone to wearing blue contact lenses when committing the crimes? Do you really care?

I know I don't.

6

Boogie Nights

When I first heard its title, I thought that *Boogie Nights* might be a documentary about the legendary San Francisco blues band, Canned Heat.

Wrong again.

Boogie Nights is actually a fiction film that revisits the seventies — more specifically, the Hollywood porn industry in the seventies. This is a pretty risqué subject for a mainstream movie, and the film definitely deserves its "R" rating. But although *Boogie Nights* explores a supremely sleazy subject, it is itself a first-class piece of filmmaking.

Ah, the seventies. Remember that polyester leisure suit decade?

Wish you didn't?

I'm exaggerating a little. The seventies weren't all bad, although any decade that pushes Cheez Whiz in an aerosol spray can on unsuspecting kids has much to answer for. Come to think of it, there was a lot of disgusting so-called food in the seventies. Remember Reddi-wip? This also came in an aerosol can, and it was the most foul-tasting whipped cream substitute I've ever had. I seem to recall that the label proudly proclaimed that it was an "edible oil product."

I'd rather not think about that.

Still, two of my favourite things emerged from the discofied, freeze-dried, Binaca-flavoured cesspool of the seventies: Steely Dan (a musical unit that got its name from a steam-powered (!) sex toy in the William Burroughs novel *Naked Lunch*) and chocolate fondue (which I tasted for the first time in about 1976). Is there anything that tastes more completely decadent than slices of just-ripened banana dipped in hot chocolate fondue?

Anyway, *Boogie Nights* doesn't have any chocolate fondue, but it does feature lots of simulated sex, frontal nudity, sexual situations, colourfully explicit language, and drugs galore (mostly cocaine). But more shocking still are the synthetic fibres, leisure suits, and disco music. Remember when Electric Light Orchestra went disco? Remember when you actually danced to crap like "Living Thing," and spent ridiculous amounts of money for watered-down drinks because you pretty much believed that you had to do the "disco thing" if you didn't want to sleep alone for the rest of your life?

Wish you didn't?

In this universe, everyone wears platform soles and pointy collars. It's quite horrible. Early on, I started thinking, "Thank God this is about porn and these people are going to take off their clothes a lot, so at least I won't have to look at these fashions for very long."

It's 1977, and Jack Horner (Burt Reynolds) (I love the character names in this film) is a porn flick director who is sitting on top of the world — or at least on top of the trash heap. Jack lives in a big house, and he's involved in a relationship with his much younger leading lady, a porn starlet named Amber Waves (Julianne Moore). Horner's entourage includes his cameraman Little Bill (William H. Macy), his leading men Reed Rothchild (John C. Reilly) and Buck (Don Cheadle), and a high school dropout turned "actress" known only as Roller Girl. Her particular claim to fame is that she never removes her roller skates, not even when she's in front of the cameras doing a torrid sex scene. The new kid on the block is a confused but extraordinarily well-endowed (or so we are told at every turn) young man named Eddie (Mark Wahlberg). Jack has "discovered" Eddie working in the kitchen of a popular disco. It seems that Jack has heard stories about Eddie's equipment and can't wait to put him in front of the cameras and make a fortune. Wahlberg is no stranger to sexploitation: I seem to recall that he was a Calvin Klein underwear model — pretty good qualifications for stepping into this role.

Eddie is introduced to Jack's milieu. He's a know-nothing kid with dreams of making lots of money, having lots of chicks, and being a star. Jack has him eating out of his hand in no time. In a chilling early scene, Jack invites Eddie to "audition" for him with a willing young lady. Jack sits in his comfy chair in his living room and the camera shows his face in close-up, a dirty old man watching two clueless kids having sex.

Boogie Nights has a very dark side, which emerges slowly as we come to realize how desperately unhappy and screwed-up all of these people are. The only one who seems in control and happy — if you can call it that — is Jack, although he longs desperately to make (in his words) a "real movie." He longs for mainstream acceptance as a filmmaker. It's revealing to note that this longing for mainstream credibility seems pervasive in the adult film business. While visiting porn film shoots to research the role of Jack, Burt Reynolds was repeatedly asked the same question by the actors on the sets: "How do I get a Screen Actors Guild card?"

In a scene at once hilarious and pathetic, Jack is editing his latest porno opus, a parody of the James Bond genre. The film stars Eddie as Dirk Diggler. As we watch clips of the movie, which features atrocious acting, badly staged kung fu fights, and superbly inane dialogue, Jack gets very emotional. Tears come to his eyes as the editor declares, "It's a real movie, Jack." Looking solemnly at the editor, Jack responds, "It's the best thing I've ever done. It's the one I'll be remembered for."

A few porn stars have managed to leave the business and obtain roles in mainstream films, Traci Lords and Ginger Lynn being the most successful examples — although Lynn (who is actually a good actress) eventually returned to doing adult films in the late nineties after having had roles in films like *Young Guns II* and even having been close to landing the role that eventually went to Sharon Stone in Martin Scorsese's *Casino*. The sobering news for the great majority, however, is that once you choose pornography, all other doors are slammed shut.

On one level, *Boogie Nights* functions as a campy, often hilarious satire of an outrageous, morally vacuous universe, a savage poke at the sleaziest of businesses. But there is an even darker side to the tale, which emerges as this world begins to unravel. The story follows the characters into the early eighties, by which time Eddie is a coke addict, and he can no longer get it up for the cameras. Jack's empire is threatened by the advent of video, which offends Jack's "artistic" sensibilities: quality adult movies, he believes, should be shot on 35-mm film.

Fascinating sub-plots abound. Jack's cameraman, Little Bill, is about to go off the deep end. In what is at first a running gag, his wife (played by a real-life porn star named Nina Hartley) enjoys having sex with other men at every opportunity, usually in public. During a party, she decides to do it with someone in front of several leering spectators. In a stunning moment of understatement, Little Bill turns to a friend and says, "That's so embarrassing." The joke soon turns to tragedy, however, when Little Bill finally snaps. Other notable sub-plots involve Amber's desperate, pitiful attempt to regain custody of her child, and Roller Girl's devastating and violent encounter with a former high school acquaintance.

As the various characters spiral down into the depths of their own excesses, the film climaxes (sorry!) with Eddie deeply embroiled in a botched drug rip-off at the house of a psychotic dope dealer, played with ferocious, maniacal intensity by Alfred Molina. This scene, reminiscent of *Pulp Fiction*, is gripping — crisply directed and tightly edited. Unlike the delusional Jack Horner, Paul Thomas Anderson has real talent. He gets terrific performances from the entire cast, and directs a great-looking movie that negotiates every plot twist with the smoothness and precision of a Ferrari.

The characters are slimy but endearing. You just can't take your eyes off this movie; it fascinates like a writhing, shifting neon snake.

Boogie Nights arrives at a time when sexually explicit or kinky mainstream movies are dying at the box office. Cronenberg's *Crash* (which I found boring in the extreme) was a box office flop. *The People vs. Larry Flynt* also did not do well in theatres. North American movie audiences seem more uncomfortable with sex than they have been in a long time, although they seem to be embracing increasingly graphic violence.

Am I the only one who finds this disturbing?

In a recent article published in *Premiere* magazine, senior editor Glenn Kenny pointed out, "It's as if the sexual revolution had been a figment of the collective imagination."

The seventies, however, were no figment. They really happened, and they left a stamp on social consciousness.

What were once considered pornographic images have slowly — I'm tempted to say insidiously — become prevalent in mainstream advertising and entertainment.

Boogie Nights asks us to reflect not only on the seventies, but on our own era as well. By showing us, in sometimes campy detail, a world that no longer exists, it allows us to see contemporary society in a different light.

But is it exploitative?

To some degree it is. Much of the movie resembles a dirty joke. We are told about Eddie's "gift" throughout the film, but it is only at the very end, with Eddie in his dressing room getting ready to shoot a scene, that we finally get to see this wonder of nature, and this dénouement is presented as the ultimate joke, because what Eddie pulls out of his pants is clearly, obviously, a rubber prosthetic.

So, what is the point? Is *Boogie Nights* saying that pornography is a lie, a fake, a cheat? Certainly. But some will feel that it should not have taken 150 minutes to make what is after all an obvious point. Still, this is an entertaining movie. The tempo is brisk; the plot throws new, ever more bizarre situations at you every ten minutes. It is perversely fascinating.

But not satisfied with titillating the audience, *Boogie Nights* also gets to the heart of the whole tragic human mess, and it does so with subtle eloquence in the scene where Eddie and Amber are preparing to have sex on camera for the first time. Eddie asks her, "Is it okay if I kiss you? Can I be tender?" Here they are, about to copulate on camera, but he's asking about tenderness.

This is where the script hits the truth about pornography: it shows all of the mechanical aspects of love in great detail, and with great fanfare and exaggeration, while capturing nothing of the warmth, and the deep, shared intimacy, of the physical act of love. In a moment of true inspiration, the director, Paul Thomas Anderson, turns the camera inward as this scene starts to unfold, and shows us only the whirring, turning gears of the camera itself, mechanically, mindlessly recording an "act of love" that is, in truth, only an "act," and contains no love at all. I thought that this was a brilliant way to convey the emptiness of the entire process: human feelings negated; a naked couple reduced to an organic Meccano set, nothing more than an assemblage of gears and wheels, spinning and clicking lustily.

7

Capote

I first came into contact with Truman Capote's writing in an oblique way. I had no idea who he was when, as a ten-year-old back in the late sixties, I first saw Jack Clayton's *The Innocents*, with Deborah Kerr. At the time of that broadcast on network television, I had never heard of Henry James or of his Victorian ghost story *The Turn of the Screw*, which was the inspiration for the film. I was immediately captivated by the eerie atmosphere of *The Innocents*. The film made such an impression on me in fact that for several weeks afterwards I had nightmares. I also loved the dialogue. I was just discovering the finer points of the English language (I still am!), and it seemed to me that this was English at a level I had never heard, or even imagined. It was only a few years later that I learned that the brilliant screenplay was by Truman Capote.

In the summer of 1973, when I was fifteen, I found a copy of Capote's *In Cold Blood*, and I was hooked from the first page. By that time I had seen Capote on *The Tonight Show* with Johnny Carson. I had been struck by how fantastically eccentric he was. In baseball terms, he was a real screwball. The exaggerated mannerisms, the lisp, and the flamboyant clothes all conspired to convey an image of a character who was almost otherworldly. "Could he be acting weird on purpose," I wondered, "because he knows it is expected of him? Is he just trying to be entertaining?" Johnny Carson certainly seemed to enjoy his company. I think that Johnny laughed more when Capote was a guest than when almost anyone else appeared on the show. Capote was weird, to be sure, but he was also obviously very bright and funny, and when I read *In Cold Blood* I discovered that he was a brilliant writer.

Genius is a word that is often abused, and I don't feel qualified to determine whether or not someone is a literary genius, but *In Cold Blood* is a helluva book. The realistic account of the brutal murder of a farming family in Kansas in 1959 and of the ensuing police investigation, it also recounts the lives of the two murderers, who eventually find themselves on death row. While reading *In Cold Blood*, I felt that terrible secrets were being whispered in my ear, and that worlds I knew nothing about — secret, frightening worlds — were being revealed to me. The book was simply more realistic, grittier, and more frightening than anything I had ever read. Just the idea that two strangers could get into a house and murder a nice, ordinary, God-fearing family was extremely unsettling. More unsettling was the fact that the murders had been committed for no reason. While the original motive had been robbery (Mr Clutter had been rumoured to keep large amounts of cash at home), there had actually been no secret safe, and the murderers found only forty dollars in the house. Why had they proceeded to kill the family? It seemed senseless, mindless, a demonstration of a brutality such as I had never imagined. And one of the victims, Kenyon Clutter, was my age, fifteen, as I was reading the book. The book also raised all kinds of complex moral questions — about the death penalty, about the cruelty of keeping men for years on death row, awaiting execution.

Capote, the film, begins in New York in 1959, when the famous author and darling of the cocktail circuit reads a brief account of the murder of the Clutter family in a newspaper. He immediately calls his editor at the *New Yorker* to express his interest in writing a story about the murder, and more specifically about its impact on the small farming community of Holcomb, Kansas, where the Clutters lived. Soon Capote is off to Kansas by train, accompanied by his research assistant and childhood friend, Harper Lee. Also a writer, Lee will soon publish the book that will make her famous, the brilliant *To Kill a Mockingbird*. Once they are in Kansas, it becomes abundantly clear that Harper Lee is going to be vitally important to the project, because Capote is so eccentric — in his attire, his mannerisms, and his speech — that no one wants to talk to him. When he approaches people, they act as if he has just arrived from Mars. Harper is a much less intimidating and bizarre presence, and she quickly gets the locals to open up and talk. A golden opportunity arises when Capote and Lee are invited to the house of Dewey, the chief investigator (Chris Cooper). The invitation actually comes from Chief Dewey's wife, who is positively thrilled at the opportunity to have Truman Capote in the house — a celebrity himself, and someone who knows Bogart and Monroe and Elizabeth Taylor. Slowly, without fanfare, Capote gains access to people working on the Clutter case, and, as they become more comfortable with his nosy presence, begins to gain access to the townspeople who knew the family.

When the two suspected killers are caught, Capote meets and talks to one of them, Perry Smith, and slowly, in the course of repeated visits, gains the man's confidence. Capote develops a strange kind of symbiotic relationship with Smith. As Smith tells the author about his hellish childhood, Capote, in order to gain his confidence, also opens up to Smith, telling him about being neglected and abandoned himself as a child. The relationship that develops is a strange, unhealthy one. Actually, "unhealthy" might be a bad choice of words: it's healthy for Smith in the sense that as long as he is alive and hasn't told Capote the whole story of the murders, Capote will do everything in his power to keep him alive, at one point hiring the best New York lawyers to obtain a temporary reprieve for both Smith and the other accused, Richard Hickock.

Without Smith's first-hand account of the night of the murders, Capote's book will be incomplete. By this point, Capote has decided that the project has evolved far beyond a magazine article. He tells his publisher excitedly that his book about the Clutter murders is going to be a very important book, a great book, a new type of literature, what he calls a "non-fiction novel." But he needs to hear the whole story of the murders or the book will not work. From Perry Smith's point of view, Capote is a rich celebrity who can help him stay alive by getting him top-notch New York lawyers. So each is trying to manipulate the other to get what he wants, with Capote definitely being the more manipulative. There are some brilliant scenes between the two. At one moment Capote may seem to be sincerely concerned about Smith, but this moment of apparent sincerity will quickly pass, as a glimmer in Capote's eyes and a subtly pointed question reveals that he really couldn't care less about Smith's eventual fate, just as long as he gets his story before the state doles out its ultimate punishment. Philip Seymour Hoffman's ability in these scenes to transform his character's mood and intensity ever so subtly, with just a look or a facial twitch, is a marvel of acting technique.

After a few legal appeals, Smith writes a series of letters in which he practically begs "amigo Truman" (as he calls him) to find him another lawyer for an appeal to the Supreme Court. At first not even acknowledging Smith's letters, Capote eventually curtly refuses any further help, telling Smith that he has done all he can. In reality, he has not done all he can, but he is struggling to finish his book, which is becoming a terrible emotional and mental strain. Capote is increasingly tormented by the idea that this book, in which he has invested almost five years of his life, and which he firmly believes holds the key to his literary success, will prove to be a failure if Smith and Hickock are not executed. What began as an exciting, if rather morally dubious, literary project gradually takes on a much darker tone, with Capote emerging as a coldly calculating exploiter, willing to manipulate these condemned men to satisfy his literary ambitions.

The high-stakes game of lying and bluffing takes its toll on Capote. He starts drinking a great deal, and begins to unravel before our eyes. The script paints a complex portrait of a man bursting with contradictions — brilliant, manipulative, self-centred, yet genuinely caring, and capable of great humanity — who is left an emotional wreck by the weight of the tactics he has employed to create his greatest literary work. Hoffman's perfectly controlled and understated performance is certainly the strongest of his career, and also one of the best by any American actor in recent memory.

Hoffman's performance reminds me of that of Bruno Ganz as Adolph Hitler in *Downfall*: it is not an impersonation, but rather an almost miraculous transformation. Hoffman *becomes* Capote as Ganz *became* Hitler. His performance goes far beyond the perfectly studied mannerisms and the lisping speech. Hoffman's Capote has that elusive but palpable quality of believability — the ring of truth —

that resonates like a fine brass bell on a clear summer morning. *Capote* is a brilliant example of the magic of cinema. Yes, even a crusty old critic like myself can be completely taken in when direction, script, and acting conspire to create film art that transcends technique and appears to give the audience something genuine and true.

8

Casino

A movie about violent people has to contain *some* violence, even a film reviewer understands that. But there are scenes in *Casino* that could set you off your popcorn right quick. This is very unfortunate, because the combination of Scorsese and De Niro is always exciting for a film buff — and believe me, I am a film buff first and a critic second.

This time around, Robert De Niro is Ace Rothstein, gambler extraordinaire. Ace has either a functioning crystal ball hidden somewhere or a golden horseshoe up the kazoo. He has an uncanny ability to correctly predict the outcome of everything from college football games to dog races.

Ace is employed by some shady characters in Kansas City, and his talents are a huge source of revenue for his employers. Soon the big boys decide to buy a casino in Las Vegas, and Ace is selected to run it. Of course, characters like these always want to hedge their bets, so they decide to keep an eye on Ace, and to make sure that nothing happens to him. To "keep Ace company," then, they send along a vicious enforcer named Nicky (Joe Pesci). There have been a number of colourful lunatic characters in Scorsese films, but Nicky takes the fruitcake. One-dimensional in the extreme, this character leaves an amazing number of dead bodies in his wake before finally coming to a brutal, horrible end himself.

Our hero Ace falls in love (or something) with Ginger (Sharon Stone). Ginger is a high-priced call girl who is looking for the ultimate free ride. Ace and Ginger get married, and then things get very nasty, very fast. Ginger is not only an alcoholic, but also a junkie, and she is still involved with her ex-pimp, Lester Diamond (James Woods).

The opening scene of *Casino* is remarkable. Ace gets into his car and starts the engine, and the car explodes in flames. As the ominous strains of Bach's *Saint Matthew Passion* wash over the scene, Ace's body falls through the air in slow motion. The principal credits then begin to roll over shots of garish, neon-illuminated Las Vegas. It's a striking and stylish overture. But what does it mean?

Scorsese is setting us up for a wild descent into a modern-day *Inferno*, with Las Vegas standing in for Hell. The plot of *Casino* revolves around three people, Ace, Ginger, and Lester, who live in what they believe to be a kind of paradise, swimming in money, power, and success. Soon, however, they will fall from grace and lose everything. Las Vegas will bring out the worst in them, and they will be consumed and destroyed by their own vices.

The entire cast is generally outstanding, although I found Joe Pesci's portrayal of the sadistic enforcer Nicky so over the top that it was hard to believe that this could be a real person.

Sharon Stone's Ginger steals the show — and anything else her character can get her impeccably manicured claws on. Stone is absolutely riveting as the totally out-of-control, self-destructive bimbo. I was reminded of Elizabeth Taylor's indelible portrayal of a vicious Fury in *Who's Afraid of Virginia Woolf?* Stone's on-screen histrionics and drunken tantrums register a nine on the Richter scale. I don't know how she prepared for this role, but she seemed to be channelling not only Elizabeth Taylor, but also Cruella De Vil and even Jessica Rabbit. Stone doesn't just steal every scene she's in, she chews up the scenery and spits out the two-by-fours. Stone won the Golden Globe in 1996 for this performance but lost the Oscar to Susan Sarandon, who won it for *Dead Man Walking*.

Casino features a soundtrack that assaults us with just about every pop song released in the seventies. The onscreen events are played out against this omnipresent musical wallpaper, and the lyrics of the song snippets seem to comment or add ironic counterpoint to the action. This struck me as a clever idea the first few times it was done, but it quickly became profoundly annoying. Also annoying is the almost unrelenting use of voice-over narration by Ace, De Niro's character. A measured dose of narration can be beneficial to a fiction film by providing a heightened feeling of realism, and this was probably the director's intent, but this much narration is quite simply overkill.

While many of his films contain brutal violence, *Casino* marks the first time that Scorsese has tumbled into sensationalistic splatter. *Taxi Driver* and *Raging Bull* (to name only those two) both contained graphic violence, but the violence served the plot. In *Casino*, the plot is often overshadowed — indeed overwhelmed — by the violence. It's unfortunate that many filmmakers chose to portray increasingly graphic violence in the nineties, as if they believed that mainstream audiences had developed an appetite for the kind of excesses previously found only in the worst exploitation flicks. The kitschy brutality and stomach-turning violence of Quentin Tarantino's *Pulp Fiction* and *Reservoir Dogs* seem to have profoundly influenced many directors. As he gets older, Scorsese may be fooling himself into believing that cranking up the graphic violence several notches is somehow going to make his films more contemporary. In reality, the excessive brutality found in *Casino* panders to the lowest common denominators of junk culture. It seems to me (and I may be old-fashioned) that just the *suggestion* of placing a man's head in a vice is sufficient to create a dramatic effect. It seems exploitative in the extreme for the director to show the eyeballs actually exploding. What is Scorsese hoping to achieve with such a scene? Is he hoping that *Casino* will one day be the featured Movie of the Week on the Autopsy Channel? If you are one of those weirdos who believe that art is supposed to be about subtlety and suggestion, then you may well be repulsed by these shenanigans. The graphic violence in *Casino* doesn't make it a more powerful viewing experience; it actually diminishes the film's impact, because the viewer becomes distracted (or simply disgusted) by the brutality. This undermines the finer elements of the narrative.

Casino clocks in at a little under three hours. In its final thirty minutes, it degenerates into a repulsive orgy of brutality. I think that it's truly a shame that a movie that could have taken its place among Scorsese's very best is ruined in this way.

9

Cellular

Q: What has become the ultimate contemporary fear in Western societies?

A: Fear of answering the telephone.

Think about it. Is there anything more mind-numbingly frightening, more absolutely terrifying these days than having to answer the phone? I mean, really think about it That could be *anybody* calling you up. It could be somebody really scary. It could be ... a *really insistent* salesperson. How do you get off the hook? How can you refuse a free trial subscription to *Curling Quarterly* or *Pet Pride* or *Bathroom Interiors International* without looking like an uncultured buffoon?

And how in heck can you refuse a free alarm system for your home without looking like a complete moron (never mind that only the installation is free and that you then have to pay $24.95 a month in service charges)?

And how will you respond when an icy, superior voice on the other end says, "It's free, dummy. What do you mean you're not interested?"

And how can you refuse more life insurance (egotist!), or a platinum Visa card?

Or giving money to worthy charities?

That's the worst. Oh, the voice stays polite — well, usually — but the tone speaks volumes: "What kind of a creep are you? You're refusing to help little handicapped children?"

Every time the phone rings, my heart pounds. In the next few moments, I may have to behave like a selfish, immoral, no-good rotten excuse for a human being and *refuse* somebody.

This is essentially what happens to twenty-something Ryan in David R. Ellis's *Cellular*. Ryan is driving along when his cell phone rings. A woman on the other end says, "I've been kidnapped. You're my only hope! Don't lose this call, please. Please, please take ten minutes of your time and go to the police and let me talk to them."

At first, of course, he's not buying it. He thinks the whole thing is a gag. After all, these things only happen in movies, right (nudge, nudge)? He even puts her on hold for a minute while he talks to a buddy. But then she says, "Just go to a police station and let me talk to a cop. It'll just take a few minutes. Please, please, please!" And so he heads off to the nearest police station. And the fun begins.

Cellular was co-written by Larry Cohen, who also wrote *Phone Booth*. What is it with this guy and telephones? I'll have to call him up at 3:00 a.m. sometime just to freak him out.

Previously, David R. Ellis directed *Final Destination 2* — which sounds pretty stupid if you think about it. I mean, if the first one was the *final* destination, how can you go any further?

The first question that comes to my mind when I sit down to watch a Kim Basinger movie is "Will I believe her in this role?" I know that she has perfected the art of portraying vacuous blondes and/or bimbos. After all, she gave a Teenage Movie Hall of Fame-calibre performance as Honey Hornée in *Wayne's World 2*, and she took the Best Supporting Actress award for her portrayal of a Veronica Lake look-alike in *L.A. Confidential* in 1997. But before outraged readers point to her Oscar as proof positive of her thespian abilities, let me mention that owning an Oscar only proves that you got more votes than the competition. For my money, Julianne Moore deserved the Supporting Actress award in 1997 for her role in *Boogie Nights*. But that's the way the egg rolls, as they say. The Oscars are not like the World Series: the best one doesn't always win. And sometimes winning an Oscar is not the best thing that could happen to an actor's ego. I can imagine that certain actors might become rather unreceptive to direction. Picture this: a director tactfully suggests a different approach to a scene, and the recently Oscarized actor yells at him, "You can't tell me how to act! I won an Oscar!"

In *Cellular*, Basinger demonstrates that she is an exceptionally good screamer. She possesses a good high pitch and plenty of volume, although I can't be completely certain that she's doing her own screaming. We *hear* her scream on the phone a lot, but we don't always *see* her screaming, so she may be using a scream double — kind of like the body double some actresses use for nude scenes, you know? Maybe there's an obscure voice actress in Hollywood who screams for all the celebrities.

What do you mean, "That's ridiculous!"? Can you prove that there isn't?

In *Cellular*, Basinger's character is very scared most of the time. Her character is also very thin, all of the time. I have to say that Basinger trembles exceptionally well. When confronted by big, evil-looking kidnappers she manages to tremble with great panache. For those of you who may be tempted to dismiss this, let me tell you that it's not easy to tremble convincingly on cue. Of course, it is possible that the director slipped some ice cubes down the back of her dress just before shooting some scenes ... we'll never know for certain. There are some directing secrets that are jealously guarded, and with good reason.

Basinger portrays Jessica Martin, a high school science teacher. Now, based on my own experiences in high school, I would never in a million years believe that a high school science teacher could look like Kim Basinger. Maybe if she was a really short bald guy ... But times have changed, so let's not dwell on it. The point is that she's supposed to be very smart, and she quickly proves it by fixing a smashed-up telephone. Never mind that she is supposed to be a biology teacher. Teachers today possess a much wider range of knowledge than they did when I was in school.

The phone was on the wall in the attic where she is being held, and she needs to repair it because it has been smashed to smithereens by the bad guys. But why have the bad guys *smashed* the phone? Why not just rip the cord out of the socket? Or simply cut it? It's much easier.

The answer is (as Hercule Poirot would say) of a *simplicité infantile*: if the cable had been cut, it would have been extremely difficult for the character to repair the phone, at least without a soldering gun.

End of movie.

Also, simply cutting the cable isn't dramatic. It is, however, *very* dramatic to have the bad guy smash the phone with a sledgehammer. This also satisfies one of the tried and tested conventions of Hollywood thrillers: bad guys smash things. When the bad guys first arrive at Jessica's house, they dramatically smash through a plate glass door. In real life the bad guys would have knocked, then quietly muscled their way in, instead of making all this racket breaking the plate glass and possibly alerting the neighbours that something unusual was going on.

Sometimes real life is just not sufficiently dramatic.

After this noisy entrance, the bad guys proceed to shoot the maid. I don't know if the maid was expensive, but she sure is expendable. She is the maid equivalent of those expendable crewmembers on *Star Trek*. Remember? "Hello. Smile at the camera. Say your three lines ... Bang! You're dead!"

Working with the broken bits of phone our brilliant kidnapped teacher manages to get a dial tone and, by repeatedly touching some wires together, place a call. She of course has no idea what number she is dialing. By an incredible stroke of luck — well, it *could* happen — she composes our hero's cell phone number. In real life, of course, if you were kidnapped and managed to get the phone working to make a random call, you'd get "Thank you for calling Bob's Plumbing and Drain Cleaning. Your call is important to us. There is no one here to take your call at the present time but please leave a message. BEEEP!"

You might be wondering at this point why a bunch of bad guys are kidnapping a high school teacher in the first place? Are they disgruntled parents severely displeased with the grades she's been giving their kids? I don't want to give too much away, but suffice it to say that it is Jessica's husband who has brought this upon his family by inadvertently videotaping a crime. And the bad guys want her to reveal the location of the video.

Even though the plot has holes in it the size of Santa Monica, the movie zooms right along with such verve that you don't really have much time to fall into them.

Chris Evans, who plays the young man who receives the call, is, I think, destined for stardom of some kind. He's got the looks, he's got the pecs, he's got the whole shebang. William H. Macy, as detective Mooney, is terrific, as usual.

Cellular only generates believability when Macy is on screen, which is just not often enough. If only the script had called for William H. Macy's character to pick up the call initially, we might have had a superior entertainment, but teenage girls undoubtedly would have stayed away in droves. Acting skills are one thing and box office is something else, and Macy's pectorals just aren't in the same league as Evans's.

Ryan, the character Chris Evans portrays, sure is a helluva driver. He must have a PhD in stunt driving, not to mention three or four St Christopher medals on his dashboard. In real life, do you know how long it would take before you were involved in a massive and fatal car crash if you drove the wrong way at high speeds on an L.A. freeway? About ten seconds. Oh, Ryan does *cause* several accidents, but the plot doesn't dwell on that. Why should it? Who cares about innocent bystanders? It's Jessica we're worried about, dammit! Ryan also manages to back out of a tunnel during rush hour and survive. I sometimes almost get totalled just backing out of my driveway!

I am now going to shock you by saying that *Cellular* is actually fairly entertaining, in its own unbelievably idiotic way. Once you stop tripping over the plot holes, things go pretty well. Kim Basinger, although awkward and self-conscious in certain scenes, does an OK job as the freaked-out but ultimately resourceful mom, and, as I mentioned, William H. Macy is always worth watching.

Here's a suggestion for the next time you are driving and almost get sideswiped by someone who is speeding while talking on a cell phone: don't get angry; relax, take a deep breath, give him (or her) a big thumbs up, and enjoy the warm, fuzzy feeling that will wash over you as you contemplate the possibility that you may just have helped to save a kidnap victim.

10

Chicken Run

To give you an idea of just how beloved Nick Park's animation really is, consider the following true story: in 1998, while he was flying home to England, the Wallace and Gromit figures he uses to make the cartoons were stolen from his luggage. Upon arriving home, he and some staff went about distributing "missing" posters showing the two characters. The posters gave notice that if the figures were not returned there would be no more *Wallace and Gromit* cartoons, ever. Two days later the stolen figures were left on Park's front doorstep.

Let's go behind closed doors now as Nick Park pitches his concept for *Chicken Run* to the assembled Dreamworks executives:

Park: Think of *Stalag 17* and *Hogan's Heroes* but with chickens! It will be very British, and it will be set in the fifties in a Yorkshire chicken farm, which will look just like a POW camp. The eventual liberator will be an American Rhode Island Red rooster named Rocky! We could get Mel Gibson to voice him.

Dreamworks executive (*wild-eyed*): Gibson? If you're gonna call the rooster Rocky, why not get the real thing? (*pointing to an assistant*) Get me Stallone on the phone! We can get him cheap, he needs the work! (*looking back at Park*) I don't know about Yorkshire, I've never heard of it. We could set the story in Philly! Do they have chicken farms in Philly? What about making it a prison for hard-boiled criminals ... Hard-boiled! Hey, now that's funny! And we could have a sadistic warden, kind of a cross between Darth Vader and Colonel Sanders. I like this. Keep talking, Nicky!

Park (*looking pale, glancing suddenly at his watch*): I forgot, I have to catch a plane back to England. Sorry. Really gotta run!

You might be forgiven for thinking that my scenario is a caricature, but you can bet that many creative people have seen their ideas hijacked and mangled by short-sighted, empty-headed executives. Luckily for us, on the strength of Nick Park's track record with his wonderful *Wallace and Gromit* shorts (which won him two Oscars), the good folks at Dreamworks were smart enough to trust his creative vision.

And what a vision it is!

What's next, I wonder? The possibilities are fantastic. Imagine remakes of every kind of genre picture, only featuring claymation chickens ... you could do a ghost story about the spirits of dead chickens haunting a Kentucky Fried Chicken restaurant and call it *Poultrygeist*, or maybe a sci-fi thriller called *Eggsistenz* ...

As the story begins, Ginger, our heroine, a particularly bright hen, is masterminding an escape attempt. Like her previous plans, this one will be thwarted by the watchman, Mr Tweedy, and his snarling Dobermans. This is Ginger's third escape attempt, and she is rewarded for her efforts by a three-day stay in solitary confinement. Not all of the chickens are as bright as Ginger, and some of them just don't quite get the drift. When Ginger emerges from the hole, one particularly dim fowl asks her, "Been on holidays, then?"

As in all escape films, there is also a brilliant, nerdy character; this one designs outlandish contraptions. And those familiar with *Wallace and Gromit* know that Park has a thing for outlandish contraptions. *Chicken Run* features some truly bizarre inventions, cooked up — I was tempted to say hatched — in the brilliant chicken mind of Bunty, a Nobel-calibre inventor who wears thick glasses and speaks with an even thicker Scottish brogue, courtesy of the great Imelda Staunton. The contraptions alone are enough to sustain my interest. Other memorable characters include Mr Tweedy, the watchman. Really not so terrible, he's actually just the long-suffering — I was tempted to say henpecked — husband of the *truly* terrible Mrs Tweedy, who is perfectly voiced by Miranda Richardson. We've all run afoul (I can't stop!) of a Mrs Tweedy in our younger lives, I think. You know, forty-something and formidable, dry as a cactus and almost as cuddly, the archetype of the crusty, unpleasant, hard-as-nails female bully.

> **Autobiographical interlude:**
> The character of Mrs Tweedy bears a striking resemblance to my grade school principal (God rest her soul), one of the most truly frightening people I've ever come across in my life. As I was watching this movie, my mind ran back to my days as a bright but frightened nine-year-old, those days when getting called to the principal's office might get you several hard whacks on the back of the hands with the large leather strap that Mrs C. kept in her desk. Notice I'm calling her only "Mrs C." She may be dead, but I'm still intimidated! Perhaps Nick Park also had a school principal like her. After all, I'm the same age as Park, and there may have been a lot of sadistic warden/punishers of this kind in charge of early-sixties grade schools.

A word of warning here. Although this movie is suitable for the entire family, a few scenes are rather intense and could frighten very young children. I'm referring, for instance, to the scene in which poor Agnes Chicken, or whatever her name is, is sent to the chopping block for not laying enough eggs. I could see a very sensitive four-year-old taking this rather badly. Heck, I almost choked up myself. Although Agnes is not one of the featured chickens, I still felt as if I knew her somehow. I mean, I didn't feel nearly as badly as I did when Geneviève Bujold as Anne Boleyn got sent to the chopping block for not dissimilar reasons in *Anne of the Thousand Days*, but still, I did feel a twinge of sorrow, albeit in a surreal, claymation sort of way.

Don't laugh, I'm serious.

Sure, okay, I've been watching too many movies, but I'm *still* serious.

Anyway, no wonder the poor chickens want to escape. They're trapped on this farm, they have to lay eggs, which are taken away from them as soon as they are laid, and if they don't lay enough they get their heads chopped off and wind up on the Tweedy dinner table. Can you blame Ginger for dreaming of a better place — a place where there are no fences, and no Mrs Tweedys, where you can feel the sunshine on your beak (!) and the grass beneath your claws, and no one's ever heard of BBQ?

To make an already terrible situation worse, Mrs Tweedy now has a devilish new idea that will turn her chicken farm into a real money-maker. She's bought a huge machine — a gigantic contraption that turns chickens into *(imagine a maniacal laugh here) ... chicken pies.* You put the chicken in one end and a pie comes out the other.

Things are looking decidedly bleak for Ginger and the girls.

Enter Rocky, a Rhode Island Red ("Just call me Rocky Rhodes") who has escaped from a circus, where he was featured as the flying rooster. In truth of course he was just shot out of a cannon, but our desperate chickens don't know that chickens can't fly — unless of course they have friends at British Airways. So Ginger gets Rocky to agree to a deal: if the chickens hide him, he'll teach them to fly so that they can escape.

Far from being a saviour, Rocky is just a shameless opportunist, and his good looks and movie-star demeanour quickly have all the hens swooning.

Do hens swoon, you're wondering? You bet.

The scenes in which Rocky attempts to teach the hens to fly are particularly inspired, with lots of flying feathers, loud, panicked squawking, and hilarious crash landings. But will Rocky actually be of any use to our heroines? Will Ginger and the gang escape? Will Ginger and Rocky eventually find love? Will everyone just end up in Mrs Tweedy's pies?

Chicken Run is a great movie. The truly great animated films are those that celebrate humanity by allowing us to see ourselves (with all of our hopes, our fears, and our aspirations) in totally outlandish characters.

I don't like to throw the term "genius" around too liberally, but anyone who can draw us into a world he has created out of clay and make us think that we are only laughing at clay caricatures, while all the while we are actually laughing at ourselves, certainly deserves the title.

11

Childstar

A lot of jokes were made about CBC television's *The Greatest Canadian* contest. After the program had droned on for many weeks, hockey-starved viewers eventually elected Tommy Douglas. While certainly not a bad choice, it was debatable whether he (or anyone else for that matter) deserved the title of The Greatest. Certainly Wayne Gretzky fans felt that any such title was nothing short of a copyright infringement. Still, as gimmicky and tailor-made to boost ratings as the contest was, it wasn't completely without merit. The process was severely flawed, however, because no women were named to the top ten. I can think of several meritorious females who would not have been out of place near, or at, the top, such as Justice Louise Arbour, astronaut Roberta Bondar, Auditor General Sheila Fraser; and I'm only up to the letter "F." What does CBC stand for anyway, Canadian Boys' Club?

Another question that begs to be posed is "Where were the filmmakers?" Although there were actors in the top one hundred — comics, mostly, with Mike Myers at number twenty, and Jim Carrey and Michael J. Fox in the middle of the pack — I have to ask, where were the directors? Doesn't anyone know how hard it is to get a movie made in Canada? Never mind getting it made, then you face the daunting tasks of getting anybody to distribute it and getting people to see it. Fact is, Canadian directors have to work their little beaver tails off to make maybe one movie every three or four years, if they're lucky. Don McKellar, who has been involved in numerous excellent films over the past ten years, certainly deserved a mention.

Of course, these "Greatest This" and "Greatest That" contests are always highly suspect unless you ask a question that has no possible ambiguity, like "What was the greatest rock band of all time?" Most people would answer the Beatles, and they would be right. Among their many outstanding accomplishments we could mention the unprecedented — and never-to-be-duplicated — dominance of the pop charts on April 4, 1964, when the Fabs occupied the top five positions on the singles chart. For any kids who may be reading this and wondering "What the heck was a single?" allow me to explain that a single was an unmarried song on a seven-inch piece of vinyl. When the singles got together on a twelve-inch piece of vinyl, they had a party and called themselves an LP.

Now, I realize that some people would say that the greatest rock band of all time is the Rolling Stones, if for no other reason than their amazing longevity. The flipside of that argument is that it's easy to have longevity when you've been soaking in Jack Daniels for thirty years. It preserves you, but look what it does to your skin.

Sorry, Keith.

Also, if you ever sat through *Rolling Stones at the Max*, then you can never erase from your memory banks the truly frightening experience of seeing a close-up of Mick Jagger in Imax.

But back to Don McKellar. At the 1998 Toronto Film Festival, Don McKellar was represented as a director, a writer, and an actor in no less than six films. Among others, he wrote, directed, and starred in *Last Night*, he starred in David Cronenberg's *Existenz*, and he wrote and starred in *Le Violon Rouge* (*The Red Violin*). Past successes include writing *Thirty-Two Short Films About Glenn Gould* — which was actually parodied in *The Simpsons*! Many will recall the *Simpsons* episode called *Thirty-Two Short Films About Springfield*. This supports my point about McKellar's being a prime candidate for greatest Canadian; in Canada, you aren't really famous unless our American neighbours pay attention to you. Not to diminish his accomplishments, but Tommy Douglas was never on *The Simpsons*.

Childstar features McKellar as Rick, a Canadian director of art films who can't find funding for his projects. Desperate for any kind of revenue, he takes a job as a driver for an American production company shooting a big-budget blockbuster in Toronto. The star of the movie is a twelve-year-old spoiled brat named Taylor Brandon Burns. McKellar says he was inspired to write this movie after meeting real-life child star Haley Joel Osment at the Oscars. This Oscar trip scores additional points for McKellar in the Great Canadian contest, I think, pretty well leaving old Tommy D. in the dust. How can you be the Greatest Canadian if you've never been to the Oscars?

In *Childstar*, the fictitious movie being shot in Canada is called *The First Son*. The plot of this effects-heavy, mind-numbing flagwaver has the President of the United States being kidnapped by terrorists and eventually being rescued by his twelve-year-old son, who quickly takes charge of the army (!) and winds up saving the Free World as we know it, along with dear old Dad.

So our hero Rick has landed the job of driving around the bratty child star and his mom, an over-the-top stage mom from hell portrayed with great panache by Jennifer Jason Leigh. Pretty soon, Rick is having a steamy affair with the mom, and through an unlikely set of circumstances even becomes the kid star's legal guardian. Then the popcorn hits the ventilation device as our child star decides that he's had enough and goes AWOL in the company of a nineteen-year-old Canadian actress/model/working girl (Kristin Adams). Production on *The First Son* rapidly grinds to a halt, and Rick is delegated to find the kid and get him back on the set. Rick also has to deal with the kid's talent agency, portrayed as a cross between the CIA and the Mob.

Thankfully, this movie is a lot better than my plot synopsis. It is a treat for Canadian nationalists/film buffs — filled with sly and sometimes just plain nasty lampoons of the American movie business, as well as acerbic comments concerning the strained relationship between Americans and Canadians. McKellar has proven in the past that he is particularly adept at throwing sharp little darts right at the heart of Canadian hypocrisy, and in *Childstar* he paints a portrait of a Canadian director who, for all his sincere artistic aspirations, is more than willing to completely compromise his ideals in exchange for a chance to get a foot in the door in Hollywood. Is this in any way an autobiographical statement? As I watched Rick transform himself into a shameless Hollywood wannabe I wondered if McKellar was satirically bemoaning the situation, or slyly advertising his own services south of the border.

One particularly sharp scene has twelve-year-old star Taylor take his date — actually a young woman someone has paid to be with him — on a late-night tour of his movie set. As they walk around the set, which looks exactly like the White House, he suggests different rooms where they could "do it." What about the Lincoln Library? he asks, or maybe the Oval Office? The girl looks at him and says, "Hey, whatever. It's your fantasy. I'm Canadian."

That's not only a good joke, it's also a timely warning to Canadians everywhere. Be careful, Canada: if we rely on Hollywood to churn out all our cinematic fantasies, our collective cultural imagination will wither from neglect, and our heads will become full of Yankee dreams and aspirations.

That's been happening for some time now, hasn't it?

Childstar also comments insightfully about the dangers of achieving stardom too young. Both Americans and Canadians seem to have an ever-growing appetite for young stars — or is that an appetite for ever-younger stars? We only have to look at Jacko's Neverland life and topsy-turvy universe to know that fame, when achieved at a very young age, can lead to total disorientation, if not disaster. The points that McKellar drives home in *Childstar* — that cultural sovereignty is a fragile thing, that parents should not seek fame for their children, that celebrity both corrupts and stifles personal growth — may be obvious ones, but I believe they are worth repeating. Unfortunately, most of us up here don't seem to really be paying any attention. Woe Canada.

12

City of God

What distinguishes a hyper-realistic fiction film like Fernando Meirelles's *City of God* (2002) from a documentary?

Both seek to arrive at the "truth" about a subject, but they take very different roads to get there. A documentary, by definition, is supposed to be a snapshot of the "real." For example, *Harlan County, U.S.A.* (1976) presents itself as a realistic portrait of a violent coal miners' strike in Kentucky. The filmmaker, Barbara Kopple, strives only to present the facts as she sees them. However, she cannot avoid being selective, and therefore subjective, in her choice of images and her editorial slant; she clearly supports the miners. This does not make *Harlan County, U.S.A.* a bad documentary, it simply underlines the fact that movies are made by people with opinions, and despite loud proclamations of journalistic objectivity, the filmmaker's opinion can usually be inferred. I wouldn't want it any other way. Anyone who believes in the objectivity of journalism is I believe living under the spell of a seductive illusion.

Some documentaries are actually boldly manipulative. I loved *Bowling for Columbine*, and I have great respect for Michael Moore, but he is more a propaganda artist than a documentarist. His films are applauded by some and vilified by others, depending on whether or not the viewer happens to subscribe to his version of reality. *Bowling for Columbine* is much closer to pure propaganda than is *Harlan County,*

U.S.A., but in each case, the filmmaker has a strong point of view. *Harlan County, U.S.A.* may *seem* more objective than the other, but it has also been shaped and edited according to the perspective — and the belief system — of the director.

City of God is a fiction film based on a novel, but it is a film that seems at once both totally realistic and highly stylized. The narrative structure is unorthodox (chronological time is not respected); the use of camera angles and visual effects is extremely dynamic; the editing creates an exhilarating nervous, kinetic energy. In no way does it present itself as documentary, it is obviously a finely calculated piece of fiction, but the performances — almost all of them by real street kids and other non-professional actors — are so perfect, the artistry so invisible, that you are completely swept up in the "reality" of it.

City of God is co-produced by Walter Salles, who directed a magnificent film called *Central Station* in 1998. Both of these films feature performances of seamless realism. By that I mean that all of the actors who appear on screen, both professional and amateur, give performances that seem to transcend artifice; they seem absolutely real, or as real as possible given the intrinsically artificial nature of film. Life sometimes imitates art, but there is a place where life and art intersect so seamlessly that the difference is not only impossible to detect, it is inconsequential. *City of God* seems so perfectly real that it transcends "art" as that term is widely understood. Not simply entertainment in the traditional sense, it is a riveting, profoundly human, totally unforgettable film experience.

> Brazilian reality has surpassed most attempts to portray it in fiction; the acceleration of social decomposition has transformed violence into a banality. — *Walter Salles*

City of God is based on the novel *Cidade de Deus*, by Paolo Lins. The author researched his subject for eight years, conducting interviews and investigating the drug trade in the housing projects, or *favelas*, in and around Rio de Janeiro. The housing project where Lins spent most of his time, Cidade de Deus, had been built with the specific aim of isolating the poor from the richer "tourist-friendly" areas of Rio. Lins wrote most of his book while living through a drug turf war that spanned the seventies and eighties. He experienced first-hand that period's violence, desperation, and death. The novel became a best-seller, and eventually made its way into the hands of director Fernando Meirelles, who was then living in Sao Paulo. Meirelles had read articles about the terrible living conditions in the *favelas* and about the violent drug culture, but he was unprepared for the impact the story had on him. By the time he finished reading it, he had sketched the outline of a screenplay that was to become *City of God*.

Most of the characters are portrayed by kids from a variety of backgrounds who were assembled at a series of workshops involving weeks of improvisation. Many of the kids — who are between five and nineteen years old — really are street kids. The movie was shot in various slums, not on movie sets. The producers often had to obtain permission from the drug lords before being allowed to film in these slums. Meirelles deserves some kind of award just for being able to pull off the logistics of this film. The making of *City of God*, which would be a riveting story all by itself, had profound consequences for many of the young actors. The experience of being in a film helped some of them turn their lives around. Alexandre Rodrigues, who portrays "Rocket," the narrator, left the slums where he had lived and went to work doing computer graphics for Meirelles's production company.

In *City of God*, eighteen-year-old Rocket has managed to stay out of the drug trade — although many of his friends are deeply involved — by nurturing a passion for photography. He finds it difficult to stay focused on his passion, however, because in the City of God guns are much more plentiful (and easier to obtain) than cameras. When the film begins, Rocket is caught between a heavily armed gang on one side and heavily armed police on the other. How did he get there? Will he escape? The story is told in flashback, with Rocket narrating, explaining how life evolved in the City of God, where everyone, including very young children, seems to own a gun. Adults with guns are bad enough, but when young children are involved, situations rapidly spiral out of control, often with tragic results. For all kinds of childish reasons, kids pull guns on other kids and blast away, the way kids in Canada throw snowballs. It is altogether amazing that any of these kids survive past adolescence. Of course, many do not.

Meirelles presents a nightmarish vision of poverty, of people living in constant fear, of children growing up in slums where death lurks around every corner. *City of God* explores the rise and fall of various small-time drug kings, who rule their neighborhoods with iron fists. At first, in the sixties, the drug lords fight it out for control of the marijuana trade, but then, in the seventies, cocaine becomes big business, bringing increased levels of violence and paranoia. The tight script crisply weaves various stories together: one young man becomes a big shot only to die a violent death; another escapes; Rocket, our hero, acquires a camera and starts freelancing for a newspaper, getting exclusive photos of the gangs, because he is well connected, and because he is the only one who is not afraid to enter the projects at night.

What is profoundly disturbing about this story is that so many of the violent acts — of murder even — are committed by children. And everyone behaves as if this was the most natural thing in the world.

When kids grow up almost totally devoid of hope, in a society in which unemployment is a staggering eighty percent; when extreme poverty exists side by side with the exciting allure of the big money generated by drug dealing, how could it be otherwise? Think about this: when the only legitimate job you can get is at the grocery store, and for minimum wage; when you see your friends buying new cars; when your role models are older gangsters who have gold chains around their necks and sexy girls wrapped around their fingers; when ignorance and brutality rule — what can be expected?

City of God doesn't sermonize, it doesn't pass judgment, it observes, records, testifies. It's a tough, uncompromising film, but one that does offer a faint glimmer of hope, and much food for reflection.

We tell our children that violence is not the answer. Every day we tell them that violence doesn't make the world a better place, and we believe that with all our hearts, don't we? Yet our institutions deliver terribly mixed signals. We have become experts at Orwellian double-talk. I read in the paper today that George Bush believes that a war in Iraq is going to make the world a better place and that his wish is to save the people of Iraq from Saddam. What he fails to emphasize is that a great number of innocent Iraqis — including many children — are going to have to die in order to be "saved."

13

Confessions of a Dangerous Mind

Back in the seventies my family used to watch *The Gong Show*. *The Gong Show* was the creation of Chuck Barris, who also hosted the program. He had previously given the world *The Dating Game* and *The Newlywed Game*.

At my house, we thought that *The Gong Show* was pretty funny. Even back then, before reality television, there was something perversely irresistible about watching people humiliate themselves to achieve their fifteen seconds of fame. Before *The Gong Show*, you were pretty much limited to watching live sporting events, the Miss America Pageant, or political debates if you wanted to see people humiliate themselves.

By 1976, when it debuted, *The Gong Show* was the only place where you could see people like Arte Johnson and Jaye P. Morgan.

Remember Jaye P. Morgan?

I always wondered what kind of "celebrity" she was. I had never heard of her before *The Gong Show*. Even my *parents*, for God's sake, had never heard of her. What had she done to deserve being trusted with the sacred gong? Many years later, when the Internet came into being, I discovered that she had been quite popular on television in the fifties, and had once even had a hit song, "Life Is Just a Bowl of Cherries," which she sang accompanied by the Frank

Devol Orchestra. Are you stunned? Isn't the Internet truly a wonderful thing?

Phyllis Diller was also a regular on the show. My parents thought Phyllis Diller was a scream. My mother couldn't believe that a woman would dare be seen at the supermarket, let alone on *television*, with a hairdo as messed up as that.

The Gong Show ran from 1976 to 1980 and became a cultural phenomenon. Snooty television critics and sociologists and a bunch of other people with PhDs and no sense of humour began to declare in all seriousness that *The Gong Show* marked the decline of Western civilization. Don't you love it when sociologists get their skivvies in a knot about television programs?

Today, *The Gong Show* seems almost quaint. Television has reached heights of embarrassment, sleaze, and schlock undreamed of in the seventies. In the seventies, we could never have imagined shows like *Geraldo*, or *Dr. Phil*, in which "ordinary" people talk about things like "My mom sleeps with my boyfriend."

Chuck Barris was a kind of visionary. He truly understood before anyone else to what depths people would gleefully sink just to get on television. *Confessions of a Dangerous Mind* is based on his autobiography, and marks actor George Clooney's directorial debut. The screenplay is by Charlie Kaufman (*Being John Malkovich*, *Adaptation*).

Confessions of a Dangerous Mind, the "unauthorized autobiography" (whatever that means) of Chuck Barris, is bizarre, to say the least. As if it wasn't bizarre enough to have created *The Gong Show*, Barris also claims in his book that he was a hit man for the CIA. He says that he was recruited and trained in the sixties, and was for decades involved in covert operations, in the course of which he claims to have killed thirty-three enemies of the United States.

MOVIES ATE MY BRAIN

Well, who knows? It *might* be true. Stranger things have undoubtedly happened.

A friend once told me that he had overheard a conversation in a pub in London about how, during Yasser Arafat's visit to London in 1999, Ringo Starr had been persuaded to impersonate the Palestinian leader by PLO operatives posing as producers for a BBC television comedy series. It seems that the PLO had received intelligence about the threat of an assassination, which was to take place during a tour of Covent Garden. Ever the good sport, Ringo agreed to pose as Arafat for the afternoon, having been led to believe that it was all just part of an elaborate practical joke being played on Prime Minister Tony Blair. The ex-Beatle didn't have to speak, only wave to the crowds and smile at the photographers, and no one would be the wiser. Still, the subterfuge was almost exposed when, as he stared at the Royal Opera House and forgot himself for a moment, "Mr Arafat" muttered, "I don't think I've been here since Paul and I dropped acid in '66."

Charlie Kaufman's screenplay treats Barris's CIA tale as if it were true, and, in a twisted way, the whole story seems to fit.

Think about it: didn't you ever wonder why the couples who won trips on *The Dating Game* went to such bizarre destinations? You might remember that the lucky contestants were accompanied by a chaperone — often Barris himself — and they went to very ... unusual destinations, such as Helsinki and West Berlin. Don't get me wrong, there's nothing *intrinsically* weird about Helsinki or West Berlin, but all of the other game shows that gave away trips sent the happy couples to places like Puerta Vallarta or Acapulco. Barris claimed in his book that the reason he arranged for the contestants to win trips to places like Helsinki was that he had received orders to travel to such places to kill foreign operatives — and there are really no dangerous foreign operatives in Acapulco.

If you remember *The Gong Show*, then you will of course remember the Unknown Comic. This guy used to come on the show wearing a paper bag over his head with two holes cut out for the eyes, and he'd tell terrible jokes: "Hey Chucky, Chucky! My first job was working in an orange juice factory, but I got canned because I couldn't concentrate. Ha, ha!"

GONG!

In real life, the Unknown Comic was Murray Langston. Langston once owned the cabaret restaurant where David Letterman got his start as a stand-up comic. When casting for *Confessions* began, a lot of actors expressed interest in landing the role of the Unknown Comic. It was reported that both Brad Pitt and Samuel L. Jackson enquired about the role, which eventually went to Halifax native Joe Cobden. It has also been rumoured that Cobden was once approached by the Conservative party to run as a candidate in Nova Scotia, but that he was discarded when he insisted that he would only run for the Conservatives if he was allowed to wear a bag over his head.

Woven into the wildly improbable narrative of *Confessions* are real interviews with people who knew Barris. They share their opinions about the kind of person he was, and speculate on whether or not his CIA ramblings were true. Even Jaye P. Morgan shows up, talking about how much fun "Chucky" really was. These real-life interviews give the movie a fascinating multi-layered narrative texture that keeps the audience off balance.

Sam Rockwell gives an excellent performance as Barris, portraying him from his young hotshot days to his demented, paranoid, "Howard Hughes" period. Drew Barrymore plays his long-suffering girlfriend, and does a fine job projecting an at times lovable naïveté and a mounting exasperation. George Clooney also directs himself, in an understated, deadpan performance as Barris's CIA contact. Julia Roberts, as a spy who has a fleeting affair with Barris, gives a performance so opaque that I can't really tell if she is any good or not. She does all of the usual things that actors do — she moves, she speaks her lines — but her "performance" seems to be the weird product of some kind of off-screen remote control device.

Confessions of a Dangerous Mind moves along nicely, and shifts gears smoothly from humour to drama. Above all, it is surreal. Clooney obviously took some notes while working on *O Brother, Where Art Thou? Confessions* is definitely permeated by a Coen brothers atmosphere. As a first-time director, Clooney seems a bit like a kid in a candy store, using a lot of flamboyant techniques, such as saturated or washed-out colour and strange camera angles ... He doesn't seem to have developed his own style yet, but he has tons of enthusiasm behind the camera, a good script to work with, and a great performance from Rockwell. Look for Brad Pitt and Matt Damon in a cameo as two bachelors on *The Dating Game*.

Confessions of a Dangerous Mind is a lot of fun. Maybe it's because I grew up in the seventies, but watching this almost made me nostalgic for shag carpets and corduroy bell-bottoms.

Almost.

14

The Day After Tomorrow

On the day after tomorrow, the build-up of greenhouse gases suddenly melts the polar ice cap. The Gulf Stream is inundated with fresh water, causing it not only to slow down but to *reverse direction* (!). This triggers a new ice age, plunging the northern hemisphere into a permanent deep freeze. The whole frozen mess is directed by Roland Emmerich, who gave us *Independence Day* and the 1998 remake of *Godzilla*.

I guess it was inevitable that after presenting Aliens blowing up the White House and a giant mutated lizard stomping on New York, Emmerich would have Mother Nature herself beat the frozen custard out of us filthy, polluting humans.

Emmerich's movies are top-heavy with special effects, and pretty much brain-dead when it comes to script and character development. What makes this one a little more interesting is that it possesses some socio-political resonance. In light of the Bush administration's recent refusal to ratify the Kyoto accord on greenhouse gas emissions, the premise of the film has become particularly timely.

Kenneth Welsh, who portrays Vice-President Becker, is an Alberta-born actor who has carved out a niche portraying American politicians. He previously played James Baker in a made-for-TV movie called *The Day Reagan Was Shot*. He bears a striking resemblance to Dick Cheney, the actual

Vice-President. This is inspired casting, considering that the script features Vice-President Becker spouting lines like "The economy can't afford to worry about the so-called greenhouse effect," or participating in the following exchange with climatologist-hero Jack Hall:

> Jack Hall: Our climate is fragile. The ice caps are disappearing at a dangerous rate.
> Vice-President Becker: Our economy is every bit as fragile as the environment. Perhaps you should keep that in mind before making sensationalist claims.
> Jack Hall: The last chunk of ice that broke off was the size of Rhode Island. A lot of folks would say that was pretty sensational.

Yes, our movie Vice-President sounds a lot like the real Vice-President, who often sounds like a first-year science dropout. This character's raison d'être is to coax the maximum amount of hisses and boos from every Democrat — and probably every Canadian — in the audience. He's the politician we love to hate.

I've often wondered why we don't make our own, Canadian-style disaster movies — and no, the John Candy vehicle *Canadian Bacon* doesn't count, that's not the kind of disaster I mean. We could have *The Day It Snowed Really a Whole Lot in Toronto*, or how about *The Day of the Conservative Landslide* (that's a scary one!), or *Night of the Living Day*, about the return of Stockwell Day from the political dead? Lord knows we've had lots of horrific or potentially horrific events up here. It's not all tulips and poutine in the Great White North, eh?

The Day After Tomorrow features some excellent special effects. It also features a scientifically silly script that lamely tries to make a serious point about the consequences of ignoring global warming. But if the script is cartoonish in its ramifications, the idea at the heart of the story is a valid and timely one. After witnessing the horrific impact of hurricane Katrina, it's hard to dismiss the relation between the growing frequency and intensity of hurricanes and the rising temperature of the oceans. The scientific data seem loud and clear. Unfortunately, political expediency and corporate profit motives are powerful forces. *The Day After Tomorrow* presents a gravely serious problem, but its Hollywood sensibilities — its concern for the box office — guarantee that the audience will take home nothing of substance. Its heart is in the right place, but its brain is missing in action.

The movie features Dennis Quaid as a paleoclimatologist, someone who studies what the weather was like back in prehistoric times. We are also unfortunately subjected to a teenage romance sub-plot that had even the teenagers in the audience giggling in the wrong places. The proverbial icing on the cake comes in the form of more disaster movie clichés than you can shake a barometer at.

Ian Holm, a great actor, shows up as a kindly and wise Scottish climatologist named Dr Rapson, but, unfortunately for the audience — not to mention the Scottish people — dear auld Scotland goes under the big snowdrift pretty early in the proceedings, and his screen time is limited.

This type of film can almost sink or swim (or freeze!) on its special effects, which, as I've already mentioned, are excellent. In the end, however, it all depends on how much pure enjoyment the viewer can derive from watching New York City get flooded, and then frozen solid. Speaking as a Boston Red Sox fan, I would say that there is definitely some enjoyment to be derived from such a scenario. I was fairly thrilled that Yankee Stadium was under seventy-five feet of solid ice. I didn't even dwell on the fact that Boston was probably in the same condition. We don't know for certain, however, because the conditions in Boston are never described. This omission is probably for the best, since New England audiences in general, and Red Sox fans in particular, are neurotic enough as it is. After all, we never really recovered from the horrific news that Ted Williams's head had been cryogenically frozen. I believe that Sox fans might suffer a complete mental collapse if a movie were ever to show Fenway Park under solid ice.

When the climate starts going screwy, we are treated to snowstorms in New Delhi, a devastating hailstorm that flattens Tokyo (what is it with Tokyo getting flattened all the time, anyway?), and even the British royal family coming under attack. The royals are killed when the three helicopters flying them to the cozy confines of Balmoral Castle in Scotland crash after a massive drop in temperature suddenly freezes up their rotors. Exactly why the royals would think they could escape bad weather by flying to Scotland remains unclear. I'm also not sure why the royal family needs three helicopters — perhaps the Queen's corgis have their own.

As things go from bad to worse, Los Angeles is destroyed by massive tornadoes. The Hollywood sign is shredded, and the Capitol Records building flies apart. We don't know whether the Dodgers were in town at the time, but hopefully Eric Gagné got out and is safe in the Bahamas. Early on there is also a news report about terribly frigid temperatures in Canada, but no one seems to pay any attention to it. We do see some archival footage of crashing waves in Nova Scotia, but after that Canada is never mentioned again. One can only assume that Canada also received seventy-five feet of snow and that the temperature plummeted to minus 100, but what else is new? Given that these events are taking place in July, it's possible that the Stanley Cup playoffs are still on, and nobody has noticed it's snowing.

If you are addicted to disaster movies, you might well gobble this up. But if you're a real student, a connoisseur of the genre, you know that the best disaster movies don't rely on special effects. The best disaster/end-of-the-world movies rely on well-developed, believable characters and literate scripts. If you want to experience a true gem of the genre, try *The Day the Earth Caught Fire*, a 1961 production from the UK directed by Val Guest. It is a gourmet disaster movie, one in which you believe what is happening, and you care about the characters. *The Day After Tomorrow* is not gourmet, it's more like a popsicle.

As uneven as it is, it does benefit from the presence of Dennis Quaid. He turns in his usual solid performance. His portrayal of a valiant dad struggling to make his way to frozen New York by snowshoe in order to save his teenage son and some friends who are holed up in the New York Public Library is almost inspiring.

A subplot that involves three young men venturing outside the Library to scrounge for medicine and food hits a 10 on the silly scale. These are supposed to be science students. The way they behave outside, it's a miracle they survive for more than five minutes. What *are* they teaching in science these days? For example, to better grip a frozen door one of the characters does what everybody knows you should do when it's bitterly freezing cold and you are trying to get a better grip on a metal door handle: he removes his mitten (!). I guess this is taking place in a parallel universe, because, impossibly, his hand doesn't stick to the metal. Will wonders ever cease? Looking for food and medicine, our clueless heroes climb aboard a Russian cargo ship that floated down Fifth Avenue on the tidal wave but is now frozen solid in the middle of the street. They are then set upon by a pack of wolves that have escaped from the New York Zoo.

This is known as sub-plot overkill.

It's not dramatic enough that the world is turning into a frozen snowball and that they are starving, our heroes have to be menaced by wolves. And it's not enough for the wolves to be just run-of-the-mill snarling, famished wolves; the special effects department has them looking so absurdly muscular that I began to wonder if they hadn't escaped from the same secret laboratory that developed José Canseco and Mark McGwire. Forget lean and mean, even their *fur* has muscles.

To make a long, cold story short, Jack does make it to the Library to save his son and his friends. But by the time the weather has calmed down, half the world has been destroyed. Vice-President Becker has become president by default and, in a nice ironic touch, the few surviving Americans are trying to cross the border illegally into Mexico.

The new president addresses the nation on the now number one-rated television channel in the world, the Weather Channel (which I guess is broadcasting from Guadalajara), and he proceeds, in a gentle voice and with a tear in his eye, to apologize for being a pig-headed moron.

Hold the phone!

Even in a suspend-your-disbelief-from-the-highest-rafters sci-fi clunker like this one, the idea that a politician could — even after his imbecility has almost destroyed the world — ever admit that he has been behaving like a pig-headed moron is beyond incredible. I almost passed out from the sheer gargantuan absurdity of the concept.

If you have to see this, wear a tuque. Your brain might catch its death.

15

Dogtown and Z-Boys

Beware of any film review that begins with the phrase "when I was a kid." The ensuing review usually gives you more information about the film reviewer than about the movie being reviewed …

When I was a kid, some friends of my parents moved to California.

California seemed like a very long way from Hull, Quebec — in my imagination California kids all had blond hair and great tans and wore those Mickey Mouse Club hats with the ears.

In 1967, when I was nine years old, these family friends sent me a weird contraption as a gift. A thick piece of varnished hardwood about eighteen inches long, it had four metal wheels bolted underneath and a really cool drawing of a shark on top. I was told that it was a "skurfboard" — a cross between roller skates and a surfboard. Pretty soon this thing became my favourite toy, and my friends and I would take turns riding it down the street. Once you got rolling on pavement, the metal wheels would send crazy vibrations up your legs, and soon your feet and then your ankles would start to get numb, and pretty soon you'd have to jump off, because you couldn't feel your feet anymore.

Rolling over a pebble or a small rock was potentially catastrophic. If this pebble or small rock got jammed in a wheel, the board would just stop ... but for a few seconds I would keep moving. Flying, actually ... This scene was repeated countless times all across North America, with thousands of kids becoming unwitting acrobats, and leaving most of their knees and elbows on the pavement. This was bad news for kids, but it was a windfall for the company that made that red antiseptic stuff that every mom reached for when kid and pavement made contact. Imagine the sales figures for Mercurochrome after skateboards became popular. The mind boggles. Forget those fantasies about what would have happened if you had bought IBM at $3.00 a share. If you had put your money into Mercurochrome in the early sixties, you'd have been able to spend the last twenty-five years enjoying your beachfront property in Saint-Tropez.

I was once told that the same people who owned controlling shares in Mercurochrome had very early on invested heavily in one of the biggest skateboard factories. Urban legend, or sinister conspiracy?

Skateboarding is now a gazillion-dollar industry, and the boards are lighter and wider and very hi-tech, and they have polyethylene wheels for a smooth ride with no vibration, and they have cool designs that the kids love, and, best of all — for the companies that make them, that is — they are expensive. And the buck doesn't stop there, because you have to buy the culture that goes with it. You need the clothes and the T-shirts and the shoes and the helmet and the pants and the DVDs and the magazines. Whew! All of a sudden, I'm feeling a little light-headed — in the wallet. Beware of what happens when the old marketing machine gets in bed with good old fashioned capitalism. Throw in a bit of greed, some zesty profit motive, and multi-million dollar marketing campaigns, and abracadabra! Mom and Dad's money just disappeared.

In the old days, skateboards were just a fun thing that some kids in California invented. You know: grab a piece of wood and bolt on some wheels and pretend you're surfing — city-surfing. But it evolved from that. Skateboarding became really popular for a while back in the sixties, but then it kind of fell off the radar until a bunch of guys reinvented the whole thing in the early seventies in a rundown neighbourhood around Santa Monica and Venice Beach called Dogtown.

The kids were mostly between twelve and fifteen, but there were some older guys, and they were surfers and surfboard designers. Together they formed a kind of gonzo renegade skating team, and they called themselves the Zephyr team — the Z-Boys. Director Stacy Peralta, now forty-five, was one of them.

Dogtown and Z-Boys is the story of those Z-Boys, and of that wild and crazy time back in the seventies when the modern, vertical style of skateboarding was created. Even if you have little interest in skateboarding, this makes for a pretty compelling story. It's also a bittersweet story, because while some of the Z-Boys — like director Peralta — became successful, others on the team tasted stardom too young, falling into the familiar traps of booze and drugs and endless parties. Some wound up in jail; others wound up dead.

If you were to visit Dogtown today, you'd see restaurants and condos. Back then it was a beachfront slum. This wasn't the California that Brian and the boys had been singing about — the soundtrack to this place and time isn't "Surfin' Safari," it's the Stooges singing "Gimme Danger, Little Stranger." Dogtown wasn't trendy, it was dirty, and sleazy, and dangerous. The surfer kids came mostly from broken homes, and they had a desperate need to be part of a group, a family, *something*. They were about to do some stuff on four wheels that no one had ever done, and throw one of the biggest gonzo parties of all time while doing it.

Ever wondered where those vertical tricks and flips that the kids do today came from? One word: drought.

There was a terrible drought in the seventies in California, and one result was that swimming pools were left empty and untended. So here come some kids looking for nice smooth surfaces to skateboard on, and — what do you know! — if you have a big round or oval pool that's empty, then you can skate in there! Brilliant! So they started skating in the old cement pond, and pretty soon one kid, a little more gonzo and fired up than the others, decided to try going higher and higher up the vertical walls, until pretty soon he was almost flying. Modern skateboarding was born.

The word spread quickly about what the Z-Boys were doing, and they became local stars. In 1975 the Z-Boys entered the Grand National Skateboarding Competition. When the judges saw what these kids were up to, they started having kittens. Nobody had ever seen tricks of the kind these guys were executing. Before the year was out some of them had signed endorsement deals. Some of them, like Tony Alva, became huge international stars. The Z-Boys became almost a brand name. Jay Adams, who was apparently the most gifted one — and the most gonzo — had a hard time adjusting to all the attention. He was interviewed for this movie in prison, where he is serving time on drug-related offences.

Dogtown and Z-Boys features inventive editing, narration by Sean Penn in that wonderful monotone of his, and some cool seventies music. With a running time of ninety minutes, it's an engaging film, and a smart piece of social anthropology about how a bunch of impoverished but creative people used some junk and the vestiges of middle-class comfort (abandoned swimming pools) to create something new that has made its way around the world.

One of the fascinating aspects of this subject is how far removed the contemporary phenomenon of skateboarding has strayed from its roots in marginalization and poverty. I have long believed that anything, no matter how creative or original, can eventually be swallowed up by capitalism and spit back out as consumer-oriented slush (or hamburgers). To paraphrase Jean-Louis (a.k.a. Jack) Kerouac (who is "safe in heaven dead"), The wheel of the greedy profit motive turns in the void of Western Culture expelling plastic food, 100-dollar skateboarding designer pants, interchangeable pop music idols, and an endless assortment of brutal weapons of mass distraction ...

I've never thought that because someone is making a ton of money it necessarily follows that whatever is being produced has no artistic merit, but it seems to me that it's not in the too-comfortable confines of the bourgeoisie that the truly creative stuff often happens, but out on the edge of town. *Dogtown and Z-Boys* illustrates this eloquently. The tone of the film is a little too self-congratulatory, though. You always have to be a little suspicious when a bunch of middle-aged guys start reminiscing about how incredibly original and creative they were in their youth. It's a bit like the stuff you hear when you coach Little League. You wouldn't believe how many dads were just like Hank Aaron until they became lawyers ...

16

Downfall

Movies are cultural artifacts. They are not created in a bubble, but are the product of a specific time and place, and are written and directed by people who have hopes and fears, beliefs and prejudices. A movie is both a window and a mirror. It allows us to gaze into a long-dead world, or into a universe that never existed, or into contemporary society.

One of the many vital functions that movies can perform is to give an audience the illusion of "setting the world right." Movies often appear to balance things out, to correct the flaws of the real world, to redress injustices. In movies, the bad guys usually — but not always — get what's coming to them. Most audience members want, in fact *need*, to see the bad guys brought to justice. Movie justice gives us the illusion of a fair and balanced universe. It's no coincidence that one of the most popular plots in contemporary film involves the hero bringing criminals to justice after traditional (read: legal) methods have failed.

We like to tell our kids that there is justice in the world. And some dictators do get caught, it's true. But others get to spend their days in comfortable exile. It's a funny world, isn't it? Martha Stewart goes to jail, but Ferdinand Marcos goes to Hawaii. And then you have dictators like Muammar al-Qaddafi. Declared time and again by Western governments to be a terrorist responsible for planning and financing heinous crimes, he is now rehabilitated. Political expediency or financial pragmatism? I sleep better at night knowing that good old Muammar is now a valued trading partner.

As bad as they are, Qaddafi's crimes pale in comparison to those of the twentieth century's ultimate bogeyman, Adolf Hitler. Hitler has been the subject of numerous films produced outside of Germany, but director Oliver Hirschbiegel's *Downfall* is different from all previous treatments. *Downfall* also marks the first time since the end of the Second World War that Hitler has been portrayed in a mainstream German film. It has taken sixty years for a German-born filmmaker to tackle the subject of Hitler head-on.

Noted Hitler biographer Sir Ian Kershaw has been quoted as saying that there is a gradual, continuing, and inexorable process at work in Germany that is slowly allowing the German people to see the Hitler era as history, and that films like *Downfall* are an important part of that process. It is Kershaw's opinion that for many Germans it has been almost impossible to entertain a positive relationship to the past. I suggest that for some Germans, *Downfall* could have a cathartic effect.

Downfall is based in part upon *Until the Final Hour: Hitler's Last Secretary*, the memoirs of Hitler's secretary, Traudl Junge. That book was also the subject of the documentary film *Blind Spot: Hitler's Secretary*, a film that paints a fascinating portrait of the woman who was Hitler's personal secretary from 1942 until his death in the bunker under Berlin in 1945. Junge witnessed first-hand the collapse of both Hitler and the Third Reich. She recounts in detail Hitler's raving tirades to his generals, which he delivered while moving non-existent armies around on maps, blind to the fact that on the ground his forces were running out of petrol and ammunition, and were being encircled and destroyed by the Red Army and the Allies. She was also a witness to the mind-boggling fanaticism that reigned to the very end among Hitler's inner circle.

What makes *Downfall* such a powerful, almost overwhelming viewing experience is the perfectly realized, absolutely believable *mise en scène*. Every museum-quality detail, every seamless performance conspires to place us inside the claustrophobic bunker. The viewer becomes a wide-eyed, astonished witness to the horror and insanity of the Reich's final days.

Legendary Swiss actor Bruno Ganz portrays Hitler. To say he *portrays* Hitler really doesn't do justice to his performance; it would be more to the point to say that Ganz *inhabits* Hitler. Several years ago, Sir Alec Guinness portrayed Hitler in *Hitler: The Last Ten Days*. It was an excellent performance, but Ganz goes beyond the image of a raving, almost cartoonish little dictator that audiences have grown accustomed to. He embodies the entire spectrum of the man. As the news from the front gets worse, and it becomes clear the war is lost, Ganz shows us a man crumbling and withering under the weight of defeat. His back becomes more bent and his eyes more glazed, while his right arm, having been permanently injured in an unsuccessful assassination attempt, is kept self-consciously behind his back, twitching uncontrollably. This is not a sympathetic portrait of Hitler, as some have suggested, but rather a portrayal that is not afraid to show Hitler as something more than a caricature of evil.

The Adolf Hitler whom we encounter in *Downfall* is obviously psychotic: he makes numerous brutal and repugnant statements not only about Jews, but about the German people, and even his own generals. In one scene, as some of his generals plead for surrender in order to avoid more useless slaughter of German civilians, he screams, "The people are weak. They get what they deserve. If we can't win this war, then no one deserves to survive!" His complete lack of compassion toward his own people is beyond appalling.

It seems obvious that Hitler was disconnected from certain fundamental precepts of human behaviour, but he was not a three-headed, tentacled Martian. It would be so much easier to understand his actions if he were. The problem one faces when trying to understand Hitler is that he often looked and behaved quite normally. When dealing with his secretary Frau Junge, for example, Hitler was positively grandfatherly. *Downfall* is a disturbing and courageous film because it dares to show Hitler as a human being, albeit one filled with terrible contradictions — a man who is uncaring about the slaughter of millions, yet whose eyes fill with tears and who can't bear to watch as an ss doctor puts down his favourite pet dog Dolly. The unsavory truth revealed in *Downfall* is that homicidal dictators are not apart from the human race; they orchestrate their monstrous crimes while hiding behind human faces.

Downfall pulls no punches in its depiction of the carnage and horror of war, but its most horrifying scene is quietly understated. As the Allies draw nearer to the bunker, Frau Goebbels, one of Hitler's most fanatical followers, enters her children's room and smiles warmly as she encourages them to drink the sleeping potion that a doctor has prepared so that they can "get a wonderful night's sleep." Later, with the children in a profound sleep, she approaches each bed in turn and ever so gently inserts a small glass vial of poison into each child's mouth. She holds the child's head, breaks the vial, and holds the child's mouth closed for a few seconds. She later tells her husband that she could not bear to imagine the children living in a world not ruled by the

Nazi party and by their glorious Führer. Her husband, Propaganda Minister Joseph Goebbels, nods in silent understanding.

The murder of the children by their mother is a scene that unfolds with quiet, unrelenting horror, and for days afterwards it remained vividly in my mind, a disturbing presence. Both cast and crew reported that they were profoundly shaken and emotionally drained after filming the scene.

Downfall manages to accomplish a rare cinematic tour de force: it completely and unequivocally draws the audience into a hidden world. By the time Hitler and his bride Eva Braun had committed suicide, and their bodies had been dragged out of the bunker, doused with gasoline, and burned, in anticipation of the arrival of the Russian troops, I was convinced that I had seen these events as they must have happened in reality. That may seem naive coming from a seasoned movie critic, but the experience of watching *Downfall* is as far removed from the normal movie-going experience as diving into an icy mountain lake is from sitting in a warm bath.

17

Eyes Wide Shut

Eyes Wide Shut, Stanley Kubrick's final opus, was certainly one of the most hyped films of the nineties. The presence of the *couple du jour*, Tom Cruise and Nicole Kidman, added a gossipy, tabloid aura to the film's launch that certainly helped it at the box-office. The pre-release rumours of numerous steamy sex scenes didn't exactly hurt either.

Cruise portrays Bill Hartford, a successful M.D. in New York. I immediately disliked this character because I felt certain that he was a Yankees fan. His wife Alice (Kidman) is looking for work after the financial failure of the art gallery she managed. The couple has a huge and undoubtedly monstrously expensive apartment on Central Park West. They also have a beautiful seven-year-old daughter. They've got the money, they've got the looks, they've got the whole American dream. But are they awake, or just sleepwalking through it? Are their eyes wide shut?

The very first scene reveals Kubrick's game plan. Alice, her back to the camera, slips out of her dress while the camera lingers on her bare bottom. Kubrick is a very smart film-maker. Right off the top he makes sure that the audience are going to keep *their* eyes wide open.

All is not well with Alice and Bill's marriage. They go to a Christmas party given by a very wealthy libertine named Victor (Sydney Pollack). Alice drinks a couple of glasses of champagne and immediately gets quite stinking, which allows Kidman to indulge in a self-conscious impression of Marilyn Monroe, complete with drunken giggling and sexy winking. She then dances with a stranger and engages in provocative banter with him, but rejects his advances. Meanwhile, Bill is propositioned by two (!) young women, who invite him upstairs, promising to show him the "pot of gold at the end of the rainbow." Just when we get the impression that Bill is about to succumb to temptation and run upstairs with the girls, he's called away by the host, Victor. Victor tells Bill that the prostitute he has been partying with upstairs has overdosed on a speedball — which, by the way, is a mix of cocaine and heroin. (Call me a square, but whatever happened to a few tokes and a glass of wine?) Bill goes upstairs with his trusty medical bag and saves the girl's life.

The point is made early on that both Alice and Bill have lots of opportunities to engage in infidelities, but they both resist. The next night, while smoking a joint (which seems to have the same effect on her as champagne), Alice admits to Bill that she once had some hot fantasies about a young naval officer she met while on holidays. The effect of this revelation on Bill is to make him "flip out," as we used to say. Bill becomes obsessed with visions of his wife having sex with another man. He quickly decides to get even (?) with his wife. Remember, now, that while his wife has only indulged in *imaginary* infidelities, Bill decides to engage in some *real* ones. Doesn't this all sound like one of those French art movies from the sixties?

Bill is soon cruising around the seamier areas of New York, excitedly looking for some action, but he just can't seem to get lucky. Finally he encounters a prostitute, who takes him up to her apartment. Just when he's about to score,

Alice calls him on his cell phone. He immediately decides that he should go home, but, being the kind of guy that he is, he pays the prostitute anyway. That's another strange leitmotif in this movie: Cruise's character always has endless amounts of ready cash in his wallet. He's like a biological bank machine. This seems an important part of Kubrick's message: having access to a bottomless wallet can only lead to ruin and ruination, especially if you're as good-looking and eager as Tom Cruise.

I wouldn't know.

Walking home, our rich and horny hero stops by a jazz bar, where Nick, a musician friend of his, is performing. Nick tells him about a private gig he's been booked to play later that night. It becomes obvious that he's talking about an orgy. He whispers to Bill that it's all very hush-hush. The people who hire him have him play blindfolded, and all of the participants are masked. Anticipating a little sexual debauchery, Bill insists that Nick give him the address and the password he will need to get in.

In anticipation of the orgy, Bill goes to a costume shop to rent a disguise, and then proceeds to the address Nick has given him. Met by a mysterious — and suspicious — man, Bill gives the password and is admitted. After our uninvited guest has wandered around in this den of iniquity for a while, he is discovered, and soon finds himself at odds with some very dangerous characters.

The orgy scene, which was much hyped, and eagerly anticipated by some moviegoers, involves numerous groups of people engaging in various sexual activities and acrobatics. To avoid the dreaded NC-17 rating, several characters were digitally added to the sex scenes after the fact in order to block the audience's view of the explicit details. I don't really know what all the fuss was about. Even without the added characters blocking the view, it seems to me that these scenes would have been relatively tame.

If you think you might be attracted to this film by the possibility of seeing Tom Cruise *sans vêtements*, disappointment awaits you. Just about everyone else in this movie — everyone female, anyway — winds up naked, but Tom maintains his *pudeur* and his underwear.

If you're sick of the F-word being used incessantly in contemporary films to add dramatic emphasis, *Eyes Wide Shut* is going to drive you nuts. The F-word is used here as a noun, verb, adjective, and pronoun. It may even be used as a prop, I'm not quite sure. I saw *something* strange during that orgy scene and I still can't figure out what the heck it was.

Some of the performances Kubrick has coaxed out of his cast are pretty awful. From all reports, Kubrick placed enormous importance on casting. Like Hitchcock, he felt that casting was the biggest part of directing. In other words, once he had selected his actors he pretty much let them run free. It may seem paradoxical, but even though he gave his actors almost complete freedom, he was notorious for demanding take after take of the same scene. Remember that scene in *The Shining* where Scatman Crothers gives Nicholson's character a tour of the kitchen and the freezer facilities in the Overlook Hotel? There isn't much going on in this scene. It's quite unremarkable. But it has been reported that Kubrick made both actors do the scene *136 times*. Talk about a long day at the office! If this is true, it's either perfectionism pushed to the nth degree, or a case for a psychiatrist. To paraphrase Dr McCoy in *Star Trek*, I'm a movie critic, Jim, not a psychiatrist. I guess if you're a genius director, you can demand as many takes as you want.

Unfortunately, I don't think that Kubrick demanded enough takes from Tom Cruise. A well-known critic described his performance as "solid." That's a good term. "Wooden" would be an even better one. Kidman's performance was deemed by some critics to be exceptional, but I'm not sure in what way. I think that Kidman is a good, sometimes even great actress, but she's been much better in other films. And it doesn't help that here she is used more as a prop than as a fully developed character. She is the catalyst for much of the action — the object of sexual desire and of obsession — but the story places the husband Bill in the eye of the storm.

As I watched this movie, a question kept resonating in my head like a Gene Krupa rim shot: "Why did Kubrick make this movie?"

What was he trying to say? He must have thought it was important. He must have known that this was pretty much going to be his last movie. What is this story really about? Is Kubrick reflecting on the general emptiness of the American Dream, and specifically on the spiritual despair that inevitably arises when people adopt consumerism as a religion?

Morally, Kubrick was a very old-fashioned gentleman, obviously inspired by the Bible. When Kidman's character tells her husband about a dream that she's had, it turns out to be a classic Adam and Eve scenario, except that in her dream the two are thrown out of paradise because of something *he* has done. She has had a feminist epiphany: "We have blamed women for ages, but what about you guys?" This is also the only scene in which the word "God" is spoken. Kubrick seems to be revisiting the Fall from Grace. Here is a couple who seem to have everything, but who are unable to experience happiness, because they always want more. Worse, the "more" that they want is a lie, what that sexy young woman in the earlier scene had in mind when she offered him the "pot of gold at the end of the rainbow." Bill rents his costume for the orgy from the "Rainbow" boutique. The characters seek their happiness and fulfilment in the physical and the material; that is to say, according to Kubrick, in the illusory.

Are we levitating yet?

I think that as Kubrick neared the end of his life he wanted to pass on a deeply felt belief that was of paramount importance to him — something like, "You're lucky to be alive. Open your eyes and look around you. Enjoy what you have, and don't waste your soul chasing self-indulgent illusions."

At the end of the film, Kidman's character says to her husband, "Let's be grateful; our eyes are open now."

Corny?

Hell, no. This is Kubrick.

18

Fahrenheit 9/11

Ray Bradbury's cautionary novel *Fahrenheit 451* (the title refers to the temperature at which paper ignites) was set in a future totalitarian state in which firemen *burned* books, and where free speech, and free thinking, were outlawed. The title of Michael Moore's incendiary opus, *Fahrenheit 9/11*, symbolizes the temperature at which freedom burns.

I have on occasion over the past twelve years been accused of being cynical.

Webster's Dictionary defines a cynic as "someone who believes that self-interest is the motive of all human conduct." While I can't deny that I believe that self-interest, or, more specifically, the lust for money, is the motive for producing most Hollywood movies, and while I believe that big-budget Hollywood films are primarily concerned about creating profit rather than art, I feel that art can be created anywhere, even in Hollywood. Some of the greatest films of all time were made under studio systems that placed profit above all other considerations, but the "art" managed to sneak in anyway.

Movies that can change our way of seeing the world, movies, such as *La Grande Illusion* or *2001: A Space Odyssey*, that make us think about things in new ways, that move us forward in some way, are very rare. Most movies (like most sporting events) are fluff. They are the culture's "weapons of mass distraction," nothing more, nothing less.

I'm not putting down the vitally important, sanity-saving role of sporting events and entertainment. Lord knows that without some entertaining fluff in our lives, we'd all quickly be going gaga. As *Washington Post* columnist (and baseball aficionado) Thomas Boswell once said, "Everything can't be big issues and heart surgery."

But as much as I love baseball, I'm still going to invoke the notwithstanding clause: Boston Red Sox fans notwithstanding, baseball is not of earth-shaking importance. Yes, it's fun, yes, it's a wonderful game, yes, it's even a great metaphor for life, but it's not in the same category as fighting poverty, or fighting for social justice, or equality, or human rights. It *is* important to some degree who manages the Red Sox (remember that Grady guy?), but it's not nearly as important as who becomes president of the United States.

In Canada, voter turnout at the federal level is usually quite good, significantly higher than south of the border. Still, a lot of Canadians don't vote, and, dare I say it, the reasons given by many for not voting are cynical reasons. You know the song: "Politicians all the same." "They're all crooks." Etc., etc.

I don't believe it.

I don't believe that politicians are all the same, and neither does Michael Moore. In fact Moore believes that cynicism is an extremely dangerous philosophical position. Cynicism gives people an "out," an excuse to watch from the sidelines — while complaining, of course — without getting involved. Cynicism also gives people an opportunity to dismiss our elected officials as just so many clowns. Okay, some of them *are* of Barnum & Bailey calibre, but these clowns have *clout*. And that is the problem. As Moore says, "Democracy is not a spectator sport." It isn't baseball. If you want things to change, you have to participate, and pay attention.

In 2000, the American presidential election drew sixty-seven percent of registered voters. That places voter turnout in the United States, the most powerful country in the world, in fifty-fifth place. Number one was Burundi, with ninety-seven percent. What do the people of Burundi understand that Americans don't? As George Dubya himself said, "A low voter turnout is an indication of fewer people going to the polls."

No argument there.

In *Fahrenheit 9/11*, Moore doesn't pretend that he's being objective. To quote John Wayne, "He calls it plain." And we like plain talk up here in Canada, eh? Moore doesn't beat around the bush (!). This movie is not so much a documentary as an editorial, and Moore's agenda is plain: defeat George W. come November 2004.*

Moore believes/hopes that his movie can make a difference in November. He also firmly believes that the Bush administration had decided to invade Iraq months before September 2001 (an invasion was the logical conclusion of his father's unfinished agenda), and that the attacks of September 11 were seized upon as an opportunity to justify a war that, as it turns out, became a fantastic business opportunity for many Bush family cronies.

Moore also accuses the Republicans of stealing the election in 2000. *Fahrenheit 9/11* begins by making the case for that accusation.

It's a pretty strong case.

To cite just one example, thousands of African-Americans who had voted in previous elections, and who tried to vote in Florida — a state governed by Jeb Bush — discovered that their names were missing from the voter rolls.

---

* We all know how that turned out.

Coincidence or despicable master plan? In fact, a large number of African-American *Democrats* found their names missing from the eligible voter roles.

On election night all the news agencies were predicting that Gore was going to prevail in Florida. Suddenly Fox News overturned the pronouncements of the other media organizations, announcing that Bush had a significant lead. Incredibly, the man put in charge of tracking the election results for Fox News in Florida was Bush's cousin, John Ellis. After Fox made its announcement of a dramatic turnaround, the other major networks began predicting that Bush would win, even though some 175,000 disputed ballots still remained uncounted!

Fahrenheit 9/11 goes on to explore the numerous connections between the Bush family and the family of Osama bin Laden, and also the royal family of Saudi Arabia. Some of this stuff seems pretty incredible, but is it true? Moore is certainly biased. He certainly leans further to the left than the Tower of Pisa, and he is even pretty flaky, but he's not careless. Every startling affirmation he makes in this movie has been carefully documented — probably much better documented in fact than the bogus claims about Saddam's weapons of mass destruction and his supposed ties to Al-Qaeda.

Critics of Moore's politics accuse *Fahrenheit 9/11* of being manipulative, and they are right. But Moore believes that he is fighting the good fight against right wing forces, who are also manipulative, and who are, he believes, stifling democracy and freedom of speech in the United States. In fact, Moore feels that these forces are not only manipulative but also scurrilously dishonest. In other words, Moore answers the charges of bias with the old adage that he's just fighting fire with fire (or, in his case, pouring oil on it).

So what, according to Moore, are the real reasons behind the war in Iraq?

His premise is simple: 9/11 was a terrible tragedy, but it was also seized upon by the Bush administration as a golden opportunity to aggressively push a secret agenda. And at the heart of that agenda — an agenda set, according to Moore, many months before 9/11 — was the invasion of Iraq. It seems clear from certain leaked documents that the war had been planned well in advance of September 11. Moore's major accusation is that the Bush administration managed, through an expertly mounted campaign of disinformation, to link Saddam Hussein with the attacks of September 11 in the public mind, even though no such link existed.

Moore goes on to say that the Bush administration borrowed a page or two from George Orwell's *1984*. In that visionary novel, the State wages perpetual (and possibly fictitious) war on one interchangeable enemy or another in order to control the population by keeping it in a constant state of fear and paranoia about enemies real or imagined.

Call me paranoid, but this sounds suspiciously like the constant vague threats and states of alert issued by the American Defense Department.

The formula is simple but effective: keep the people scared, tell them that you are the only one able to protect them, and they will follow you, and accept a reduction in their basic freedoms and rights in the name of National Security.

Thousands of young men and young women are serving — and dying — in Iraq, Moore continues, for ulterior motives. The war is really all about controlling huge quantities of oil, and about giving non-tendered rebuilding contracts worth billions of dollars to friends of the Bush family, thereby generating mind-boggling amounts of money for companies connected to Bush and close cronies such as James Baker and Donald Rumsfeld.

In a word, the war is not about fighting terrorism, but about generating Big Bucks.

The emotional centre of the film is attained when Moore interviews a military mother who has lost her son in Iraq. This is a woman, a proud American, who believed her president's words, who believed the justifications given for the war, and who was proud that her son was serving. On camera, she tearfully, but without excessive sentimentality, explains that she now feels not only crushed by her loss, but betrayed by her government. This is strong stuff, and one can't help being moved by it.

In another powerful moment, Moore is back in his hometown of Flint, Michigan, interviewing young unemployed black men who are being aggressively recruited by the Marines. Recruitment, Moore explains, is much more aggressive — and effective — in the poor neighbourhoods than anywhere else. In Bush's war to enrich the already wealthy, it is the poor and uneducated who must give their lives.

At one point Moore pulls what his critics have dismissed as a stunt: he confronts various congressmen and asks them to consider signing up their own children to serve in Iraq. If this is a stunt, it certainly is nonetheless effective in underlining a simple fact: the offspring of the rich and powerful have less chance of winding up in harm's way than do less well-connected young Americans. If you've always taken this fact for granted, perhaps you should ask yourself why it should be so.

19

Far from Heaven

If you were a kid in the fifties, as soon as you had the slightest sniffle or cough your mom would grab you and break out the Vicks VapoRub and spread it all over your chest and back until you felt really icky and your cotton pyjamas were stuck to you and you were glued to your bed. This "treatment" didn't actually do anything to make you any better, but it kept you from moving around, so it was useful for mothers of sick children: if they can't move, it's easier to keep an eye on them. Your mom would then install the dreaded VapoRub Inhaler Machine, spoon some VapoRub into it, plug it in, and your room would be filled with ethereal VapoRub mist. I knew one kid who actually got addicted to this stuff, and who used to *eat* it. He would sneak spoonfuls of it when his mom wasn't looking. God knows what happened to him later in life.

When many forty- and fifty-something adults look back at their childhoods, they see everything not through a haze of nostalgia, but through a haze of Vick's VapoRub.

The fifties also mark the true birth of the consumer-driven society, and, by the way, it's pretty much exclusively television's fault if we are now mindless, drooling, consumer zombies.

In the fifties, everybody got a television set. Without warning, TV brought all kinds of stuff into your house, and it didn't even wipe its feet first. Pretty soon everybody wanted to have in real life the wonderful, totally artificial life they saw on the small screen. It was a life filled with exciting new appliances; people began to crave yellow telephones and green refrigerators, not to mention leopard skin sofas. It was mind-boggling.

But the great thing about the fifties was the food.

Sugar Pops, cyclamates in diet sodas, frozen fish sticks, TV dinners, Rice-A-Roni, Jiffy peanut butter: all kinds of junk to stuff into our eager mouths while we watched Don Messer or *Hockey Night in Canada*. But the real Kahuna, and perhaps the greatest food creation of all time, the towering achievement of the fifties, was Cheez Whiz, which I used to love on crackers while watching Ed Sullivan. Much later, when I moved into my own apartment, I discovered that Cheez Whiz was highly effective for patching up holes in plaster walls. You just scooped it in there, let it dry, and then sanded it and painted it over. In my twenties, I came to think of that favourite childhood food as orange Polyfilla.

Yes, the fifties was a cheezy-whizzy kind of era.

I sometimes think about what all of that artificial stuff may have done to my physical and mental development.

I try not to think about it too much, though.

A more frightening thought is that many of the political leaders of the Western world grew up stuffing their faces with Cheez Whiz. This may explain in part why things are such a mess: the Cheez Whiz may have permanently gummed up their neurons.

The 1950s were also a time when America prided itself on being free and democratic, in stark contrast to all of the Soviet-controlled countries. Paradoxically, it was also a time of great conservatism, and there was great pressure on everyone to conform. You were expected to know your place and to stay there contentedly. Women belonged in the home, blacks belonged at the back of the bus, and kids belonged in bed before *Bonanza*.

Far from Heaven, which is set in 1958, is a homage to the films of Douglas Sirk, who directed a series of very popular films in the fifties that used to be known as "Women's Movies." These were splashy Technicolor melodramas — some would call them soap operas — with titles like *All that Heaven Allows*, *Written on the Wind*, *There's Always Tomorrow*, *Summer Storm*, and *The Tarnished Angels*. His stars of choice were Jane Wyman, Rock Hudson, Barbara Stanwyck, Fred MacMurray, Lauren Bacall, Robert Stack, and Dorothy Malone.

The characters in his films are usually neurotic, overwrought, frightened people grappling with terrible secrets, who were born into dysfunctional families rife with dark, guilty passions. In a Douglas Sirk melodrama emotions run wild; situations don't just come to a head, they explode into histrionic fireworks of love and lust. Characters are inevitably faced with terrible choices; they struggle with social boundaries that they must not transgress for fear of becoming outcasts in a society that seems intolerant of any individual quest for happiness that deviates from the strait and narrow.

In *Far from Heaven*, director Todd Haynes has lovingly crafted a movie that looks and feels and sounds like a fifties melodrama, but explores themes that are much closer to reality than one could ever find in Sirk's films. On the surface, *Far from Heaven* seems artificial, but as the story unfolds and the dramatic situations become ever more realistic, they are played out against a backdrop of formal, contrived cinematic conventions.

Julianne Moore portrays Cathy, a perfect 1950s housewife. She looks perfect, her kids look perfect, her 1958 house with its brick fireplace looks perfect, and she looks perfectly happy with her perfect husband Frank (Dennis Quaid), a highly successful marketing executive with Magnatech electronics, makers of state-of-the-art (for 1958) Magnatech television sets.

Frank doesn't spend much time at home. He attends numerous "working" lunches (always well-lubricated), and very often works late. When his body is home, his mind seems to be somewhere else. In typical 1950s style, the offspring of this perfect couple are treated as if they were cardboard cut-outs rather than real people with real needs. Frank's son David, who is nine, is pathetically desperate for Dad to pay attention to him, as is his daughter Janice. Frank has other priorities.

Mother Cathy does pay attention to the kids, but it's a businesslike kind of attention that takes the form of "Put your bike away, and I told you not to go outside without a sweater." When little David verbally revolts ever so mildly by saying "Geez," he is strongly rebuked with the "That's not the kind of language we use in this house, young man, and leave your father alone, he's very tired" speech.

And Dad *is* tired. And he drinks a lot, but this is perfectly in keeping with the era of martinis for lunch and bourbon before supper. The women drink too; when Cathy has some female friends over for afternoon gossip, they all sip daiquiris. No wonder TV dinners were so popular in the fifties: Mom can't cook anything up. It's three o'clock and she's on her third daiquiri. Mom is blotto.

Luckily for the kids, the family has a maid. She is black and her name is Sybil (Viola Davis). It is the maid who keeps the family functional; she takes much better care of the kids, more *loving* care, than the parents do.

One evening, wishing to surprise Frank at his office, Cathy surprises herself when she spies her husband kissing another man. Later, when she confronts him, he agrees to see a psychiatrist.

What?

Well, remember, this is the fifties. Frank is ashamed, and he is also just as misinformed about homosexuality as the rest of the population. The psychiatrist discusses various forms of "therapy," including something called Heterosexual Reconversion Therapy (!), and even Shock Avoidance Therapy (?).

Sounds like the shrink has been sniffing very large amounts of VapoRub, doesn't it?

Unfortunately, this was the kind of nonsense they used to throw at people who were confused and desperate enough to consult psychiatrists about their sexual orientation back in the Cheez Whiz era.

But stay tuned, the plot hasn't even begun to thicken yet. Cathy befriends her gardener (Dennis Haysbert), a tall, attractive widower, a black man to whom she had never before paid anything but perfunctory attention. A genuinely kind man, Raymond will eventually console Cathy, although the relationship remains platonic and completely innocent. Small-town Connecticut being what it is, however, it only takes two shakes of a lamb's tail before the gossips are out in force. Pretty soon Cathy is ostracized from her narrow-minded bourgeois milieu. The gardener Raymond fares no better: the black community is no readier than the whites to accept friendship between a white woman and a black man.

The relationship between Cathy and Raymond is several shades of grey. It is based on trust, respect, and a shared need for communication and moral support, and it completely baffles people unaccustomed to perceiving relationships between men and women with any nuance. No one is capable of believing, or even imagining, that the relationship between Cathy and Raymond isn't sexual.

I found myself enjoying the subtle irony of the *mise en scène*, how cleverly the production values underline and amplify the sub-text. The cinematography uses spectacular, almost garish colours for ironic effect: except for Cathy and Raymond, all of the inhabitants of the town see everything in black and white, just as it appears on their Magnatech television sets.

After seeing *Far from Heaven*, we in the twenty-first century can all feel good about ourselves. After all, haven't we finally built a much better society, one in which racism has been eliminated, and in which there is no longer any stigma attached to sexual orientation? Thank goodness that in the modern world we have solved all of the problems of ignorance, narrow-mindedness, and hypocrisy that poisoned the lives of these characters in 1958.

Pass the VapoRub, please.

... I'm looking forward to feeding the reindeer on Christmas Eve. Maybe I'll leave them some celery sticks with Cheez Whiz like last year ...

20

The Fog

Part of my honeymoon was spent driving down the east coast of Nova Scotia in August. It was a part of the world we had never seen, and at every scenic spot along the coast that our pocket guide recommended we stopped excitedly, filled with anticipation of the beautiful sea views we had been promised.

Fog.

Fog, fog, fog.

Eventually we purchased a bunch of postcards and held them out at arm's length while we faced the sea, in order to get an idea of what the view was supposed to look like. Actually it was kind of romantic, standing at Blue Rocks, holding our postcards, hearing the waves crash, smelling and tasting the salty air, listening to the lonesome sound of the foghorn moaning in the grey morning.

BUUUUUUUUHHHHH!

In the Maritimes, the fog is part of the culture, like fiddle music and chowder. Fog seems to appear magically, anywhere, and at any time.

I understand that back in the fifties there was even a theme park called "Fog World" near Yarmouth, Nova Scotia, but it went out of business, because the tourists couldn't find it.

John Carpenter's cult classic *The Fog* (1980) is set not in the Maritimes, but rather in a small fishing village off the

California coast called Antonio Island. On the hundredth anniversary of its founding, the town is besieged by a mysterious fog. The village was built on the site of a leper colony, and the fog that is rolling in is the ghostly manifestation of the spirits of the colony's inhabitants. Very soon, the fog begins to dispatch the inhabitants "with extreme prejudice." Carpenter's film features a crafty script, creepy special effects, and way above-average — by horror film standards at least — performances from the cast, which includes Adrienne Barbeau, Jamie Lee Curtis, Janet Leigh, and Hal Holbrook. Also, *The Fog* has almost no graphic violence or gore. It is an intelligent, *restrained* horror flick. In a word, it is almost diametrically opposed to the 2005 remake.

BUUUUUUUHHHHH!

When it comes to scary movies about fog (or about anything else) there isn't really anything new under the sun. Good horror movies are going to be remade forever. It's just too tempting; there is just too much money to be made. Twenty-five years after Carpenter's film, there is a whole new generation of teen-aged moviegoers out there just ripe for the picking.

Rupert Wainwright, the director of this new *Fog*, previously directed several rap music videos, and also, in 1999, a very bad, and very noisy, rip-off of *The Exorcist* called *Stigmata*. If you still haven't seen that mess, keep it up; you're on the right track.

Wainwright attended the prestigious UCLA film school, where he seems to have majored in loud noises. To get the full effect of Wainwright's talent, you have to experience *The Fog* in a theatre in which Dolby surround is cranked up to Nirvana. I don't want to play amateur psychologist here, but Wainwright has a thing about loudly shattering glass. It's an obsession at the very least. I don't know if he was locked in a room as a child and forced to watch the House of Mirrors scene from *The Lady from Shanghai* over and over again or what, but in *The Fog* glass shatters — very loudly — every ten minutes.

But why does the fog make all manner of glass shatter?

Well, this malevolent fog is *alive*, its very essence comprised of vengeful spirits, ghosts of the lepers, who had been brutally murdered by the founding fathers of this little coastal village. And now the spirits have returned to wreak terrible vengeance on the descendants of the murderers — and to blow their eardrums out with the sound of shattering glass in Dolby. After the first half-dozen incidents involving shattering glass, the effect becomes extremely silly, not to mention extremely annoying.

Time now for a little quiz to test your horror movie IQ Ready?

Q: It's night, and four men in a rowboat are moving away from a large wooden ship that is on fire. The ship is filled with screaming people, and some are jumping off to escape the flames. The four men have just robbed the ship and are rowing furiously in order to escape with the treasure. Suddenly the rowboat gets stuck, possibly on a sandbar. One of the men leans slowly over the side, his face inches away from the dark water, trying to see. What happens next?

(a) nothing;

(b) there is a sudden loud sound of shattering glass;

(c) Flipper comes up out of the water and kisses him on the nose; or

(d) a skeletal hand comes out of the water, grabs him by the throat, and pulls him in.

If you answered "b," you may be suffering from the same obsession as the director. If you answered "c," don't despair, you may yet play an active and useful role in society, but only if you agree to years of risky experimental treatment.

Q: Having just been told by her boyfriend that there is a dead body below decks, attractive blonde Elizabeth immediately goes below to check things out for herself. With razor-sharp deep-sea fishing hooks dangling dangerously at eye level, she noses around in the semidarkness until she spots a large freezer. She approaches it, grabs the handle of the door, and opens it suddenly. What happens next?

(a) nothing: all the freezer contains is several boxes of frozen fish sticks in a light tempura batter;

(b) when she opens the door, we hear the loud sound of shattering glass;

(c) Frosty the Snowman jumps out at her and offers her a frozen treat; or

(d) she screams at the sight of the frozen corpse of a missing crewmember.

If you answered "b" again, you need to close this book *immediately* and call for professional help. Don't panic. Take deep breaths and repeat to yourself, "I have a problem, but I *can* be helped." If you answered "c," you probably have the munchies by now, so you should go to your refrigerator. But remember to open the door slowly, because there may be someone, or some *thing*, in there.

Judging from the trailer, I fully expected this to be a foggy, soggy mess of a remake, but I went anyway. The horror fan in me, the eternal childlike movie-lover, always thinks that there is just a chance that a horror movie — *any* horror movie — will contain at least one scene of real suspense and terror that will make the whole exercise almost worthwhile.

And, surprise! There is!

As the fog rolls in and surrounds the house where little Andy and his Aunt Corrie are staying, Auntie is doing the dishes. Suddenly the water goes slurp down the drain and the sink is empty. In the next shot we are looking up from under the dishes and we see the woman peering down into the drain. This is a good shot; it keeps the audience off-balance, in anticipation of what may happen next — or perhaps it simply gives us the perspective of Josephine the plumber. At any rate, as Auntie slowly lifts the dishes, a skeletal hand comes out from the drain and grabs her by the throat. Yes, it's *The Creature from Beyond the Drain*! I know this sounds hokey, but it's the most effective scene in the entire movie.

That being said, it's not difficult for an even minimally talented director to successfully pull off a "jump moment." For those of you not familiar with the intricate inner workings of the horror movie industry, allow me to explain that a "jump moment" is a moment designed specifically to make people jump and spill their popcorn. Later, when the cinema is empty, the staff will go around sweeping up the spilled popcorn so that it can be re-bagged and re-sold. If you think that there are obscene profits to be made selling ten cents worth of popcorn for four dollars, imagine the fortunes to be generated by *re*-selling the same popcorn.

The mind boggles.

This is one of the industry's dark secrets, something not talked about except in hushed tones behind closed doors. But now you know. Next time, before you buy popcorn at the movies, think about it.

And stay out of the fog.

21

The Game

Let me put my cards on the table right now: the following film review is in reality a rant about the fact that Hollywood is shredding its last vestiges of artistic integrity.

Once upon a time, in the days of the movie moguls, such all-powerful studio executives as Jack Warner or Sam Goldwyn could take a completed movie out of the hands of its director and modify it by re-editing it, or re-shooting scenes, or changing the ending. This would happen whenever the big cheese came to the conclusion that a picture just didn't "work" — in other words, when he thought the picture wouldn't sell enough tickets or enough popcorn. This could of course be a terribly traumatic and profoundly insulting experience if you were a director, and you saw your work taken away from you and presented to the public in a "butchered" form.

It happened to Orson Wells. In 1942, RKO pictures took over his film *The Magnificent Ambersons* and re-edited it (Wells always said "butchered" it), snipping out huge chunks and destroying much of the character development and ambience, not to mention the internal logic of the film.

Welles never forgave anyone even remotely involved.

Why am I telling you this? Because similar events still occur today. Director Robert Altman ran into problems in 1997 when his film version of the John Grisham novel *The*

Gingerbread Man received negative feedback from a test audience. Worried that they had a major flop on their hands, Polygram hired an editor to re-cut the film. When the new version received even worse reviews from preview audiences, Polygram relented and released the director's cut.

Director Spike Lee also clashed with his studio bosses in 1992, before the release of *Malcolm X*, when he refused to submit the film to what he called "idiots in a focus group."

The sad fact of the matter is that studios are terrified of having a flop on their hands. As you can imagine, risking fifty million dollars or more on a movie makes some people skittish. But nowadays, rather than have movie moguls make the decisions, the studios "test" the film. They test, and test, and test. They test titles, they test trailers, they test endings. They conduct "research screenings." This may ensure that the film will be better received by mainstream audiences, but is it the way to create "art"? Can you imagine Picasso "testing" one of the most influential and progressive works of art of the twentieth century, *Les demoiselles d'Avignon*, before exhibiting it? I can imagine the feedback he would have received: "too weird"; "poorly drawn"; "I don't get it"; "would make a great dart board"; "sick"; and so on.

Which brings us to *The Game*.

The Game is, for its first hour at least, a tight, gripping thriller. It is then ruined by an excess of silly plot twists and an ending that seems to have been hammered together after feedback from a focus group at a test screening.

The Game tells the story of Nicholas Van Orton (Michael Douglas), an incredibly rich modern-day Scrooge, who lives alone in a huge mansion surrounded by security cameras. Douglas's characterization is at best cartoonish, a portrait of a man who seems to live in constant fear that the slightest smile will permanently damage his face. Nicholas, haunted by the memory of his father's suicide, is alienated from his past. He is alienated from his ex-wife and alienated from his only blood relative, his younger brother Conrad (Sean Penn), a ne'er-do-well ex-druggie.

On his birthday, our Scrooge agrees to lunch with his brother, who offers him an intriguing birthday present, a business card from a mysterious organization called "Consumer Recreation Services." "What is it?" Mr Van Orton asks. "You'll see," says Conrad. "Call them. It's a profound life experience. It's The Game." So Van Orton calls and makes an appointment. He is subjected to a battery of psychological tests and a physical examination, only to be told by phone a few days later that his application has been rejected. Well this guy has never been rejected in his life, and he just can't believe it — and neither can we. Pretty soon things start to get weird. He arrives home one night to find a body in the driveway in the same spot where his father was found years before after jumping from the roof of the family home. Upon closer inspection, it turns out that the body is a mannequin, a clown. Even more intriguing, the clown has a key in its mouth. What is the key for?

The Game has begun.

Our hero is soon swept away on a terrifying rollercoaster ride filled with progressively stranger and more dangerous events. At first The Game seems exciting, but not particularly sinister. Pretty soon, though, it looks as if someone is out to kill him and steal his fortune. But is this really a sinister plot, or is it just "a game"? Who is behind it? Could it be his brother? Or his only trusted business associate? Or perhaps the mysterious blonde (Deborah Kara Unger) who seems to show up at the most opportune moments?

As I mentioned, this works beautifully for about an hour; however, there's nothing worse than a thriller with too many plot twists.

The script for *The Game* was originally written by the same people who did the Sandra Bullock thriller *The Net*. But then David Fincher, the director, brought in Andrew Kevin Walker, who wrote *Seven*, to re-write the screenplay. This is where the problems start. *The Game* has an intriguing premise. The story grabs you and keeps you on edge, keeps you guessing, for at least an hour. Trying to add that extra bit of excitement, the script piles on plot twists, incredibly contrived coincidences, and hairpin curves to the point that it destroys its own internal logic. For a thriller to work, the story has to maintain some level of internal logic and believability. When it threw in everything, including the proverbial kitchen sink with garbage disposal unit attached, the script actually threw everything out the window. The ending is absolutely ridiculous. It smells (stinks, actually) of … *test screenings.*

The Game would have been an excellent film if it had respected its own logic and come to a conclusion at the point where its own plot dictated that it should do so. I don't want to spoil the movie for anyone who might want to watch it, but I will say that near the end there is an opportunity for the story to come to a stunning, film noir, slap-in-the-face conclusion. Instead, the story continues, and it concludes on a sour note of monumental proportions, an incredibly hokey cop-out of an ending that left me feeling completely ripped off. But, of course, test audiences tend not to like stunning, film noir, slap-in-the-face endings, so there it is.

Imagine this: at the end of *Rear Window*, it turns out that the character played by Raymond Burr hasn't really killed his wife and cut her into pieces, but rather that she has been visiting her sister in Poughkeepsie; Jimmy Stewart and Grace Kelly have just been imagining things; it's all just a silly joke, and the characters all get together over champagne and have a good laugh about it.

Yuck.

Well, this is essentially what happens in *The Game*. The ending will have you ranting and raving for your money back.

22

Godzilla

If you believe that size really doesn't matter, you may be underwhelmed by the return of *Godzilla*. And if you believe that things like plot and dialogue *do* matter, you will be bitterly disappointed.

Even the most skeptical moviegoers have to acknowledge that "old Atom Breath" (as he is affectionately called by his legions of fans) has been a lucrative movie staple since his first screen incarnation back in the fifties. It's interesting to note that director Roland Emmerich is not a fan of the original *Godzilla* movies. He agreed to direct this latest version only after he was promised that he would be allowed to do whatever he wanted with the creature and the storyline. However, Toho Co. Ltd., the copyright owners, had only agreed to allow an American version to be made if Tristar Pictures promised that certain guidelines would be followed to ensure that the film would respect what the Japanese called the "spirit of *Godzilla*." The American end-product managed to ignore practically every single guideline proposed by Toho.

This latest instalment in the *Godzilla* saga arrived riding a tsunami of hype. Teasers began appearing in theatres almost a full year before the movie was finally released. The world premiere took place in Madison Square Garden with twelve thousand people in attendance. Yes, this was The Big

One. Big budget, big hopes, big dollar signs flashing in those beady, greedy little corporate eyes.

Godzilla first captured our collective imagination in 1956. Quickly becoming a franchise, the *Godzilla* series of movies were a real pop culture phenomenon. As I write this, there are numerous websites and fan clubs devoted to the creature that flattened Tokyo. If you're interested, you can check out "Barry's Temple of Godzilla," and "Mario's Godzilla Page" on the World Wide Web. These sites are chock full of *Godzilla* lore, innuendo, and rumour. For example, I discovered by browsing the net that Godzilla received an MTV lifetime achievement award for his many films. There's a strong rebuke for people who think that the Internet is filled with useless information. The story didn't mention whether he had flattened the studio or any spectators when he arrived to receive his prize.

In this 1998 version of *Godzilla*, Matthew Broderick portrays Niko, a young scientist who must confront the hordes of military nincompoops who try to take over when Godzilla arrives on the scene. In true B-movie fashion, the army winds up blowing up every great building in New York, including the Chrysler Building and the Flatiron Building, in its attempt to defeat the creature. Jean Reno plays a French Secret Service agent who leads a team of crack commandos whose mission is to destroy Godzilla. The French wish to atone for the South Pacific nuclear tests that created old Lizard Breath in the first place. Between bouts of getting our heroes out of tight spots, Reno spends much of the movie complaining, in stereotypical French fashion, that you can't get a croissant or a decent cup of coffee in the States.

Maria Pitillo portrays wannabe TV-reporter Audrey Timmonds, who bravely tries to get the story while renewing a sappy love relationship with Matthew Broderick's character. This love story contributes much of the inane dialogue that pollutes this movie at every turn.

Stellar examples include:

He: We've got to evacuate Manhattan.
She: But there are three million people in Manhattan. Has that ever been done before?
He: I don't think so.

Or how about:

He: You left me eight years ago without so much as a note or a phone call. That hurt.
She: Well, that was eight years ago. Can't you let it go? Some people change.
He: Most people don't.

And some directors never change either: after all, Roland Emmerich previously committed *Independence Day*. It was a huge financial success, but also a critical turkey of gargantuan proportions.

Strike one.

He then went on to direct *The Day After Tomorrow*.

Strike two.

I should be careful. I may wind up as a caricature in one of Emmerich's movies, just as critics Roger Ebert and Gene Siskel do in this one. You see, Emmerich never forgave the pair for mercilessly panning *Independence Day*. In *Godzilla*, the mayor of New York is a Roger Ebert look-alike. He is also an incompetent who spends his time barking out silly orders and stuffing his face with chocolates. Mayor Ebert also has an incompetent sidekick named — guess what —

Gene! I can almost imagine a salivating Emmerich muttering under his breath, "Trash my movies, eh? I'll get you, damn know-it-all critics! And *Godzilla* is *still* going to make a Godzillion dollars. Nyah, nyah, nyah!"

There is actually one solid scene in this mess. It takes place in Madison Square Garden, where Godzilla has laid dozens of eggs. Our heroes are trapped inside the Gardens when the eggs begin to hatch. They must outrun and outwit the baby Godzillas in order to escape. It's a pretty good scene, and it produces some chills and suspense, but unfortunately it doesn't appear until over an hour into the proceedings. By that time you may already have died of boredom, or possibly choked on the incredibly stupid dialogue.

The only truly interesting thing about this film is the technology that went into its creation. The monster was animated using a process called Motion Capture. An actor dressed in a suit equipped with some seventy-two light-reflecting markers mimes Godzilla's movements. These movements are exactly reproduced by the image of the monster on a computer monitor. The director watches his monitor and sees Godzilla crunching through the streets of New York, copying the actor's moves exactly. He can say to the actor, "Okay, lift your arm and hit that building!" And onscreen, Godzilla lifts his arm and punches a hole in the Met Life Building — a move that might draw applause from audience members particularly annoyed with insurance companies. The result of this virtual reality puppeteering is that the monster moves much more naturally than he did in the earlier movies, because he's no longer a guy in a rubber suit.

Speaking of the guy in the rubber suit, Japanese actor Kenpachiro Satsuma, who portrayed Godzilla in several movies between 1985 and 1995, apparently walked out of an advance screening, complaining that the film had all but destroyed the spirit of the original.

There's no denying that the look of the monster has changed dramatically. Godzilla used to be kind of cute and clunky. He now looks like a cross between the creature in *Alien* and a raptor from *Jurassic Park*. And he is just so damn big that the whole concept becomes silly.

I suppose that sounds strange.

I mean, the concept always *was* monumentally silly, wasn't it? But now, believe me, it's off the silly scale. The new Godzilla is four hundred feet tall or something. I'm willing to suspend my disbelief, but at that height I get a nosebleed.

At the advance screening I attended I overheard one disheartened fan mutter in disbelief, "Where's his atom-mist breath? They've taken away his atom-mist breath!" For fans of the real deal, taking away Godzilla's radioactive breath is like deciding that Superman can't fly anymore. How dare these people muck about with our sci-fi icons in such a cavalier fashion!

In the wake (or was it the tidal wave?) of *Titanic*, Hollywood is going to continue to think that bigger is better, and that special effects are enough to justify expensive blockbusters, and that elements like well-plotted stories and intelligent dialogue can be dispensed with.

Strike three.

23

Grace of My Heart

Once upon a time Carole King's *Tapestry* (1971) was the biggest-selling LP in pop music history. Do you know *anyone* who didn't own a copy back in the seventies? When everyone switched over to CDs in the late eighties, *Tapestry* became the most often-sighted LP at garage sales, along with such yard-sale staples as the Tijuana Brass and the Bee Gees.

What many casual listeners who bought *Tapestry* way back then did not know was that from the late fifties to the mid-sixties, Carole King was one of the most successful writers of pop songs in America. Working alone, or with her then-husband Gerry Goffin, she wrote an amazing number of hit songs for many now legendary artists, including Aretha Franklin, the Shirelles, and the Drifters. A very small sample of songs King either wrote or collaborated on includes "Chains," "Go Away Little Girl," "The Loco-Motion," "I'm Into Something Good," "One Fine Day," "Up on the Roof," and "(You Make Me Feel) Like a Natural Woman."

King wrote these hits back in the days when the American music industry was rigidly specialized; that is, singers were expected to sing songs written by professional songwriters. In 1961, the Brill Building — located on Broadway just north of Times Square — enjoyed its golden era. Songwriters, music publishers, and record producers occupied almost every inch of its ten floors. There were hundreds of them, many in offices so small they could barely contain a single piano and a few chairs, and all were working to create what they hoped would be the next big top-ten hit. Many supremely talented people toiled in the Brill, and the jumbled sounds of piano and vocals drifted from under dozens of doors, a raucous, joyful cacophony that tickled the ears of anyone who might happen to be walking down a hallway on any given day. And if a visitor were really lucky, he might hear works in progress by Bert Berns ("Twist and Shout") or Neil Diamond ("I'm a Believer"), or by song-writing teams — some of them married couples — such as Jeff Barry and Ellie Greenwich ("Be My Baby"), or Barry Mann and Cynthia Weill ("On Broadway"), or Burt Bacharach and Hal David ("The Man Who Shot Liberty Valance"), or Tommy Boyce and Bobby Hart ("Last Train to Clarksville").

Starting in 1964, the Beatles ushered in a revolution in popular music: groups and singers would soon be recording their own material almost exclusively. In a very short time, personal expression became of paramount importance, and "true" artists could no longer be expected to perform songs written by someone else. The music business changed almost overnight, and even the very best songwriters were faced with tough choices. Many would turn, with varying degrees of success, to recording and releasing their songs themselves rather than selling them to others. By 1967 a golden era of popular music, which had seen the flourishing of professional songwriters working in tandem with producers and hand-picked vocal groups, was almost dead.

I discovered pop music at a very early age, thanks to my older sister's small record player — a "pick-up" we used to call it — and the dozens of 45-rpm records that were always lying around. The first sounds that I truly loved were, I learned much later, created in the Brill Building, or in similar environments in Chicago, Memphis, and L.A. I was too young to read the titles when I discovered these little records, but I learned to distinguish the songs by their labels. Aside from being captivated by the sounds they made, I was also fascinated by how they looked as they spun around. As seen from directly over the spinning turntable, the orange and yellow swirl label of Capitol Records was truly hypnotic. When I got to be a little older and learned to read, I discovered that the singers and bands I loved had such names as "Ray Charles," "Turtles," "Beatles," "Four Seasons," "Young Rascals," "Shirelles," "Dion and the Belmonts," "Lovin' Spoonful," "Wilson Pickett."

Grace of My Heart, written and directed by Allison Anders (*Gas, Food, Lodging*), is somewhat different from the other films discussed in this book in that it is neither a great movie nor a particularly bad one. It is actually no more than an entertaining, if rather contrived and overly sentimental, viewing experience. But, more importantly, it is a wonderful celebration of the pop music I discovered as a child, and still love today.

Rather than fill the movie with classic songs from the sixties, the producers have enlisted the formidable talents of Larry Klein, Elvis Costello, Burt Bacharach, Gerry Goffin, Los Lobos, and Joni Mitchell to compose songs in the *style* of artists like Leslie Gore, the Supremes, and the Beach Boys. Larry Klein, the film's musical director, has also recruited some of the veteran studio musicians who played on many sixties hits to record the new tracks, while arranging for the songs to be recorded in Capitol Records' legendary Studio B. It takes exceptional musical ability and sensibility to successfully recreate earlier musical styles, and Klein and company do a superb job. The soundtrack they have crafted for *Grace of My Heart* is one of the best to be heard in any American film produced in the nineties.

After winning a local talent contest in 1958 in Philadelphia, heiress Edna Buxton (Illeana Douglas) decides, against the wishes of her family, to move to New York to pursue her dream of a singing career. She wins a modest recording contract for one single, and then records a romantic ballad she has written herself called "In Another World." After listening carefully to her performance — and complimenting her on the quality of her song — the producer gives Edna the bad news: "Not only does everyone in town have a singer like you, Toots, but everyone is trying to get rid of the singer they have like you. Male vocal groups are in, girl singers are out!"

Down but not out, Edna meets a fast-talking, savvy record producer and music publisher named Joel Millner. As portrayed by John Turturro in yet another quirky, hilarious screen incarnation, Joel overwhelms Edna with his energy and takes her under his wing — "*hijacks* her" would be more to the point — quickly convincing her over a couple of cheeseburgers to try writing songs for the artists he's currently managing. Horrified to discover that her name is Edna and, worse, that her family is none other than the incredibly rich Buxtons of Philadelphia, he imagines a new identity that he feels will give her more street credibility in the music business. Somewhat reluctantly, Edna becomes "Denise Waverly from the slums of South Philly."

"Denise" is soon at work in a cubbyhole office in the Brill Building writing pop songs. Before too long she has written a hit, and has met and fallen in love with another songwriter, Howard Cazatt (Eric Stoltz), who writes socially relevant lyrics. Inspired by the sad tale of a young black girl's pregnancy, they compose "Unwanted Number," a terrifically catchy tune that echoes, in real life, the Supremes' "Love Child" and Goffin-King's "Will You Still Love Me Tomorrow?" "Unwanted Number" becomes a controversial hit, pushing Denise and Howard onto the covers of the most influential music trade magazines. They are now the hottest song-writing team in New York. Soon they are married, and the hits just keep on coming.

In its first half, *Grace of My Heart* parallels the lives of Carole King and her husband Gerry Goffin pretty faithfully, up to and including their divorce, and this first hour saves the movie. The girl-group, doo-wop, Brill Building era is lovingly recreated, and we are given a wonderfully evocative portrait of a simpler, more innocent time in the music business. Highlights include Bridget Fonda — in an amazing, hair-sprayed, back-combed, homecoming queen "flip" hairdo — as a Leslie Gore look-alike singer who harbours a desperate secret love.

Denise's divorce from Howard coincides with the arrival of the British Invasion bands in 1964, and also marks the point where *Grace of My Heart* begins to wander off into melodrama, with decidedly mixed results.

The movie becomes more dramatically overwrought and predictable when Denise hooks up with a Brian Wilson-John Phillips hybrid character, a young hotshot producer-songwriter from California named Jay Phillips (Matt Dillon). Despite having enormous success with his surf-type group the Riptides, Jay has become "psychedelicized," and dreams of going "really far-out" with a concept album. Unfortunately, the script stumbles badly at this point, and allows Jay to make a painfully anachronistic statement. During the course of a televised interview that is supposed to be taking place around 1965, Jay explains how he is trying to push the boundaries of traditional popular song lyrics. He then cites the example of John Lennon, who has recently, Jay says, "written a song about a walrus."

Hey, wait a minute, man.

Like just about everything else concerning the Beatles, the year that Lennon wrote "I Am the Walrus" is well documented, and it is 1967. A mistake like this may well go zipping over the heads of most moviegoers, who either won't catch it or don't really care one way or the other, but for me it's like a flaming dart to the forehead. The re-creation of an era in a believable way is a delicate process, one that can be noisily shattered by this kind of sloppy faux pas.

That being said, Matt Dillon does a fine job portraying Denise's new surfed-up, spaced-out boy-genius husband, but as we move deeper into the psychedelic sixties, the plot gets increasingly (and annoyingly) groovy, man. A totally unrecognizable Peter Fonda shows up in one scene as a psychiatrist trying to rescue Jay from a particularly bad trip. Fonda's performance gets dangerously close to caricature, but he somehow manages to recite every hippy-dip, stoner line of pop-psychology dialogue with enough panache to pull off a successful, if a bit wobbly, performance.

The movie descends into cheesy melodrama when Jay commits suicide and Denise is left to wander around without a compass until Joel rescues her from a commune and shakes her into resuming her music career, this time as a singer. Eventually her LP *Grace of My Heart* is released, to rave reviews, and the movie ends with her finally tasting the personal success that had always eluded her.

Although it is uneven, *Grace of My Heart* is one of those movies that I just can't help enjoying. As hokey as it is in places (and is it ever!), it still holds up remarkably well to repeated viewing. For readers who may be nostalgic for the good old 45-rpm days of impeccably crafted three-minute musical gems shimmering with infectious, memorable melodies, groovy beats, and catchy, poppy lyricism, *Grace of My Heart* is pretty much irresistible, as is Illeana Douglas in the role of Edna/Denise.

24

The Hitchhiker's Guide to the Galaxy

Douglas Adams (1952–2001) said that the idea for *The Hitchhiker's Guide to the Galaxy* came to him when he was hitchhiking around Europe in the early 1970s, carrying around one of those "Europe on ten dollars a day" guides (which by now must be called "Europe on seventy-five euros a day"). Lying in a field in Austria after having generously sampled the local beverages, Adams thought, "Wouldn't it be great to have the same kind of guide to the Galaxy? I'd be off like a shot."

Well, who knows if humans won't be travelling around the Galaxy some day? But if we are, let's hope that we improve our manners and pick up our garbage.

The problem with visiting the universe — as opposed to visiting Moncton, for example — is that it's so darned big. As Adams points out in the *Guide*, the universe we live in is of a size beyond human comprehension. The human mind just isn't very good at wrapping itself around concepts of galactic scale. I was excited to hear a while ago that a team of astronomers working with a very large telescope in Chile had captured the first photographic proof of a planet beyond our solar system. The planet that was photographed is in the galaxy of Hydra, some two hundred light years from Earth.

Two hundred light years.

I don't know why this was not front page news all over the world. A discovery like this seems to me to be of paramount importance. Astronomers have long inferred the existence of other planets, but this is proof of it, and, as former prime minister Jean Chrétien once said so eloquently, "A proof is a proof ... and when you have a good proof, it's because it's proven." And this should be just the beginning. Let's face it, where there's one planet, there's a bunch, maybe millions, maybe billions!

But two hundred light years! This planet is so far away that the light from it, travelling at 186,000 miles per second (or 700 million miles per hour), takes two hundred years to get to us. It's almost impossible to imagine.

Now 502 feet I can understand. That's the longest home run Ted Williams ever hit at Fenway Park. I can visualize 502 feet. But my puny mind can't really wrap itself around two hundred light years.

The Hitchhiker's Guide has had several incarnations. It started out as a radio play — a radio series, actually — produced by the BBC. It then became a book, and then another book, and then a television series, which aired here in Canada in the eighties on TVO. It's also been a computer game. About the only thing that *The Hitchhiker's Guide* hasn't been is a breakfast cereal. It's had more incarnations than Shirley MacLaine.

Douglas Adams was always both thrilled and deeply worried about his *Guide* being turned into a Hollywood movie. He moved to Santa Barbara with his family in 1999, and he was working on the movie project at the time of his death. He once compared the process of having a Hollywood film made to "trying to grill a steak by having a succession of people coming into the room and breathing on it." He did finally finish the script, but, sadly, died before the film was made. The script was written in collaboration with Karey Kirkpatrick, who wrote the brilliant *Chicken Run.*

A word now about the Infinite Improbability Drive, the drive system that allows a spaceship to travel instantaneously to any point in the Galaxy. Without it, you really aren't going to be able to travel much further than Moncton, cosmically speaking of course. One weird temporary side effect of engaging the Infinite Improbability Drive is that during the short time it takes for a ship to "jump" to another point in the universe, the people on board are subjected to a series of bizarre, seemingly random transformations. You might suddenly turn into a sofa or a cupcake before re-integrating your human form. This is disconcerting for the space traveller, but a constant source of outlandish, sometimes hilarious sight gags in the movie.

The hero of *The Hitchhiker's Guide* is Arthur Dent, a thirty-something British Everyman. As is the case in numerous blues songs, Arthur wakes up one morning to find his little house surrounded by bulldozers ready to demolish it to make way for a new bypass. Then, still in his pyjamas, Arthur is visited by his friend Ford Prefect, who gives him even worse news: *Earth* is about to be demolished to make way for a new intergalactic expressway. "But all is not lost," Ford continues. "We have twelve minutes. Let's go for a few pints at the pub."

Unbeknownst to Arthur, his buddy Ford is actually a galactic researcher who has been visiting Earth to write a chapter for an extremely popular galactic publication called *The Hitchhiker's Guide to the Galaxy.* Ford wants to save Arthur's life, because Arthur once saved his. When he first arrived on Earth, Ford, thinking that automobiles were the dominant species, tried to shake hands with an oncoming car, and Arthur pushed him out of the way in the nick of time. The character's name, Ford Prefect, comes from a car model made by Ford for the English market. The nuts-and-bolts Ford Prefect was apparently a lemon, along the lines of the infamous Ford Pinto.

Seconds before Earth is destroyed, extra-terrestrial Ford grabs his human friend Arthur and hitches a ride aboard a huge spaceship that is overseeing Earth's destruction. The ship is piloted by creatures called Vogons. These critters are the bureaucrats, the functionaries of the Galaxy. They don't decide anything, they just execute orders. We are told that, like many functionaries here on Earth, they have no imagination, they just run things. Their mission is to eliminate Earth to make room for a hyperspace highway bypass.

To picture the Vogons, imagine lumpy, greyish, seven-foot-tall Muppets with very bad, very yellow teeth, big, rubbery, purple lips, and absolutely no sense of humour. And not only are they ugly, the Vogons are absolutely the worst poets in the Galaxy.

By the way, why do you think it is that Alien races so often have names like Vogons, or Metrons — or that band that just couldn't stick together, the Teflons — names that make them sound like either sixties surf bands or doo-wop vocal groups, as in "Reach for the steam iron, we're being invaded by the Rayons!"?

Anyway, Arthur and Ford escape the Vogons and are picked up by another ship, captained by the President of the Galaxy, Zaphod Beeblebrox. Zaphod is a loud, egocentric, two-headed creature — both heads empty — but he is a friend of Ford Prefect, so our heroes are safe, at least temporarily. Also on board the ship is Trillia, the only surviving Earth woman (Zooey Deschannel), whom Arthur had met previously at a party and has a crush on. She is also attracted to him, but she is currently involved with the demented

Zaphod. Also on board is a manic depressive robot named Marvin, who is voiced in a hilarious, depressed monotone by Alan Rickman. Marvin, who has many of the best lines in the film, displays generous quantities of the celebrated dry British wit, which is not to be confused with the equally celebrated wet British weather.

Zaphod is on a quest to learn the ultimate answer to life, the universe, and everything. In the absurdist universe of *The Hitchhiker's Guide*, it seems that the answer to life is already known, having been revealed by a supercomputer millions of years previously, but the question that goes with the answer is still being sought. And in case you're wondering, the answer to the meaning of life, the universe, and everything is ... 42. Baseball fans will find this interesting: 42 was Jackie Robinson's number. As the number of the first black player to be accepted into Major League baseball, 42 could be seen as a symbol of racial harmony and integration. It is fitting, then — although certainly completely coincidental — that Adams chose that number as the answer to everything. If integration and racial tolerance don't constitute the ultimate answer, then I don't know what does. In reality, Adams seems to have arrived at the number 42 purely by chance. When asked about his choice, he declared that the number had just popped into his head while he was contemplating his garden one morning. I'm certain that author and ex-ballplayer Bill Lee, a.k.a. The Spaceman, could have a field day with the Jackie Robinson coincidence — he has for years expounded on the notion that baseball has profound cosmic significance.

The Hitchhiker's Guide to the Galaxy is absurdist satire of the highest order. It satirizes bureaucracy, British society, organized religion, and even science-fiction itself. But it's difficult to adapt something like this for the screen, because people expect a movie to be about "getting somewhere." This movie, like most hitchhiking trips, declares the pleasure to be in the trip itself, and in its unlikely detours. Hollywood being what it is, elements were added to jazz things up and inject suspense, and also to keep things moving along at a brisker pace than Adams intended. For example, the character of Trillian, Arthur's love interest, becomes much more important than she is in the novel; the romantic sub-plot (which doesn't work as well as it could) has been thrown in, I suppose, because one of the producers felt that it would make the film more appealing for some audience members. Also, a sinister Alien character, portrayed by John Malkovich, appears. I'm not really sure what he's doing here, but his unnecessary albeit colourful presence seems like an attempt to inject more suspense into the proceedings. Stale elements are borrowed from *Star Wars* and other films — for example, Trillian is kidnapped by the Vogons and has to be rescued (the old damsel-in-distress-in-space motif) — but they don't really add anything of real value to the plot. Generally, these tacked-on elements feel, well, tacked on.

The cast is excellent. Mos Def is Ford, Sam Rockwell the clueless Zaphod, and Martin Freeman the solidly English and endearing Arthur. The special effects are first-rate also. This is a very good-looking movie. It is also funny. The animated sequences that explain the *Hitchhiker's Guide* itself are superb, and feature terrifically entertaining narration by Stephen Fry (of *Harry Potter* fame).

The Hitchhiker's Guide to the Galaxy captures the benign spirit of Adams's satire, which celebrates with great wit the utter zaniness and absurdity of human existence. Not having read the book, I brought no expectations to the film. More serious connoisseurs and purists might have major quibbles, but my advice to them, and to all Earth creatures, is the following: Don't Panic!

25

House of Wax

In *The Wizard of Oz*, the Wicked Witch of the West (Margaret Hamilton) famously screamed, "I'm melting!" After watching the 2005 version of *House of Wax* I felt as if my brain was melting.

The *House of Wax* that most people are familiar with is the 1953 3-D version. It featured an icon of B-movie horror, Vincent Price. One of the gimmicks the studios looked to in the fifties to tear people away from their newfangled television sets and bring them back into the theatres was 3-D. It was fun, but it was also a bit of a flop. If anything "saved" Hollywood in the fifties, it was arguably the drive-in. But that's another story.

House of Wax (1953) was not the best 3-D movie ever made. The director, André de Toth, didn't seem to truly grasp all of the possibilities offered by the process. His movie just didn't have enough things jumping out at you. This is perhaps explained by the fact that André de Toth only had one eye.

Really.

Can you say "depth perception"?

No wonder he didn't get this 3-D thing. Only in Hollywood would someone assign a one-eyed director to direct a 3-D film.

The 1953 *House of Wax*, with Vincent Price, also marks the screen debut of Charles Buchinsky, who portrays a hunchbacked assistant. Now here's an opportunity for you to impress your friends and family around the dinner table with your superior knowledge of darned-near useless Hollywood trivia:

> Q: Following this first screen appearance, what name did Mr Buchinsky adopt for the remainder of his movie career?
> A: Charles Bronson.

More trivia: Charles Bronson inspired a certain Mr Arroyo, who loved Bronson's movies, to name his son Bronson.
Go Sox!

The 1953 *House of Wax* was a remake of a 1932 film called *Mystery of the Wax Museum.* In it Lionel Atwill portrayed a sculptor, horribly disfigured in a fire, who goes on a murderous spree, encases his victims in wax, and exhibits them in his museum.

The newest *House of Wax* is directed by Jaume Collet-Serra, who has previously directed television commercials. I don't know which ones, but if they're anything like this movie, I'll bet you they're full of really annoying people.

By the way, am I the only one who thinks that the nosy, know-it-all, supposedly helpful neighbour in those Canadian Tire commercials is really annoying? You know, that grey-haired guy with the glasses and the little goatee who keeps popping up out of the hedges and shrubs with all kinds of advice about car repairs and lawn care. You have a moron who can't get his lawnmower started, and then this guy pops up and says, "You can get a three-hundred horsepower Mastercraft six-speed lawnmower with reversible do-it-yourself appendectomy drill bit for only $599.00 this week at Canadian Tire."

Whenever I see him, I yell at the television, "Don't listen to this guy! Nobody needs a $600.00 lawnmower! All you need to get the darned thing started is a three-dollar spark plug!"

And then, adding insult to injury, they throw that jingle at you: "I'll start with you ..." Every time I hear it I think, "Listen, buddy, *don't* start with me!"

Anyway.

House of Wax should have starred Cher. After all, she is already at least partly made of wax, so this movie would have been a natural for her. Unfortunately, we get Paris Hilton instead.

Paris and her friends (not to be confused with *Rocky and His Friends*) are travelling in two vehicles: Paris and her boyfriend are in a four-by-four and another couple and friends are in a car. On their way to a big football game, they stop and camp for the night out in the middle of nowhere. The next morning, they discover that the fan belt on one of the vehicles has been cut.

Unfortunately for them, that annoying neighbour from the Canadian Tire commercials doesn't pop up to help them.

From this point onward, every stupid slasher/splatter movie cliché we can imagine is thrown in our faces. Early in the proceedings, one of the moronic young heroes points a camcorder, which has been running constantly, at Ms. Hilton. In mock anger, she yells, "Put down that camera!" I found myself wishing that the director of this meltdown had done exactly that and stopped production, but he didn't.

While looking for help to repair her boyfriend's car, Elisha Cuthbert (from the television series *24*) wanders into a decrepit-looking town and is promptly captured by the homicidal maniac twins who have converted the place into a real-life chamber of horrors. The two brothers have apparently killed off everyone in town, encased them in wax, and put them on display. Some unlucky locals are displayed in their living room windows, while others are dressed in their Sunday best and sit neatly in church. There is even a small movie theatre, which screens *Whatever Happened to Baby Jane?* night after night for its waxen, permanently transfixed audience.

At the mercy of her psychotic captors, poor Elisha gets part of a finger cut off and has her lips glued together with Crazy Glue. One young man who goes looking for her is decapitated with very nasty-looking knives. Another young man has an equally nasty knife stuck in his throat.

What else? Oh yes, one guy is encased in wax while still alive and then has half of his face peeled off by a well-meaning friend who is attempting to liberate him from his wax envelope. The friend doesn't have time to dwell on the horror of what has just transpired, however, because he is summarily decapitated.

As the Beach Boys would say, "Fun, fun, fun!"

But the absolute highlight — in a movie filled with highlights — is certainly the moment when Paris Hilton herself pokes her head up from her hiding place only to be very rapidly skewered by a two-foot metal bar that punches its way unequivocally through her forehead like a javelin through cheddar. Anyone who can throw a metal bar with such pinpoint precision and velocity is wasting his time as a homicidal maniac. He should be recruited immediately for the javelin throw by the US Olympic team. A gold medal is assured.

Did I mention that the homicidal maniacs dwell in a house that is literally made out of wax, and that at the end of the movie, when it burns down in a fiery crescendo of excitement, the whole thing turns into a gooey, steaming puddle?

Other highlights include Paris looking for her lip gloss while her boyfriend is driving his truck — at least that's what her character *says* she's doing down there — and Elisha Cuthbert slipping down a slippery slope and landing face down in an assortment of roadkill. This, perhaps the most "colourful" scene in the film, is designed to coax the maximum "yuck factor" from the teenaged girls in the audience while getting the teenaged boys to declare gleefully, "All right! Gross!" while laughing at the cringing teenaged girls, who are at this point turning various shades of green.

The mostly inane dialogue attains its zenith when Elisha Cuthbert confronts one of the homicidal brothers, a psychotic sculptor, with the immortal line, "You don't have to do this. You're an artist!"

Given the choice between sitting through this again and having that Canadian Tire guy move in next door, I would rather sit through this again. That being said, this is one of those rare movies (I see maybe one or two a year) that have no perceivable positive qualities. Well, okay, maybe one. Ms. Hilton's death scene was pretty funny, but because I don't want to be accused of being a sadistic critic I won't dwell on it.

If you ever get the urge to rent this when it appears on DVD my advice would be to take the five bucks, buy some candles instead, light them, and watch them slowly melt. You will get more entertainment from that experience than you will from watching this gooey concoction.

26

I Am Sam

I respect Sean Penn. He was remarkable in 1995 as the condemned man awaiting execution in *Dead Man Walking*. He was also remarkable in 1999 as the morally vacuous self-centred guitarist in *Sweet and Lowdown*. He has been consistently excellent throughout his career.

He has also directed. He has written scripts. He has behaved badly in public. He has punched photographers. He once served a month in jail for punching an extra on a movie set. He is on the record as having called Oliver Stone a "pig." If he had called Stone a "paranoid psycho-pig" he might have been eligible for a Pulitzer Prize. Penn has a son named Hopper Jack, after Dennis Hopper and Jack Nicholson. He is an "actors' actor." He has often accepted roles in films that did not pay him a lot of money. In other words, the man is an artist.

Unfortunately, he also seems obsessed with flamboyant, over-the-top roles that appear designed to win him a Best Actor Oscar.

But he's not alone. Consider for a moment the case of one of the great actors of his generation, Dustin Hoffman. Hoffman has won two Best Actor Oscars, one for *Kramer vs. Kramer*, and one for *Rain Man*. In that one, Hoffman played an idiot savant, an autistic man with very special talents. He blew the competition to smithereens at the Oscars.

The members of the Academy of Motion Picture Arts and Sciences love tender, sentimental, funny portrayals of mentally challenged people.

Consider the case of Ingrid Bergman. She was a wonderful actress who was completely overlooked by the Academy during the last twenty-five years of her career, except in 1975, when she won a Best Supporting Actress Oscar for her portrayal of — you guessed it — a wonderfully loving and sincere, but mentally challenged woman in *Murder on the Orient Express*.

Or think of Jack Nicholson's obsessive-compulsive curmudgeon Melvin Udall in *As Good as It Gets*. Same type of character, same result: Oscar. Or what about Russell Crowe's brilliant paranoid-schizophrenic in *A Beautiful Mind*? Oscar.

The point here is that Sean Penn may have taken the lead role in director Jessie Nelson's *I Am Sam* as a career move, if not an Oscar grab. I know that sounds cynical, but moviemaking can be a cynical business. I would like to give Sean Penn the benefit of the doubt and think that he went for the role of Sam Dawson because he felt that it was a challenge to his acting skills and that he could make an artistic statement while at the same time pointing a finger at the societal prejudices that hinder the mentally disabled. But this is one of the phoniest, most manipulative movies I have seen in a very long time. Is Penn good in it? Yes he is. In fact, he positively shines. He shines so intensely that you may want to wear shades. (Hmm ... "shines" ... that reminds me of another movie ... Yes! *Shine*, with Geoffrey Rush! Rush took home the Best Actor Oscar for his portrayal of an idiot savant pianist. Do I detect a pattern here?)

Unfortunately for the audience, *I Am Sam* isn't set in the real world, although it's supposed to be. What we really get is a gooey "feel good" alternative universe, a shiny Spic-n-Span Starbucks world, filled with Kodak moments and product placement, and brimming with the sound of Beatles music. Beatles songs are everywhere in this movie. They are used as background music, they are used as foreground music, they are sung by the characters — especially by Sam, who reveres them — and the lyrics are quoted constantly, and on and on, and Obladi Oblada …

In this Pepperland world, Sam Dawson has fathered a child with a homeless woman. We learn that immediately after giving birth this woman left Sam to look after the baby girl by himself. It's not explained how or why Sam had sex with a homeless woman, and it's a good thing that it's not, because, like a lot of other things in this movie, this is about as believable as the one about the hen that laid the golden eggs or the Iraqi weapons of mass destruction. Pointing out all the holes in this script would take longer than counting the ones in Blackburn, Lancashire.

Sam, as I've mentioned, is obsessed with Beatles music, so obsessed, in fact, that he has named his daughter Lucy Diamond Dawson, after the John Lennon song "Lucy in the Sky with Diamonds." Sam explains every event in his life by quoting Beatles lyrics. Even for the most dedicated Apple Scruff, this is overkill. Worse, the songs we hear aren't even the original versions. They are cover versions by artists like Aimee Mann and Rufus Wainwright. It seems that the producers of *I Am Sam* felt that it would have been just too expensive to pay for the rights to reproduce the original recordings. Not that the cover versions are all bad — some of them are quite good — but the quality is uneven at best.

Sam seems to have only very minor problems dealing with the first six years of his daughter's life. Despite possessing the intellect of a seven-year-old, he seems to manage beautifully. He has a wonderful apartment, and access to quality day care while he is at work; indeed he appears to have no problems whatsoever. Everything is fine. And why shouldn't it be? Most seven-year-old children could raise a child, couldn't they?

Things only get complicated when little Lucy approaches her seventh birthday, and she begins to tire of Dad wanting to read to her Dr Seuss's *Green Eggs and Ham*. Soon, little Lucy begins to fail intentionally at school, because she doesn't want to seem smarter than her dad. Quick as you can say "Mean Mr Mustard," the powers that be want to take little Lucy away from Sam, because they have come to the conclusion that he's not up to the task of raising her, and it's all very sad, and what a sad critic I am, green eggs and spam.

Michelle Pfeiffer enters the story as Rita (lovely Rita?), a bitchy, self-absorbed lawyer who gets embarrassed into doing some pro-bono work on Sam's behalf. Pfeiffer's character has a son, but her marriage is in trouble. Her husband's main fault seems to be that he is of average intelligence. According to the logic of this film, he can't be doing a good job as a dad, because dads with average or above average intelligence don't do a good job. From the screenwriter's point of view, mentally challenged Sam *would* do a good job if given a chance, and he should therefore be given custody of his daughter.

Laura Dern pops in as sweet and bubbly Randy, a potential foster mom for little Lucy. Randy seems as if she would be a great mother. She has begun to spend time with Lucy, and obviously loves the little girl very much. The problem with Randy is that her husband Brad has average intelligence. Consequently, the script never gives us one single scene between him and little Lucy. Why? Because he might be a good potential dad! We couldn't have that, because the script has decreed that Sam is her dad, and only Sam should raise her. Oh what a bored and frustrated critic I am, green scripts and jam.

After a series of court scenes in which the bad guys try to take little Lucy away from Sam, I began to fume. What *is* wrong with these judges and lawyers, I thought to myself. Don't they know that all you need is love?

Everything in this movie — every silly, sappy, vapid piece of dialogue, every situation, every misuse and abuse of Beatles music and lyrics — is contrived to make the audience feel mushy and liberal.

I saw this movie on a Monday afternoon, and only about twelve people were in the cinema. Strangely, several of them couldn't help repeating every line of dialogue, and reading aloud everything that appeared on the screen. There were actually some better performances in the audience than up on the screen. Also, three ladies behind me sniffled a lot during the proceedings. No wonder. The script was pushing all of their emotional buttons at once, playing them like a Kleenex salesman at an onion-peeling contest. But, cranky critic that I am, when a movie tries to push all of my buttons like this, I get ... well, cranky.

This is one of those movies that piles on the emotional manure so thickly that the fumes alone can be enough to paralyse certain critical functions of the human brain.

Where are those Blue Meanies when we really need them?

27

Jurassic Park III

I'll admit to having a soft spot in my head for movies with dinosaurs in them. I just can't help it. A rotten movie with dinosaurs is far superior to a rotten movie with no dinosaurs.

Usually.

I always loved those old comic books like *Star Spangled War Stories*, in which Second World War soldiers stumbled onto the "island that time forgot" and did battle with colourful dinosaurs. Think about this: if the producers of *Jurassic Park* had been really smart, they would have united their efforts with the producers of *Pearl Harbor* (one of the true brontosaurian-sized turkeys of our times) and have *dinosaurs* attack the American battleships, not Japanese planes. This would have been fun. I can see the snarling dinosaurs chomping on 50-mm cannons and spitting the live ammunition back at Ben Affleck.

IMPORTANT NOTE TO WOULD-BE SCREEN-WRITERS: bad dialogue doesn't matter so much when you have pterodactyls knocking fighter planes out of the sky.

Several years ago Joe Johnston directed a movie that I liked a lot called *The Rocketeer*. It was a solid, spiffy, old-fashioned adventure movie that really worked. He also did *Jumanji*, a pretty good fantasy-adventure — my then seven-year-old son loved it, and it's always hard to find good movies for young kids — and, later, *October Sky*, an entertaining, even invigorating, family movie.

That was the good stuff.

Bring on the dinosaurs.

Sam Neill is renowned paleontologist Dr Alan Grant. Anxious to obtain research funding for his new theory of velociraptor intelligence, he is persuaded by a wealthy adventurer (William H. Macy) and his wife (Tea Leoni) to undertake an aerial tour of Isla Sorna, the infamous island that was once InGen site B. Remember? Cast your mind back to the first *Jurassic Park* and it will come back to you. Site B has now become both a primordial breeding ground for John Hammond's magnificent creations and a magnet for thrill-seekers eager to encounter them. In other words, it's a theme park. Welcome to Dino World.

Who's for lunch?

When a tragic accident maroons (surprise!) the party of seven, Dr Grant discovers the true reason his deceptive hosts have invited him along. They are actually searching for their son, who crashed while parasailing too near the dangerous island. In the ensuing perilous attempt to escape with their lives, the ever-dwindling group encounters terrifying new creatures undisclosed by InGen, and Grant is forced to confront first-hand the dreadful implications of his raptor intelligence theory.

Let me now reveal the dreadful implications of Dr Grant's raptor intelligence theory: the raptors — the carnivorous ones, not the slow-footed basketball ones — have become so intelligent that they are now able to write scripts for bad movie sequels themselves. The good news is that they seem to be evolving at such a rapid pace that they'll be intelligent enough not to get involved with *Jurassic Park IV*, if ever, God forbid, someone thinks that we need another one of these. One well-known critic (I'm not telling!) has stated that this movie operates on the intellectual level of a twelve-year-old. If I was twelve, I would sue for slander.

A word about Sam Neill as paleontologist Dr Alan Grant: this is almost perfect casting. All of his facial muscles seem to be fossilized. Neill is without a doubt the most wooden actor since Charlton Heston. He is the Pinocchio of adventure heroes.

If you're looking for suspense, look elsewhere. This movie is the cinematic equivalent of an amusement park haunted house. You walk in, and it's really dark, and you wander around, and at every turn a luminous plastic skeleton is shoved in your face and a recorded scream blares "EEECKKK!" in your ear. Not only is the movie version incredibly annoying, but it also becomes incredibly expensive. Every time the lady next to me jumped out of her seat and hit me with her elbow, I spilled my popcorn. Total cost for popcorn: $24.50 (3 bags).

Whom do I sue?

The first *Jurassic Park*, based on Michael Crichton's novel, at least had some intriguing and almost plausible-sounding science in it. Here the pseudo-scientific jargon goes off the scale. For example: velociraptors are now able to vocalize, to produce a range of sounds of varying pitch and volume that allows them to "talk" to each other. I can just imagine what they said when they realized during production what a monumental turkey of a movie they were involved in: "*Talk* to my agent, man? As soon as I find him I'm going to *eat* him!"

28

Kinsey

Alfred Kinsey became a kind of sex guru for Americans in the 1950s, thanks to his well-publicized, statistically weighty reports on human sexual behaviour. He grew up in a strictly conservative Christian household dominated by his father, a fiercely religious man who enjoyed giving dramatic sermons at the local Methodist church. In an early scene in *Kinsey*, his father is shown blasting the congregation about the evils and dangers of ... well, just about everything. Building up a full head of steam, he severely criticizes the zipper as a profoundly immoral invention, an evil device of decadent modernity that allows males to succumb more quickly to their baser impulses.

You had no idea that the lowly zipper could have caused such a stir, did you? Imagine the gentleman's reaction to Velcro, had he lived to see that abomination ...

Later, fleeing his father's stifling influence, and against his wishes, Alfred enrolled in university to undertake the study of entomology. He became a teacher, and after studying gall wasps for some twenty years, "Prok," as he was affectionately known to his students, had accumulated the world's largest collection of the little critters. Feeling that he had pretty much exhausted the subject, he began to shift his focus to humans, who are, let's face it, a lot more interesting. Kinsey had a colourful way with words: he once described humans as "mammals in search of an orgasm." In 1947 he founded the Institute for Research in Sex, Gender and Reproduction at Indiana University in Bloomington.

A few years ago, director Bill Condon (close, but no cigar!) was responsible for *Gods and Monsters*, an excellent film about James Whale. It explored the situation of a gay director in the days when homosexuality was hushed up, and gays often blackmailed. Whale, a great director (*Bride Of Frankenstein*, *The Invisible Man*), was offered very little work in Hollywood after his reputation was damaged by gossip about the wild parties, attended largely by young men, that took place at his home in the thirties.

Here Condon tackles a movie about an entomologist turned sex researcher who seeks to get to the truth of American sexual behaviour in a purely scientific way. When Kinsey published his first study, *Sexual Behavior in the Human Male*, in 1948, it became a best-seller, even though it was a hefty scientific textbook filled with statistical analysis and graphs and charts. It was a bit of a chore to browse through, but people couldn't resist discovering what was really going on in the bedrooms, the truck stops, and even the bus stops of America. Many readers were shocked to learn that there was actually a lot more going on — and in much greater variety — than anyone had previously thought, although according to the surveys Kinsey conducted the missionary position was still the only one as far as seventy percent of American males were concerned.

Kinsey's method was simple: interview people one on one and get them to reveal their sexual histories in detail, and then compile the masses of data. Many of the best moments in *Kinsey* occur during the course of these interviews. There are several humorous moments, and also some shocking ones, but what emerges globally from this film is a message of tolerance, specifically with regard to homosexuality. In that respect, *Kinsey* is extremely relevant to our own times. In 2004 the United States went through a presidential election that placed gay rights in the forefront of public debate, and a huge chasm between different attitudes was revealed. Back in the 1940s and 1950s, Alfred Kinsey hoped that by demonstrating scientifically and statistically that certain behaviours were not unnatural, his research would promote greater tolerance toward alternate lifestyles. Over fifty years later, North Americans are still struggling with the same social debate.

Kinsey tells its story chronologically, in a pretty straight fashion (no pun intended). Liam Neeson portrays Kinsey as an exceptionally bright scientist, but something of a social misfit, in turns annoying and endearing. He teaches a course that could be called "everything you ever wanted to know about gall wasps" to mostly bored students. We learn that Kinsey has become "one the world's foremost authorities on the gall wasp."

Excuse me?

I found it amusing that he was only "*one* of the world's foremost authorities on gall wasps"; how many authorities on gall wasps were there, for God's sake? It seems to me that one person would pretty well have that field covered.

He becomes involved with one of his students, Clara McMillen (Laura Linney). She is attractive and bright, and they develop a relationship that is affectionate, albeit totally platonic. A tireless observer of nature, he is obsessed at this point with collecting specimens of wasps, and their dates consist mostly of just wandering around in the woods talking about nature.

Eventually a passionate moment occurs when he offers her ... a pair of hiking shoes. If you're a young man reading this, take note: if you want to really impress your girlfriend, forget all of that nonsense about expensive restaurants, flowers, diamonds, and furs: buy her a pair of really ugly, clunky hiking shoes.

This gift of sensible shoes from our hero sweeps Clara off her feet. Giggling with excitement, she puts her hands inside them and pretends to walk gently over his chest. In response, he kisses her — rather clumsily, and not very passionately; this is not exactly *Romeo and Juliet*. Sitting in the audience, witnessing this shameful display of raw human sexuality being acted out on the screen, I found myself speculating about the nature of Alfred and Clara's future sexual activities. I concluded that the seeds of an outlandish shoe fetish were being sown right before my eyes.

Riding the wave of their "shoe high," they decide to get married.

On their wedding night, Alfred and Clara can't seem to find their instruction manuals. Both are virgins, and they spend most of the night fumbling around. This is a great irony, considering that he is going to become one of the foremost authorities on sex in America. For the moment, however, he is a rookie. To use a baseball metaphor, they find their wedding night about as satisfying as a rain delay.

After a while (practice makes perfect!) their sex life does improve considerably. Alfred is launched on his new career as sex analyst and connoisseur when he begins to teach sex education at Indiana University. At first, he is appalled at the lack of pedagogical material available — he has trouble finding a textbook that even mentions sex — and also shocked at how profoundly ignorant about sex most of his students really are. At this time, in the late 1930s, sex education at university consists of a mishmash of moralistic disinformation sprinkled with religious scare tactics served up with horror stories about venereal disease. The teacher who was responsible for the course before Kinsey took over, when asked difficult (read: embarrassing) questions about sex by the students, had invariably called for abstinence. After making his case to the Dean for better sex education, Alfred is allowed to teach a "marriage course." The highlight of the class, as far as the students are concerned, is the explicit slide show he has put together as a teaching aid. Word of mouth spreads quickly, and enrolment in Kinsey's class practically explodes.

Riding the spectacular success of his marriage course, Kinsey persuades Indiana University to fund his sex research project. He starts to develop a questionnaire intended to reveal its subject's entire sexual history. In order to fine-tune his questions, he invites student volunteers to answer the questionnaire. He hires an assistant to help with the ever-increasing workload, a young, attractive male student named Clyde (Peter Sarsgaard). The project gets bigger, and Kinsey convinces the Rockefeller Foundation that it should support it financially. He soon hires more assistants and begins to travel the country interviewing thousands of people about their sexual experiences.

Kinsey at first focuses on the relationship between Kinsey and his wife Clara, but then shifts, and explores the developing relationship between Kinsey and Clyde, which eventually becomes sexual. In real life, Kinsey and his wife Clara were involved in a kind of ménage-à-trois with Clyde for several years. *Kinsey* fails to explore in any depth the hedonistic ambience that existed (according to all accounts) within the team of young researchers employed by Kinsey. The film does hint at wife-swapping, but in reality it seems that the research group was a veritable sexual circus of exploration and adventure. I don't want to imply that Kinsey abused his position, or that he was running some kind of sex colony, but the reality was a lot spicier than what the film is willing to reveal.

When the first volume of his research, which explored male sexuality, is published, Kinsey becomes a media celebrity. Predictably, some accuse him of "preaching to the perverted," but things really heat up in 1953, when he publishes the second volume, dealing with female sexuality. At this time the Cold War is raging, and McCarthyism is poisoning the social atmosphere. Kinsey is quickly branded as a communist by the right-wing establishment.

It seems particularly interesting to me that some would make a connection between a better understanding of female sexuality and communist plots to undermine America's morals. My explanation of this outright hostility toward Kinsey is that after taking one look at his report on female sexuality, a lot of the men in power at this time were scared out of their skivvies that their wives would suddenly wise up to the fact that they were being short-changed, and that the sexual status quo was largely a big, boring, one-way street.

A word to those who may be attracted to *Kinsey* thinking that a movie about a sex researcher would be erotic. It's a logical assumption. The movie has to walk a fine line between *its* subject, Alfred Kinsey, and *his* subject, sex. On one level, the movie is definitely about sex — it almost comes across as "Sex 101" in a few scenes — but it contains few truly erotic scenes. There is an encounter between Kinsey and Clyde in a hotel room, there is an encounter between Clara and Clyde, there is suggestion and innuendo, and there are some graphic images, but mostly there is a lot of talk about sex — explicit, to be sure, but not erotic; "clinical" would be a better word. I didn't personally find *Kinsey* erotic. To paraphrase Mark Twain, "Sex is like a frog; you can dissect it, but it tends to die in the process." Rather, the appeal of this movie is in the way it tells us the story of this character by exploring the social tapestry of the era. The story of Alfred Kinsey is also the story of the beginnings of the sexual revolution, and of the emergence of new attitudes toward sex and the sexual empowerment of women. The script is literate and coherent, and it flows smoothly. There are perhaps a few too many sub-plots — the script tries to say too much — but the film benefits from some excellent performances, particularly from Liam Neeson and Laura Linney.

By the way, if the sexually explicit photographs shown during the sex education class in *Kinsey* were to appear in any other film, it would surely receive the NC-17 rating in the US, which is normally reserved for pornographic films (no one under seventeen admitted *under any circumstances*). *Kinsey*, however, is rated R in the US (it received a 14A rating in Ontario, a 13+ in Quebec), which means that no American youngster under seventeen is admitted unless accompanied by an adult. If it's not an oxymoron to talk about "enlightened censorship," it seems that in the case of *Kinsey* at least, the American censors have taken into account the context of the story being told, and have refrained from giving the film the dreaded NC-17 rating. NC-17 is usually the kiss of death at the box office. I can think of only two films rated X (the old rating prior to its being replaced by NC-17 in 1990) that went on to have mainstream commercial success, the highly regarded *Midnight Cowboy* and *A Clockwork Orange*. More recently, in 1995, MGM/UA mounted a splashy advertising campaign in support of their decision to release *Showgirls* in its NC-17 version, but the film was so savagely and universally trashed by the critics that it quickly died at the box office. It went on to win that year's Worst Picture and Worst Director "Razzie" awards from the Golden Raspberry Award Foundation. Ironically, *Showgirls* is one of MGM/UA's top-selling home videos.

Kinsey is an entertaining film — well, how boring could it be? it's about sex, after all! — but it is also particularly timely, because the issues of sexual intolerance it raises remain largely unresolved as we enter the twenty-first century.

29

The Lord of the Rings: The Return of the King

As Charles Schultz (a very wise man) once said, "Summers fly but winters walk."

No kidding. Especially if you're a baseball fan.

Some movies fly too, and some movies walk, and some crawl. Crawl ... crawl ... like an exhausted Hobbit, it does, yesss, Preciousss. Forever walking, climbing, crawling toward Mordor, into Mordor where the shadows lie, crawling for 201 long minutes to Mount Doom. And we know how it turns out, don't we? And unequivocal fanatics of Tolkien's saga love it and gobble it up.

It's actually a pretty good story. As a baseball fan, I could relate to the little hero who's forced to leave home and undertake a perilous odyssey around the bases. He's on a journey filled with peril, but with the help of his *nine* teammates (just like a ball team!), and the benefit of some wise decisions and a few tricks from his manager, crusty old Gandalf, he makes it safely back home.

Classic stuff.

But the question remains: does this movie work? And perhaps more to the point, does it matter whether or not I think it works? Because, you see, some movies are critic-proof. They are "Harry Potterized"; that is, no one gives a hoot what the critics say. The throngs will flock (and the flocks throng) and they will enjoy, critics be damned. This is okay, but critics are only human (really!), so they're not immune to being influenced by huge waves of positive public sentiment. And nobody wants to be the Grinch Who Stole Christmas. This critic thing can be a terrible burden. Yes, a heavy burden it is, Preciousss, to be a lone voice crying in the critical wilderness. But we must be brave, Preciousss, be a brave little critic, and say what we think.

Given that this is one of the most ambitious film adaptations of a literary classic ever attempted, let me borrow from Act III of *Julius Caesar*:

> I come here not to bury Peter Jackson, but to praise him.
> It was said that he was ambitious, true, and he had brought
> Many captive film buffs and fans of the trilogy to the Cineplex,
> And many said it could not be done, that you couldn't adapt
> This massive work ... But he had guts, my fellow citizens!

And if you've seen pictures of him, he's even got a beer gut, so he can't be all bad, mate!

Jackson envisioned two films. He believed that it would be more exciting if the story, which was a trilogy in its original literary form, were broken up into two parts. But the producers did not agree; they said no, you've got to make three. Why? Because there are three books, and three movies can generate more dollars than two movies. We can sell three events instead of two.

So three it was, for a total of approximately nine hours of film. Not to mention the extra footage and deleted scenes available only on DVD. Several scenes featuring Christopher Lee as Saruman, including an apparently terrific death scene, were cut from the theatrical release but are included as "bonuses" (that is, justification for the overblown retail price) on the DVD.

I don't mean to suggest that the theatrical version has been edited with an eye on raking in the big bucks with the DVD release. Never would I suggest such a thing. And the business of making incredibly expensive movies being what it is, you'll forgive me for even mentioning the possibility.

I'm sorry, but I'm still bitter about having my VHS collection declared obsolete and being pressured into purchasing all those movies all over again in the more expensive DVD format. As a consumer (and a film lover), I feel as if I'm being taken for the proverbial long ride down the short pier. I look back fondly at the good old days when DVD meant "Dick Van Dyke," not "double your video debt." I mean, have you *seen* what they're asking for these deluxe DVD box sets? Are you not annoyed that they try to justify the outrageous prices by cramming them with ridiculous "extras," like voice-over commentary from giggling actors telling us how really, really cool it was to pretend to be Hobbits, or a documentary about how many pairs of Hobbit feet were used during the shoot and how incredibly hot and uncomfortable it really was to wear big furry prosthetic shoes?

Give me a break. Humbug!

Here's a quotation from Peter Jackson, explaining why he cut about ten minutes of Christopher Lee from *The Return of the King*: "The longer the film was, the less strong it got, because you felt like you'd been there for too long and it lost its impact."

Okay, but instead of cutting scenes that feature a great actor (and Christopher Lee *is* great, and I don't want any arguments, got it?), why not cut some battle scenes? Lord knows there are enough of them.

I loved the first film. I thought it was a brilliant rendering of Tolkien's world. I felt that in the second instalment too much time was devoted to battles and not enough to character development.

This one, quite simply, is worse. We get lots and lots of battles. Epic battles. Amazing battles. Brutal battles. Fantastic battles.

Battles, battles, battles.

My problem is simple: after about two and a half hours, the movie starts to feel endless. Or, to quote Yogi Berra, it gets late early out there. In defence of Jackson, I'm sure he was under enormous pressure from the producers to serve up a super-sized portion of action and blood and guts and special effects, and endless battle scenes, and I do not deny that this is a film of outstanding quality. It is filmmaking on a monumental scale, even if much of the monumentality is computer-generated. But it is too long. And it is bottom-heavy with battle scenes and light on character development. But so are the books, so whose fault is that?

Technically, however, it is an impressive, sometimes breathtaking tour de force, made even more so when we consider that Jackson delivers nine hours of film for about the same budget that James Cameron sank into his three-hour *Titanic*.

There are moments of real emotion, but also a fair bit of rather gratuitous bawling. If, as Jimmy Dugan said in *A League of Their Own*, there is no crying in baseball, there sure is a lot of crying in Middle-earth. It's been said that real men don't cry, but Hobbits do. A lot. Look, I'm not one of these old-style macho guys who thinks that Hobbits shouldn't be in touch with their feelings, but must they cry when they are apart and then cry again when they get back together? Must they cry when they're happy and then cry when they're sad? If human life is, as the saying goes, a vale of tears, for Hobbits it's a wading pool.

It's too bad that the female characters in general, and Liv Tyler in particular, don't get more screen time. The movie spends very little time at all on elven Arwen giving up her immortality for the love of Aragorn, which is one of the great themes of the book. Shades of Cupid and Psyche! This potentially powerful dramatic theme is left mostly unexplored.

The entire human cast is excellent, but I have a problem with Gollum. I don't think that a computer-generated character (CGC) can be nearly as powerful as a real actor. It's true that a real actor named Andy Serkis did the voice and the physical movements, but later in the process a CGC was superimposed onto the images of Serkis. This bothered me in the second film, and it bothered me even more in the third one. I know that many directors feel that this is the way of the future — and won't it be great not to have to deal with real actors and their real agents and real egos — but for me, this Gollum was not entirely believable, and that's a big chunk of the movie.

Computer-generated artwork *is* spectacularly effective when it comes to creating imaginary landscapes and vast, sweeping vistas. As much as seventy-five percent of the sets in *The Return of the King* are the product of computer-generated imagery and matte paintings, and they capture all of the splendour and beauty of Tolkien's Middle-earth. The panoramic views are stunning, the immense scale of the sets often breathtaking.

This film trilogy is an astonishing accomplishment, but there was something intangible in the books, something mystical and magical, which I felt in the first film, but which was missing from this final instalment. The first one remains my favourite.

Where is Christopher Lee when we really need him?

30

Lost in Space

Riddle me *this:* why make a movie based on a classic television series if you're going to jettison most of the elements that made the series successful in the first place?

Screenwriter Akiva Goldsman, who wrote the wretched *Batman and Robin*, also wrote *Lost in Space*. It's interesting to note that the space suits worn by the Robinsons look as if they're hot off the rack of a *Batman and Robin* post-production memorabilia sale. The suits feature moulded rubber pectorals, but (thank God) no rubber nipples like the ones on the dynamic duo's suits. Anyway, just what was wrong with those great silver suits they wore in the original series? I thought those were the coolest space suits I had ever seen. Every year at Christmas during the four-year run of the program, I actually asked for a silver space suit just like the one Bill Mumy wore.

I never got one. I'm still dealing with the disappointment.

The original *Lost in Space* series was campy fun. The movie version is a confused snooze-fest. At the heart of the original series was the strange and often amusing triangle of young Will Robinson, his faithful robot, and the devious but cowardly — and ultimately inept — Dr Smith, the stowaway-saboteur on the *Jupiter 2*. In the movie version, the robot sports a high-tech design that in no way resembles the original. The robot is voiced by the actor who did the original, Dick Tufeld, and he does have some of the best lines in the movie, for example the following corny robot joke: "Why did the robot cross the road? Because he was carbon bonded to the chicken."

That's actually a pretty funny joke, especially of you repeat it a few times in your head.

Unfortunately, Hollywood (yet again) shoots itself in the foot by trying to make a movie that will please everybody. For starters, the producers are trying to please the folks like me, who grew up in the sixties and who were hooked on this show. Secondly, the producers are trying to cash in on just about every financially successful sci-fi film of the nineties.

The first ten minutes of *Lost in Space* represent a veritable festival of sci-fi clichés, an obvious rip-off of everything we were subjected to in *Independence Day* and every other sci-fi blockbuster that has been thrown at us in the last decade. Leaving no gimmick unturned, *Lost in Space* also introduces a cuter-than-cute cuddly little Alien pal, which seems solely designed to create a sense of need in the kiddies. Dollar signs in their eyes, the producers hope to trigger a rush for the plush toy version of this little pal, which will undoubtedly soon be available at Wal-Mart. This insidious bit of casting is known as "spin-off merchandizing," and it is only one of the devious ways by which crummy big-budget movies attempt to recoup their (projected) losses. Expect to receive a little plastic version of this big-eyed cutie with your next Happy Meal.

After the *Jupiter 2*, our heroic family Robinson's space ship, is sabotaged by the evil Dr Smith (who has snuck aboard, funded by some nefarious foreign power), it crash-lands on a strange planet, where our heroes are soon confronted with a creeping time bubble that threatens to engulf not only the ship but also probably the entire observable universe. Things get very wacky very fast, and when Dr Smith finally enters the time bubble, the plot — or what has survived of it after the crash — becomes an interstellar mess that manages not only to completely confuse the kids in the audience, but also to make any adult science-fiction aficionados in the theatre whimper with despair. About halfway through the story, a substantial portion of the audience joins the Robinsons in being hopelessly lost. The big finale features Dr Smith transformed into a disgusting, slimy spider-monster. At the same time, our young hero Will must confront an adult version of himself (!). Meanwhile, the audience is attacked by huge globs of gooey sentimentality.

On the plus side, the spider-monster is quite creepy, and manages to scare the wits out of the same seven-year-old kids the movie has been targeting with cuddly spin-off merchandise up to that point. Then, if I remember correctly, the planet explodes and becomes a black hole (!) or something. Actually, it's all a bit fuzzy, and I may have been nodding by that point.

William Hurt (who needs no introduction) delivers an extraordinarily wooden performance as Dad Robinson, practically sleepwalking through the movie. It made me wonder if he ever really awoke from suspended animation after the *Jupiter 2* was launched. Mostly he seems dazed, perhaps an understandable state of mind if you have to say lines like "There's a lot of space out there to get lost in."

The best that can be said for Heather Graham is that she is cuter than cute as Judy, Marta Kristen's character in the original series. Like Hurt, Matt LeBlanc as Major Don West also seems stuck in suspended animation, except when his hormones are raging after Judy. The interplay between the two, stale as it is, pretty much represents the sum total of their character development.

In the original series, the sheer fun that young Will had just *being* in space — lost or not — was one of the attractions of watching the program, at least for me. Jack Johnson does a good job as young Will Robinson, but the script has him spending too much time agonizing over the fact that Dad doesn't pay enough attention to him. Where's the fun in that?

Only Gary Oldman seems to really be having a good time with his character, a darker, more sinister Dr Smith than the one we were accustomed to originally. But as terrific as Oldman is, his performance becomes, as the French say, *peine perdue*, sucked into the black hole of Goldsman's script. My biggest disappointment? We never even once see Dr Smith gesturing contemptuously to the robot while uttering the immortal line, "Come along, you ninny." Too bad.

Some of the original cast members agreed to appear in cameo roles. Marta Kristen and Angela Cartwright appear as journalists covering the launch of the *Jupiter 2*. Bill Mumy wanted to play the role of the adult Will Robinson caught in the time bubble, but was turned down. And after the producers offered Jonathan Harris a bit part, he declared that he would not be involved unless he could reprise his role as Dr Smith. Good for him. This movie is a stain on the memory of a fun-filled, imaginative, sometimes silly, and ultimately thoroughly enjoyable piece of my childhood.

The good news is that plans to film a sequel have been indefinitely scrapped.

*Star light, star bright,
First star I see tonight,
I wish I may, I wish I might,
Have the wish I wish tonight:
I wish some cable channel in Canada would run the original* Lost in Space *series . . .*

31

Lost in Translation

I have been lost in translation many times.

In real life (whatever that is), when I'm not being a know-it-all film critic, I actually make a living as a translator. But I translate stuff like electronics manuals. Easy stuff. I have enormous respect for the brave souls who tackle the really complex, almost impossible jobs. Take for example this little gem: "A proof is a proof. What kind of a proof? It's a proof. A proof is a proof. And when you have a good proof, it's because it's proven" (Prime Minister Jean Chrétien, on finding no Iraqi weapons of mass destruction).

Something would inevitably be lost in the translation of *that*, believe me.

If translation can be excruciatingly difficult, communicating with an audience via radio presents its own set of difficulties. For starters, you have to know how to pronounce names. And it's not like the old days, when actors had easy names like Gary Cooper or Tony Curtis. I remember the first movie I reviewed that had Gary Sinise in it, I had no idea how to pronounce his name. Two minutes before going on air I broke into a sweat, and I wound up calling him Gary *Sin-easy*, which made him sound like the sleaziest of the Seven Dwarfs. Thank goodness this movie has actors with easy names like Bill Murray. It also has actors with names like Akiko Takeshita in it, but not Hideki Matsui or Ichiro Suzuki. Too bad.

Lost in Translation is directed by Sofia Coppola. There's another tough one. Is the emphasis on the first syllable or the second? It's probably not easy being a filmmaker who is also the daughter of a great filmmaker. Of course it could have certain definite advantages, but think how embarrassing it would be if your work wasn't any good. What's worse, the Coppolas are related to the Cage family, which means that when your families get together at Christmas, you might have to put up with your cousin Nicolas breaking into his Elvis impersonation.

Here's some trivia: remember the christening scene in *The Godfather*? The child who portrayed Connie Corleone's baby boy was actually Sofia Coppola, in her first screen appearance! Throw *that* out casually during your next family movie night and watch the eyes widen in admiration.

Sofia Coppola made her first film, *The Virgin Suicides*, in 1999. It was a very good, albeit very dark, film. A real bummer as they used to say. But don't you *have* to make a dark bummer of a movie if you're going to be taken seriously as a filmmaker? After you've done one of those, you can lighten up.

Lost in Translation is light years removed from the typical Bill Murray vehicle. This is not *Charlie's Angels*, or even *Groundhog Day*. It is Bill Murray turned down several notches, and he is just plain excellent.

Murray portrays Bob Harris, an aging Hollywood actor who hasn't made a movie in years. His action movies are still hugely popular in Japan, however, and he's in Tokyo for one week to shoot some whiskey commercials for Japanese television.

Dressed in a tuxedo and sitting in a wingback chair in the Japanese television studio, Bob stares coolly at the camera and purrs, "Suntory Whiskey, that's what I drink." The young Japanese director never seems quite happy; he coaches Bob loudly in Japanese, which is of course complete gibberish to Bob, and keeps asking for another take. It doesn't clarify things that the interpreter on the set seems to be giving Bob a much-shortened account of what the director is actually saying. "More Loger Moole," the director says. "Loger Moole?" asks Bob. Then, finally getting it, "Right, right, Roger Moore, okay," says Bob. Always the consummate professional, Bob smiles and smiles and keeps delivering take after clueless take, much to the director's annoyance. This is one of the finest moments of movie comedy I have seen in the last twenty years. Five stars.

For someone who is so popular in Japan, Bob seems to know very little about the culture, and doesn't seem at all eager to learn. He just wants to get the job done and go home. Bob is not only lost in translation, he is lost in Japanese culture, lost in Tokyo, lost (we suspect) in his own life. Bob's wife keeps sending him faxes — the machine in his room starts up at all hours — asking his opinion about the colour of the carpeting to be installed in the den she's renovating at home. He couldn't care less. The phone conversations with her give us a picture of a long-married couple who are only going through the motions.

Bob is jet-lagged and can't sleep. He spends all his free time in the hotel bar. This is where he meets Charlotte (Scarlett Johansson). Charlotte is a pretty, young woman half his age. Recently married, she is in Tokyo because her husband is photographing a rock band, and she's come along for the trip. It's not much fun, though — her husband is out shooting all the time. She is alone, and she too can't sleep. The two insomniacs hit it off right away. Emotionally, they are like two victims of a shipwreck clinging to the same pieces of debris — afloat and adrift in a world that is alien, culturally and linguistically.

Scarlett Johansson is excellent as Charlotte. Only nineteen, she already has some fine performances to her credit. She was believable and moving as the ingenue in the Coen brothers' absurdist film noir *The Man Who Wasn't There.* She was excellent also in *Ghost World*. Here, although she looks like many of the empty-headed and self-centred young contemporary women we see so often in films, we soon realize that Charlotte has brains. She is also sensitive to her cultural environment. Charlotte is curious about Japanese culture, and she is also allergic to the artificial, vacuous world her photographer husband inhabits. Charlotte is searching for meaning; she is searching for her self.

And she is fascinated by Bob.

In her eyes, Bob is a mature, guru-like figure. She doesn't see that Bob's detached, cool attitude may be the result more of mental fatigue than enlightenment. Bill Murray plays his role like a virtuoso. We believe in this blasé, cynical man. We feel his attraction for the young woman; we feel his longing and his loneliness. But this is not a traditional May–September romance. *Lost in Translation* gives us more than the usual clichés, it gives us moments of truth.

At thirty-two, Sofia Coppola possesses some of the calm, astute observational skills I admire in John Sayles. In a Sayles film, time and place become an integral part of the story. Sayles gives you a real sense of where you are, whether it be Florida or Texas or the Bayou, and he takes the time to develop his characters, he allows them to live and breathe. Like Sayles, Coppola is profoundly interested in loneliness and alienation. She's interested in how people connect, and what it really means to be *with* someone. Although Tokyo is a unique city, it also serves as a more general metaphor for everything that keeps people from truly connecting in the geared-up, manic modern world. Experiencing Tokyo nightlife together, our lost heroes are thrust into the exciting yet ultimately shallow ambience of an overcrowded funhouse. The filmmaker's point is clear: giant cities like Tokyo offer only the illusion of shared experience, of community; under its neon veneer, the bustle and the crowds of this dazzling city actually manage only to distract its inhabitants, and ultimately to disconnect them from each other. E.M. Forster put it best: "Millions of people always running around, running around, trying to connect, only connect."

Lost in Translation offers us a portrait of two people who do *truly* connect for a short time. All too soon, however, it becomes achingly clear that the relationship has nowhere to go, and the audience is left with that terrible empty feeling that comes from having to say goodbye. Remember ... that one real friend you made at summer camp? The bus is waiting, and you hug and try to smile, but you are sick with the knowledge that you will never meet again.

This movie breaks your heart, but it does so without undue emotionalism. The tragedy of Bob and Charlotte's chance encounter is that each has met the right person, but at the wrong time. *Lost in Translation* reminds us gently — without hysterics — that we are all just passing through each other's lives, and that there's a big difference between a shared vacation in Tokyo and real commitment.

Lost in Translation made me think of a young woman I met many years ago during a very long bus trip up to northern Quebec. We were immediately comfortable — and honest — with each other in a way that would have taken us years to achieve under different circumstances. Sympathetic strangers are often better sounding boards for existential ruminations than old acquaintances. You can speculate a bit more, be a bit more open perhaps, because you know that the new confidante will soon — and permanently — depart from your life. There are no consequences, no strings attached.

But what if you were to fall in love with your new friend? What would you do if you had commitments back home, a wife, a husband, children? Then you would have to face your moment of truth.

Here I am talking about truth again. As a hardened movie critic, I should know better. After all, it's just a movie, isn't it? But this movie lingers in your mind, because that's what great movies do: they linger, and simmer, and bounce around up there in the old brain box for a long time. Or, to paraphrase that wisest of Yogis: even when it's over, a great movie ain't really over.

32

Mission to Mars

I remember that when Brian De Palma's *The Untouchables* (1987) was first released, one scene was singled out for special praise for its kinetic energy, complex choreography, and editing. You may recall the scene. It involves a runaway baby carriage on a large staircase in a train station. The scene is indeed a tour de force, and I don't want to diminish De Palma's artistry in any way. But the scene is not wholly original. It is actually an extremely clever reworking of the "Odessa Steps" sequence from Russian director Sergei Eisenstein's 1925 silent film *Battleship Potemkin*. There is nothing intrinsically wrong with borrowing a famous scene from a classic movie, and De Palma has always owned up to his influences. In this scene, he uses Eisenstein's basic idea and montage techniques in a contemporary way to brilliant effect. Sometimes, however, a film can get so bogged down in borrowed ideas that it turns into a reheated mish-mash with all the appeal of a three-day-old tuna casserole. *Mission to Mars* is such a movie. What's worse, it has the appeal of a three-day-old freeze-dried NASA-issue tuna casserole.

The screenplay is by John Thomas, Jim Thomas, and Graham Yost (the last-named also wrote the screenplay for *Speed*). When I saw three names on the script, I immediately suspected that this mission was in trouble. Based on my observations, when it comes to scripts, three's a crowd. Over the years — and remember that there are exceptions to what I'm about to say — it has seemed to me that the very best scripts have been written by one or two people. Usually, the addition of more input tends to muddy the waters, kind of like the old joke about a camel's being a horse designed by a committee. After watching this movie unfold — or unravel — I became convinced that these guys had been heavily inspired by a case of tequila and some rented science-fiction movies: space clichés and astrobabble abound.

Mission to Mars is set in the not-too-distant future, at a time when the first manned mission to the Red Planet has been launched. When contact with the mission is lost, commanders Woody Blake (Robbins) and Jim McConnell (Sinise) are recruited to head up a rescue mission. Weird things seem to be happening on Mars, and NASA suspects that the first crew may have run afoul of some Aliens. Even worse, once the rescue mission is launched and on its way to Mars, the ship is invaded not by bug-eyed Aliens, but by ... *product placement*. Suddenly, without warning, all kinds of convenient marketing situations arise. For instance, when the rescue craft's hull sustains a puncture from some micrometeorites, the weightless interior rapidly begins to fill with swarms of free-floating M&Ms (!) and globular masses of Dr Peppers (!!). And you thought that astronauts survived in space on dehydrated broccoli and Tang! Now you know the foul truth NASA has been concealing for decades: it's junk food heaven up there. Later, when the rescuers finally land on Mars and deploy their equipment, we are subjected to the equivalent of a Kawasaki Mars Rover commercial. Product placement may be an unfortunate fact of life in big-budget movies, but this, as Duck Dodgers would say, is ridiculous.

Once the crew leaves the earth's gravitational pull, the actors seem to succumb rapidly to some bizarre form of space virus. Tim Robbins comes down with a particularly severe case; he speaks each of his lines as if he's trapped in a state of suspended animation. Even Gary Sinise — another great actor — seems to have been affected by prolonged weightlessness. His mouth just doesn't seem to be connected to his brain in any functional way. Still, it's tough not to look like a cartoon when you have to deliver dialogue like "I don't know what's going on, but we're not leaving until we find out!" in extreme close-up with huge beads of perspiration rolling down your forehead.

Let's see, what else goes on here? Oh yes. In one scene that almost generates suspense, Commander Woody (Robbins) gets to sacrifice his life for the crew. To make a long story short, he's on a space walk and he begins to tumble into the Martian atmosphere. He's about to burn up, but he can't be rescued because the other crew members, who are also outside the ship and are wearing those little jet packs, don't have enough fuel to reach him and return to the ship. This is not a bad scene, but I'm sure that there is something wrong with the science. I'm no expert, but I dimly recall, from second-year physics, something about applying force to an object in the void ... like if you give something a push in space, won't it keep going forever? So why do you need all that jet pack fuel to get around up there? One little jet, as they say, goes a long way.

I may be wrong about this, and I'm sure not Isaac Asimov, but I recognize a smelly script when it crash-lands in my popcorn.

Like poor Commander Woody, this movie just keeps spiralling down and down into oblivion. And it's too bad, because there are some intriguing ideas in it about the origins of life on earth. And the visuals are pretty good, too. Until the Aliens show up, that is. Then the movie commits the fatal — and in my opinion unforgivable — mistake of borrowing from the Steven Spielberg extraterrestrial design handbook, and everything goes all googly-eyed and mushy. Call me old-fashioned, but Aliens should look like Michael Rennie in *The Day the Earth Stood Still.* They should not look like electronic Christmas tree ornaments purchased for $1.99 at Radio Shack. Oh! Sorry! Now *I'm* guilty of product placement!

The music poses another serious problem. Ennio Morricone is one of the great composers of film music, but his work here is the aural equivalent of those Kraft melted marshmallow recipes my Mom used to spring on us at Easter. Two of those sugar bombs and my fillings would start buzzing and ringing. Painful.

Once, when a reporter asked about his slow rise to stardom, Gary Sinise answered, "Careers, like rockets, don't always take off on time. The trick is to always keep the engine running." Never mind taking off, this mission should have been aborted.

33

Mulholland Drive

I'm usually the first to say that people should not be held responsible for mistakes they committed in their youth, but even a cursory look at David Lynch's early work is enough to make your head spin. He made his first film in 1966, at the age of twenty. A short film called *Six Figures Being Sick*, it consists of endlessly repeated shots of people vomiting. And their heads are on fire! The film is projected onto a specially sculptured screen that features twisted three-dimensional faces in various stages of puking. Really.

Thank goodness he didn't stop there.

Eraserhead followed, in 1977, a film experience some people (myself included) find almost unbearable. I've tried — Lord knows I've tried! — to watch it to the end, but I find it so disturbing, so repulsive, that I just can't make it to the finish line. This is a terrible admission for a film reviewer to make, but then I've never actually had to review *Eraserhead*. It's still on my list of movies to revisit, but I don't think I'm ready just yet. Maybe when I'm older — like eighty.

The Elephant Man (1980) was elevated by the stunning black and white compositions of cinematographer Freddie Francis — of Hammer Horror fame — and by the tour-de-force performance given by John Hurt in the title role. It remains a dark, powerful, and poignantly humanistic film. *Blue Velvet* (1986) stands out as a masterpiece of twisted, nightmarish Americana. More recently, *The Straight Story* (1999), with the late, great Richard Farnsworth, turned out to be a wonderful, totally atypical Lynch film. Many fans of Lynch's *oeuvre noire* found it too pedestrian (pun intended), too traditional. I found it to be slow, certainly, but the very nature of the story dictated its leisurely tempo. It is a perfectly constructed and perfectly realized work, and it gives more to the viewer upon each successive sitting. The moving story of a man who has almost reached the end of his life and who feels a desperate and pressing desire to reconcile himself with his estranged brother, it is perhaps Richard Farnsworth's finest hour, and also I think one of the finest American films of the 1990s. It is also so far removed from *Mulholland Drive* that it seems not only to have been directed by someone else, but to have been created on a different planet.

Lynch has never apologized for his weirdness. Why should he? Rather, he defiantly flings it in our faces. With Lynch, you don't just get a movie, you get mystery, sex, pizzazz. You get to scratch your head. You sometimes get scenes so profoundly strange that you don't know whether to laugh or scream. In fact, you get the whole zany sideshow. When you go to a David Lynch film, it is not so much as if the circus has come to town, it is more as if the circus has invaded the town and liberated the asylum. Look ... up there sitting on top of the elephants, marching defiantly down Main Street, the sexy women with big, bushy eyebrows, and over there, the dwarves, the sociopaths, the rock 'n' roll casualties, the assorted acrobats — all of them tormented souls, with attitudes akimbo and body parts on parade. A David Lynch film presents the human zoo in all its rich pageantry.

But the question begs to be asked: what is it about bushy eyebrows, really? Have you seen Isabella Rossellini in *Wild at Heart* (1990) as a blonde with dark, bushy eyebrows? Do you find those eyebrows bizarre, or is it a look that turns you on? And if so, why? And if not, why not? On second thought, let's not go there.

In a 1996 interview published in *Kinorevue* in Czechoslovakia, Lynch explained something of his methods:

> Mysteries are everywhere and it is wonderful to feel that there are things we know absolutely nothing about. Anyone of us can become a scientist or investigator. The mysteries in film work like a magnet to attract people. But the answer can be disappointing because they are not complete, and sometimes you will learn something that turns into another mystery. Mysteries are what I love.

Agatha Christie once said, "I love a mystery but I hate a muddle."

Lynch is a brilliant, quirky filmmaker, but he often loses his footing and slips down the slippery slope of mystery only to wind up face-down in a muddle. Sometimes the muddle is positively mesmerizing, but a muddle is still a muddle.

To understand Lynch — if this is possible — you have to understand how he constructs his films. Another quotation may be useful:

> A film consists of many parts, which are all of the same importance, I believe. Sometimes the visual imagination leads to a change in part of the story. At other times the story leads to visual creation. It works both ways, everything flows together. There are no rules, but in the end all the parts must fit together precisely. That is the only way to create something interesting.

While it may be almost futile to describe the plot of a two-and-a-half-hour movie in which the plot becomes almost totally irrelevant in the last thirty minutes, here are some of the more intriguing story elements found in *Mulholland Drive*:

A young fresh-faced kid named Betty, from Deep River, Ontario (!) (Naomi Watts), arrives in Hollywood for her first movie audition. While staying in her aunt's apartment, she discovers another young woman, hiding in the shower. It turns out that this young woman has been in a car crash and is suffering from that most cinematic of afflictions, amnesia. She also has a suitcase full of money, lots of money. Spotting a poster for the Rita Hayworth movie *Gilda*, the woman decides to call herself Rita until her real name occurs to her. Our heroine Betty decides to play Nancy Drew and help Rita discover her identity. At this point Lynch introduces one of his favourite devices: he suggests that the key to Rita's identity may actually be in the hands of a mysterious and influential dwarf in a wheelchair, who seems to spend all of his time inside his glass-enclosed office. Lynch loves to sprinkle meaningless "clues" throughout his stories, and he is positively famous for his nebulous use of dwarves as red herrings. Here he also introduces a herring of a different hue in the form of a blue key that "Rita" discovers in her purse. What is it for?

A young director named Adam (Justin Theroux) is casting a new movie, and two mafia types, the Castigliane brothers, are insisting that an actress named Camilla Rhodes (Laura Harring) be given a major part. Adam steadfastly refuses. Our hard-headed director is then invited to a midnight meeting, at which a mysterious and menacing cowboy issues a vague warning about the consequences of not casting Camilla Rhodes. Without giving specifics, the cowboy suggests that Adam's directorial career will be severely shortened. The cowboy tells Adam to "do good and you'll see me once more, do bad and you'll see me twice." I don't know what the heck that is actually supposed to mean, but it certainly *sounds* ominous.

At this point in the proceedings, I knew Lynch was probably playing a very elaborate practical joke on the audience, and that most of this so-called plot was just inspired gobbledygook, but he still had me completely hooked. My head was spinning; questions whirled around in my bewildered brain: who was the dead and decomposing female corpse in the apartment? Was this actually Betty's alter ego? And what about the guy with the ridiculously bushy eyebrows (again!) who had been having nightmares about a hideous man lurking in an alley behind Winkie's Diner? And what about the blue key, and later the strange blue box the key is designed for? How did those pieces fit the puzzle?

Mulholland Drive is blessed with terrific atmosphere. It oozes atmosphere. It also sparkles in gorgeous cinematography. As a treat for film buffs, sly references to many classic Hollywood films are seamlessly woven into the surreal and opaque plot. And the acting is excellent. Naomi Watts is believable and attractive as the small-town girl, and Laura Harring, doing double duty as both the amnesic bombshell Rita and as Camilla Rhodes, is spectacular, in tight, flashy red sweaters. She deserves a special Oscar for "Best performance by an actress in the style of Rita Hayworth." Sensational! Two graphic, electric sex scenes between Betty and Rita are also memorable. Depending on your point of view, of course, these scenes are either highly exploitative or absolutely vital in advancing the plot. You decide.

In what may or may not be a sly homage to Orson Welles, Lynch has inserted an enigmatic leitmotiv that is reminiscent of the oft-repeated "Rosebud" in *Citizen Kane*. At several points in the story, our attention is focused on various female characters whispering with great intensity and sensuality the single word, "Silencio." But what does it mean, jellybean? Is this a crucial piece of the plot/puzzle that would, if properly decoded, put everything into crystal-clear focus? Or is it just Lynch playfully suggesting to the audience that everyone in the theatre should shut up? We'll never know, but, like everything else in *Mulholland Drive*, it is strangely compelling.

Lynch originally shot *Mulholland Drive* as a pilot for a television series. He presented it to a group of executives at ABC, but they had absolutely no idea what to make of it. Predictably, the project was put on a shelf, where it sat for months, congealing, until a French production company approached Lynch about turning it into a feature. He agreed, shot a bunch of additional scenes, and edited the whole thing together. He then proceeded to win the Best Director Award at Cannes for his concoction. *Sacré bleu*, they are *crazee* those French people, *non?*

When I watch this film, it reminds me of a drawing by Dutch artist M.C. Escher called "House of Stairs." It has creepy-crawly insects moving through what looks like some kind of castle with impossible perspectives — stairs leading up and down simultaneously. The top half of the drawing is a mirror image of the bottom half. It doesn't make sense, but it's fascinating.

This movie leads us in circles, as we crawl around inside Lynch's brain like the creeping bugs in Esher's drawing. *Mulholland Drive* is a cinematic "House of Stairs." It is also an enigmatic exploration of the idea of Hollywood as a destroyer of identity. Hollywood offers us images, offers us seductive, almost plausible worlds, but Lynch cautions us that Hollywood is profoundly corrupt — that it consumes those it makes famous, that it eats its young. The image-making machine has an insatiable appetite for fresh faces, and the faces are ultimately disposable.

And what of the impact of movies in general on popular culture? Is our collective obsession with images and with celebrity driving us to the edge of madness? There's an old saying, "Those whom the Gods would destroy, they first make mad." *Mulholland Drive* can be interpreted as a cautionary tale — although a severely warped one — concerning the dangers of letting our revved-up-to-warp-speed image-generating machines run away with us.

If you, like me, are sick to death of movies that talk to you as if you had the intellectual capacity of a small soap dish, you might find *Mulholland Drive* strangely attractive. It may not be totally coherent, but at least Lynch treats the audience as if it has brains — and then, with great panache, proceeds to scramble them.

Scrambled brains with panache. Sounds like something that might be on the menu at Winkie's Diner, don't you think?

34

Open Range

Cowboy up, Sherman!
Set the Wayback Machine to 1873. That's the year Daniel E. Kelley wrote his most famous song, inspired by a poem written some years earlier by Brewster Higley of Kansas. It's a song familiar to Canadians, although like many other things familiar to Canadians, it's fundamentally and deeply American …

> Oh, give me a home, where the buffalo roam,
> Where the deer and the antelope play
>   [*and the rabbits!*] …
> Where seldom is heard a discouraging word,
> And the skies are not cloudy all day.

"Home on the Range" is the official song of the state of Kansas. It celebrates the myth of a pure, unspoiled American West, and the beauty of the pristine wilderness. It is a song that calls to Americans in a voice nostalgic for simpler times, when a man was his own boss, free to move his cattle from pasture to pasture, when you could ride for days without meeting another soul, when the water was clean and the air was pure, and Mad Cow disease and Income Tax had not been heard of. It was a time when the only weapon of mass destruction was a six-gun, and cowpokes woke with the morning sun, and guys with scruffy beards who looked just like Kevin Costner rolled their own cigarettes and said, "Guess we better rustle up some grub."

Did anyone ever really say that?

Who knows? But it sounds authentic, doesn't it?

Anyway, we are talking about the good old days, pardner. Or rather, the good old days as portrayed by Hollywood in a gazillion westerns.

Open Range, Kevin Costner's epic tale of the Old West, was shot in Alberta. Well, why not? Alberta is an excellent place to shoot movies, to say nothing of moose, grizzly bears, pheasants, and ducks. Alberta is gorgeous, too, and here it's made even more so by some stunning cinematography. But the process of making *Open Range* in Alberta wasn't without controversy. You might recollect that after shooting was completed, Robert Duvall made negative remarks about some of the Canadian actors who play supporting roles in the film. So much for "seldom is heard a discouraging word."

In an interview published in February 2003, Duvall said that some of the actors up here weren't very good, and that he would never shoot another movie in Canada. News of this apparently came as a complete shock to the actors involved. Their take was that Duvall had been very friendly during the shoot, and even very complimentary. Hmm ... Duvall isn't getting any younger. Maybe all those endless hours in the saddle gave him a pain in the sassafras, and he was feeling a mite ornery by the time the whole rootin' tootin' rip-snorting shindig was over.

Open Range is based on a novel by Lauran Paine, and sports a literate, tight screenplay by Craig Storper. Some are calling this Kevin Costner's comeback film, although I'm not sure why. I didn't realize that he had gone anywhere that he needed to come back from. Costner is an actor blessed with amazing resilience. Who else could survive such financial and critical fiascos as *Waterworld*, *The Postman*, and *3000 Miles to Graceland* and spring back with such gusto? *The Postman* alone would have been enough to terminate anyone else's directorial career, "with extreme prejudice."

With *Open Range*, Costner wisely revisits a genre he knows well; if he knows anything, he knows westerns. Remember that in 1994 he was directed by a master, Lawrence Kasdan, in *Wyatt Earp*, and that he himself had a huge success with *Dances with Wolves* in 1990.

Thanks mainly to the very intelligent story, *Open Range* has a bit more going on under the surface than your typical John Wayne vehicle, although this critter is well aware of its roots — sly references to classics like *The Man Who Shot Liberty Valance* and *High Noon* abound.

Duvall is Boss Spearman, a crusty, tough-as-nails old cowpoke who owns a herd of cattle. Costner is Charlie Waite, Spearman's right-hand man — and, as we later understand, his surrogate son. They've been riding together for ten years. As "free grazers," they don't own any land, but move their herd along from pasture to pasture, selling the cattle a few at a time in towns along the way. This is a classic roaming cowboy lifestyle, and by the year 1882, which is when the story is set, it's a lifestyle that is already disappearing, as America moves toward a more urban culture. Land is being bought up, and rich landowners are becoming very powerful. More and more, free grazers like Spearman and Waite are perceived as free*loaders*, even though free grazing is still legal.

It becomes clear early on that Costner's character Charley has several skeletons in his mental closet, although no details are given until later in the film, when we learn of his gunslinger past. While at least superficially reminiscent of

Clint Eastwood's character in *Unforgiven*, Charley is actually much closer in spirit to Gregory Peck's world-weary Jimmy Ringo in the excellent *The Gunfighter* (1950) — a man who can deliver death swiftly and seemingly without remorse, but who really wants nothing more than to be left alone to live a quiet life. And unlike William Munny in *Unforgiven*, Charley has never taken innocent lives — at least none that we know of — so has less to be "unforgiven" for.

There are two other hired hands along for the ride: Mose, a big gentle bear of a man, and a young Mexican kid named Button. Before long, Mose will be murdered and Button left for dead by gunmen in the service of a rich landowner named Baxter. Baxter owns not only a huge parcel of land, but he also owns the sheriff. Unopposed, he uses his hired guns to terrorize the town folk. Baxter soon has his eye on our heroes' herd, and things can only go from bad to worse. Constructed in the tradition of the classic western, the plot of *Open Range* escalates the violence until the final, inevitable shootout. This final bloody confrontation can only be described as a "humdinger," an impeccably choreographed and brilliantly edited dance of death that is one of the very best I have ever seen in a western movie. For aficionados of westerns, the shootout alone is worth the price of admission.

Annette Bening is Sue Barlow, the local doctor's sister and Charley's love interest. Bening is a fine actress capable of delivering outstanding performances, as she did in *American Beauty*, and she does an excellent job with the material at her disposal here. Her understated portrayal of a still beautiful woman trapped in a one-horse town, watching her dreams, and herself, slowly but inexorably fading away, rings true. The scenes between Sue and Charley are very well played. Costner has a wonderful gift for projecting a believable awkwardness under his tough-guy image.

By presenting a moral situation that is not black and white, but rather various shades of grey, *Open Range* veers off the conventional western trail. Our free-grazing heroes are motivated by dark feelings of revenge for the murder of their comrade. Old boss Spearman, as portrayed by Duvall, is essentially a good man fighting for freedom — as he understands the concept — but he is also a man out of step with the changing face of the American West, forced to defend his beliefs in a land where money and guns increasingly decide the winners. Duvall's character represents an earlier era, when principles were placed above profit. He personifies the communal spirit, the ideals of "Share the land," and "Live and let live." Baxter and his hired guns are the new face of America: a place where power is available to whoever can afford to hire the most brutally effective enforcers.

The literate script includes several good speeches and memorable lines, but the film's philosophy is perhaps best summed up when Duvall's character says, "Cows are one thing, but telling a man where he can go in this country is something else." In *Open Range*, it all boils down to a simple truth: when push comes to shove, you had better be able to shoot straight and shoot faster than the other guy. Our hero didn't start the fight, but he sure as heck better be able to finish it.

The violence in *Open Range* is not over the top, but it is gritty, realistic, and unpleasant. The film demonstrates clearly that while it may sometimes be necessary to shoot someone right between the eyes, it's also very messy. The music is a little messy also in places, swelling and squawking and drawing attention to itself, but I've heard worse. This is a well-crafted, engaging western elevated by its intelligent, nuanced script and by very strong performances from the entire cast, Canadians included.

35

Open Water

Open Water was made for about $160,000. Director Chris Kentis shot it entirely on video during a Caribbean vacation. You have to admire anyone who can make a movie for about $160,000. Heck, that's probably less than Conrad Black spends on beluga caviar and lobster tails in a year. The problem with this kind of video, however, is that you lose resolution and clarity. This would have been a better movie with crystal-clear, high-resolution cinematography. As it stands (or floats), it is a rather muddy, murky viewing experience.

I do have respect for Blanchard Ryan (who plays Susan) and for Daniel Travis (Daniel), who wore chain mail under their wet suits and spent days bobbing around in the water pretending to be scared while real sharks swam around them. Okay, maybe they weren't just pretending. But they certainly *seemed* to be pretending, which was a problem. Where is Robert Shaw when we really need him?

In the opening scene we meet Daniel, who is in his early thirties, and has an athletic build and very white teeth. His teeth are so white in fact that they are practically a special effect. Daniel has just finished packing the car, and he is waiting to leave for the airport for a tropical vacation. While sitting in the car, he calls up his wife Susan on her personal cell phone. She answers, and we notice immediately that she too has spectacularly white teeth. No wonder they need a vacation, they must be pooped from all that brushing and flossing.

Susan takes the call from her husband on one cell phone while she is having a business conversation on her other cell phone. People like this drive me nuts. It used to be that just having a cell phone was a status symbol, but now, to have real status, you have to have more than one cell phone, and you have to be receiving calls simultaneously on all of them. We then realize that she's in the house, and he's in the driveway. Sue and Dan are what we used to call Yuppies. Another term I've heard is DINKs (double income, no kids). The crux of the matter here is that these DINKs will wind up going on a dive with a group of strangers, and they will be left behind, forgotten, helplessly floating in the water — a horrific situation to say the least. In real life, events like this one have apparently occurred more than once.

We all have primal fears: fear of getting lost, fear of being left behind, fear of the unknown. Personally, I cannot swim in a lake, never mind the ocean. As soon as I get in the water my mind goes *tilt*, and I start imagining things. I suspect that this is a direct result of being scared silly watching *The Creature from the Black Lagoon* when I was seven years old. Now, as an adult, I imagine all kinds of slimy things swimming around below me. So here is an important message for parents: don't let very young children watch scary movies, they might never fully recover. Or they might become movie critics.

That being said, our family goes to Maine every summer and I have no problems. Why? Because in August, in Maine, the water is very, very cold and sharks dislike cold water. Also, we are told, sharks are not too bright. That may be true, but they are still smart enough not to go swimming in fifty-four-degree water, which is more than you can say for the tourists. Conclusion: Maine is safe. I enjoy it.

Now, if I was floating in the middle of nowhere with no help in sight, I believe I would behave differently from the couple in this movie. It's interesting that not once during this ordeal do either of these people invoke God. They are truly the products of a consumer culture that has replaced God with money. Money is invoked, as when Daniel yells out in exasperated panic, "We actually *paid* to be here!" But God? Never.

The characters also throw various recriminations at each other, which does give the movie some taint of realism. After all, if a husband and wife were in this situation, and diving had been the guy's idea, it wouldn't take long for the wife to point out, "I wanted to go skiing!" Try fielding *that* comment while several sharks are closing in for brunch. If you want to find out how durable your marriage really is, try getting stuck out in shark-infested waters. Or, if you want a test of marital compatibility that's less risky, try putting up wallpaper in the bathroom. Either way, guys, you lose.

If I were floating in the middle of the ocean with no rescue in sight, I *would* appeal to the Almighty. I would try something like, "Hey, God, remember me? Did pretty well on my confirmation when I was ten, remember? Went to midnight mass a few years ago. Listen, Big Guy, I've got a little problem here with some of your other creatures ..."

Of course, a can or two of shark repellent wouldn't hurt either. But then, you would never have gotten me into the water to begin with unless I was in a submarine armed with laser-guided anti-shark torpedoes.

Open Water does deliver suspense in a few places, but let's face it, if you crank up the ominous music and a few sharks suddenly splash around just a few yards ahead, it's not

MOVIES ATE MY BRAIN

too difficult to get the audience's adrenalin pumping a bit. What really would have made a difference here is a stronger identification with the characters, which I didn't feel. I wasn't exactly cheering for the sharks, but I didn't really like these people. Throw Jeff Bridges and Helena Bonham Carter in the water and it'll be a completely different story — heck, I'll jump in there with my harpoon gun myself — but I found these characters to be rather distant and spoiled and unappealing. Obviously, the sharks disagree.

Susan, the wife, has top-model good looks to go with her incredibly white teeth, but she seems to be a bit of a cold fish, if you'll pardon the expression. The night before their diving expedition, she rejects Daniel's sexual overtures. She wants no part of his scuba gear, if you see what I mean. I wondered about the purpose of this scene, because, as I'm fond of saying, there are no accidents in movies. If the director chooses to include a scene, there is a reason for it — unless the director is Michael Bay (*Pearl Harbor*), in which case it's anybody's guess.

In this case, I think the director included the strained bedroom scene in order to underline the point that this couple is not on the best of terms, and they are about to be thrown into a situation that would strain even Paul Newman and Joanne Woodward. Can Susan and Daniel hope to survive if they are not extremely close? I also think that the director does not really want us to like these people very much. This might sound odd, but it's my impression that we are supposed to feel a little detached from them, at least at first. After all, if they were very friendly and outgoing, if we the audience really liked them, then surely the other people on the boat would also like them, and ... they would not be forgotten and left behind! But this is a self-contained couple; they keep to themselves — and that is essential to the plot.

Think about it, we could never believe that Tom Hanks and Meg Ryan would be left behind, could we? They're just too nice.

Over all, these dubious plot contrivances wouldn't matter so much if the acting was outstanding, but it is not. The actors are barely adequate. When the situation starts to call for real drama, they only just manage to keep their heads above water — artistically speaking of course.

Open Water may eventually be remade using big-name actors. My suggestion would be to reunite Ben Affleck and Jennifer Lopez. They would be perfect. They probably wouldn't even have to act too much when things got strained between them. I can see the director motivating them by saying things like, "Think about your divorce settlement," and J-Lo could throw one of her famous tantrums and scream at Ben, "You brought me on this dive and they're not even serving Crystal champagne!" Yes, with Ben and J-Lo bobbing around, the audience could cheer for the sharks without feeling too guilty.

36

Pollock

I'm a musician — a drummer, to be more specific — and abstract art is for me the form of painting closest to music. Like instrumental music, abstract art is about emotion, not ideas. When I look at an abstract painting — a Jackson Pollock, for example — it can suggest a whole range of thoughts, but, being a musician, I invariably ask myself, "What does this painting sound like? Is it jazz, rock, blues, electronic music? Is it sad, frenetic, joyful? Is it a medium-tempo stroll in the park, or a manic, headlong shot out of a cannon?"

Jackson Pollock loved Gene Krupa's complex, often frenetic drumming. Was Krupa's drumming (and showmanship) perhaps one of the influences in the development of Pollock's improvised drip-and-splatter painting technique, along with the Native American technique of sand painting that Pollock was familiar with? Watching actor-director Ed Harris as Pollock creating one of his abstract works — with the canvas stretched out on the floor and the artist walking/dancing around it, dripping and flinging paint from *sticks* and *brushes*, or directly from the paint cans — I imagined him as a kind of Krupa of paint, transported by the intensity of the creative moment, disappearing into his work, totally absorbed by the *rhythm* of the painting being born. *Pollock* reminded me just how wildly original and unique, how surprising and shocking — at least to the general public, and even to some critics

— Jackson Pollock's paintings must have seemed back in the late forties and early fifties.

Artists are sensitive, and great artists have especially sensitive antennae; they "pick up" things — ideas, concepts — long before the rest of us. The ones we identify as geniuses seem to possess the ability to see beyond the visible world. Like the shaman in traditional cultures, they can travel to — or create in their minds — alternative worlds, filled with wonders and terrors, which they interpret through their art. Geniuses often do things that no one has ever tried to do, or even thought of doing, before. Their creativity is not always celebrated or applauded, at least not at first. In fact they may be so far ahead of their times and of popular tastes that their talent is not appreciated until many years after they have died, leaving them to suffer great hardship during their lives. And even if they do achieve financial or critical success, that is no guarantee of happiness.

By the early fifties, after years of personal and artistic struggle, Jackson Pollock did become enormously successful, but his success did not banish his demons. The enormous pressure to maintain his financial and critical success took a huge toll. The expectations placed on him by the public — by 1951 he had been popularly anointed "America's most famous artist" — and by many art patrons and critics, who viewed him primarily as a "creative machine" rather than a human being, would have been hard enough for an emotionally stable person to handle, and Pollock was considerably less than stable. Pollock's extreme sensitivity and fragility left him incapable of dealing with the demands of success — which he may never have felt that he even really deserved in the first place, such was his insecurity — and he retreated into booze. Pollock had battled alcoholism all of his adult life, but during his last five years alcohol abuse gnawed away at his talent, alienated him from his friends, and fuelled the disintegration of his marriage under the weight of his boozy infidelities. Like Charlie Parker before him, Jackson Pollock wasn't a genius *because* of his addiction, but in *spite* of it. A socially awkward introvert who was racked by feelings of inferiority, Pollock used alcohol to deaden (read: protect) himself. Herein lies a terrible paradox: the extreme sensitivity that allowed Pollock to achieve greatness also left him broken, battered, and incapable of functioning in a universe where thick skin is a basic survival tool. This is unfortunately the reality for many artists. At the height of her popularity, two years before her death of a heroin overdose, Janis Joplin told a friend, "The best feeling is no feeling at all." To quote Quebec music icon Robert Charlebois, "Fame is a dangerous game. The more you give, the more they want."

Prior to directing *Pollock* in 2000, Ed Harris had been thinking about a film based on the life of the abstract expressionist painter for about ten years, ever since his father, impressed with how much his son physically resembled Pollock, had given him a copy of *Jackson Pollock: An American Saga*, by Steven Naifeh and Gregory White Smith. One look at a photograph of Pollock and you are immediately struck with the resemblance. Physically, Harris is a perfect candidate to portray the artist, and he lives up to the challenge by giving one of the strongest performances of his career.

Harris surrounds himself with a talented cast, including his wife, Amy Madigan, who presents us with an amusing portrait of Peggy Guggenheim, the New York gallery owner who, in the 1940s, mounted Jackson Pollock's first exhibitions. Marcia Gay Harden won the Best Supporting Actress Oscar for her role as Pollock's wife Lee Krasner, in real life a very talented painter. Her work, like that of many talented woman artists (Frida Kahlo, the wife of Diego Rivera, immediately springs to mind), was overshadowed by her husband's — at least during his lifetime. Krasner outlived Pollock by almost thirty years, and did eventually receive the critical and popular recognition that had previously eluded her.

Jackson Pollock was perhaps the first American-born "star" of the art world. In August of 1949, inspired largely by the raves of art critic Clement Greenberg (portrayed in the film by Jeffrey Tambor), who was to become his most enthusiastic champion, *Life* magazine did a major story on Pollock. His abstract canvases quickly became familiar to people all around the country, an easily identifiable "standard" of modern art in the popular mind.

Pollock is a gorgeous film. Lisa Rinzler's cinematography spectacularly captures every nuance and explosion of colour, and the editing is razor-sharp — full of kinetic energy that mirrors the movement and intensity of Pollock's own action paintings. Unfortunately, *Pollock* suffers from a flaw that is all too common in movies that explore the life of a "tortured artist" — it seems more interested in exploring the torture than the art.

There are of course many artistic geniuses not so tormented and self-destructive as Pollock, but no one seems really interested in making movies about them. I suppose they just don't offer the same dramatic potential. Time and again, in movies like *Bird* (about Charlie Parker) and *Life with Judy Garland: Me and My Shadows*, the oeuvre of the artist is overshadowed by his or her substance abuse and personal problems. The Garland bio-pic, which features a wildly histrionic performance by Judy Davis, was a particularly unfortunate example, its script more interested in showing Judy's alcohol- and pill-fuelled rages — in one scene she sends the Thanksgiving turkey flying across the living room — than it was in celebrating her often transcendent performances of classic tunes from the Great American Songbook. I don't know what it is about Thanksgiving that brings out the worst in some people, but there is a scene in *Pollock* in which the Thanksgiving dinner table — complete with turkey and trimmings — is overturned in spectacularly messy fashion. Perhaps it's in the nature of the Thanksgiving holiday to underline most painfully just how little some people feel they have to be really thankful for.

At any rate, pills and booze and turkey are an explosive mix. Watch out for the flying cranberries!

Jackson Pollock once said that "every good artist paints what he is." Consequently, his paintings were explosive, tempestuous, sometimes confused, overwhelming, filled with emotional fireworks — the stuff of life in all of its glory, drama, and contradiction. It is understandable that a scriptwriter, faced with the daunting challenge of exploring Pollock's life on screen, cannot truly dissociate the "art" from the "person." And *Pollock* does almost achieve that razor-fine balance between obsessing on the artist's emotional and mental states and celebrating the beauty that was born in the dark recesses of his soul. But ultimately, *Pollock* fails in the same way that *Bird* fails. After viewing *Pollock*, I was extremely happy that someone had taken the time to craft a film of high quality about this subject, but I was also saddened that the script had focused more on the artist's personal demons than on the art he created. On the other hand, *Pollock* isn't a documentary, so how could it really be otherwise?

In the end, *Pollock* is an emotionally and intellectually engaging failure, a film that, like Pollock's paintings, reveals new depth with every viewing.

37

Psycho

When I first read that a remake of Hitchcock's *Psycho* (1960) was in production, I reacted the same way I did when I first learned that George Martin was producing a CD of Beatles classics sung by people like Jim Carrey and Céline Dion. I thought, "Why? ... Why? ... Why?"

It seems that Gus Van Sant had been trying for almost ten years to convince Universal to let him remake *Psycho*, but every time he approached the studio about it the answer was a resounding "No!" Then Van Sant had a huge hit with *Good Will Hunting*. The answer, suddenly, was "Yes!"

Funny how these things work.

The relatively cheap price tag, $25 million, helped to green-light the project. Here in Canada, a $25-million movie would not be a trifle, but in Hollywood it's no big deal. Just imagine for a minute how many films Canadian director Don McKellar could make for $25 million ...

Answer: about twelve.

In my opinion, remaking *Psycho* was a terrible idea. Let's see how Gus Van Sant justified the project:

> I felt that sure, there were film students, film buffs and people in the business who were familiar with *Psycho*, but that there was also a whole generation of filmgoers who probably hadn't seen it. I thought that this was a

way of popularizing a classic. Like staging a contemporary production of a classic play while remaining true to the original.

Well, not really.

The way to popularize a classic movie is to re-release it. If kids these days don't want to watch black and white movies, we need to educate them to the fact that black and white is not just colour's impoverished second cousin. The play analogy doesn't work either. If you want to present a play, you *have* to mount a new production, it's the nature of the medium. A film is preserved for all time.

I return then to my little idea: this is Van Sant's commercially focused way of paying homage to Hitchcock while peddling cheap goods — although $25 million isn't *that* cheap — to an unsuspecting and unaware (read: too young to remember the original) segment of the population. In remaking *Psycho*, Gus Van Sant has taken great pains to re-create the original shots. He has used the same camera angles, the same framing, the same lighting techniques.

Let's compare the two.

After an advance screening of the original *Psycho* for studio bigwigs, Hitchcock was strongly "encouraged" to return to the editing suite and rethink the brilliant shower scene in order to reveal less of Janet Leigh. Some Universal executives were concerned that a substantial portion of the audience would be offended by so much exposed flesh. In the early sixties in America, some film producers believed that audiences could deal with a homicidal maniac slashing an attractive young woman to death in the shower, but a major scandal would surely erupt if anyone caught a glimpse of her bare derrière while she was being slashed. Before you get too smug, dear reader, and roll your eyes and declare how totally archaic and wrong-headed those 1960s executives were, I will suggest to you that in mainstream movies today, in twenty-first century America, brutal violence is *still* considered more acceptable than nudity and sexual situations.

Here's a piece of trivia that might well win you the admiration of your friends the next time you are discussing movies: *Psycho* was the first American film to show a toilet being flushed.

Aren't you glad I threw that in?

Van Sant's remake is slightly more risqué than the original. We see a little more bare flesh in the shower scene. Not much, but a little. The biggest difference between the two shower scenes is colour. The original *Psycho* was in black and white; the remake is in colour. This makes the shower scene in the new version bloodier. Film buffs will recall that Hitchcock filmed the original in black and white primarily because he was concerned that the shower scene would be too repulsive in colour. But Hitchcock did want the scene to look realistic to a point. After several tests using the stage blood traditionally used in movies, it was decided that *chocolate sauce* actually looked better in black and white. The blood you see in the original *Psycho* is actually chocolate.

Yummy.

In general, the remake of *Psycho* also contains a little more graphic violence than the original, but it is to Van Sant's credit that he hasn't gone overboard with brutal violence. The main problem I have with this remake is that the casting is wrong. Vince Vaughn is the wrong physical type to replace Anthony Perkins, although he is much closer than Perkins was to Norman Bates as author Robert Bloch described him in the original novel, which was published in 1958. Bloch conceived Norman Bates as a chubby, baby-faced mamma's boy. When Joseph Stefano adapted Bloch's novel for the screen, he agreed with Hitchcock that even though Anthony Perkins didn't fit Bloch's description, he would still be perfect for the part — his angular features and gaunt look lent a haunted, hunted quality to the character. Hitchcock and Stefano transformed Norman's character into a sleek bird of prey. By casting Vince Vaughn as Norman, Gus Van Sant has chosen to respect Bloch's original vision, but it's a choice I disagree with.

Because Vaughn is such a different physical type from Perkins, it's unfortunate that he often appears to be trying to mimic Perkins's performance — Norman's nervous laugh, for example. Rather than imitate Perkins, which is impossible anyway, Vaughn would perhaps have been more successful playing Norman as a completely different type of character. This would have helped distance Vaughn from the inevitable comparisons with Perkins. I want to stress, though, that Vaughn is only miscast; he does not give a poor performance.

It is useful to remember the enormous importance Hitchcock placed on casting. He felt that casting the right actor — the right "type" — was crucial in achieving precisely the right effect, such that the audience was able to *believe* the character.

Birds are a leitmotif in *Psycho*. Numerous verbal, visual, and musical references to birds are woven artfully through the fabric of the film. Even the doomed heroine's name is a little inside joke. Think about it: Marion Crane ...

"You eat like a bird," Norman remarks to Marion as she chews on a sandwich he has prepared for her. And what is Norman's hobby? Stuffing birds. The parlour where they sit together for Marion's last meal is decorated with the winged victims of his taxidermy. His next trophy will be a (human) crane. Hitchcock reinforced Perkins's bird-like characteristics by strategically lighting the actor's face to emphasize its angularity. In one scene, the cinematography even makes Perkins's nose look like a beak. According to various interviews, Hitchcock was fascinated with the ambivalence of birds: on the one hand they are soft and delicate, yet, with their sharp beaks and talons, they can be killers, beautiful agents of doom. Having explored this idea in *Psycho*, he then took it to a logical, nightmarish conclusion in his next film, *The Birds*.

In Van Sant's remake, Anne Heche portrays the doomed Marion as a worldly-wise cynic, a tough cookie. The gentleness and vulnerability that Janet Leigh brought to the role, which made her violent death all the more shocking to the audience, are absent in Heche's performance. Heche is not a bad actress, but in comparison to Leigh she is unconvincing in several crucial scenes. Take another look at the scene where Marion is pulled over by a traffic cop. Leigh is brilliant in the original, Heche in the remake is merely very good. Brilliant is better.

The original *Psycho* is a landmark film. The shower scene alone will be studied and analyzed until the last film school has crumbled to dust. Gus Van Sant may well have had good intentions, but we all know where good intentions often lead, don't we ... ?

If you want to really get to the bottom of this discussion, I suggest that you rent both versions and view them back to back. I also suggest that you begin by watching the remake first. Always better to end on a high note, don't you think? And while we're at it, why doesn't Green Day remake *The White Album*?

38

The Rock

The Rock is a $65-million-dollar movie (remember those cheapies?) possessed of a silly script, brutal and gratuitous violence, loud, obnoxious music, and more explosions than occurred during the entire Vietnam War. Sounds like a box-office winner, doesn't it?

Retired General Frank X. Hummel (Ed Harris) is a disgruntled war hero. The General is in a major snit — or should that be a general snit? — about the lack of recognition the US government has given to brave young Americans who have lost their lives while involved in covert activities. Because the operations in question were "covert," the government is unwilling to acknowledge the participants publicly. The General is also profoundly displeased about the lack of financial compensation given to the families of the men and women involved in the aforementioned covert activities. After deciding that picketing the Defense Department just won't do it, the General assembles a team of crack ex-marines. The plan is to steal some missiles armed with very nasty chemical and biological stuff, storm the island prison of Alcatraz (now a tourist attraction), and take a group of tourists hostage.

Makes sense so far.

The General then threatens to launch these deadly missiles on San Francisco unless the government agrees to pay compensation to the families of the dead soldiers, and also to fork over several millions of dollars to the General and his gang of mercenaries.

The FBI is called in.

Enter our hero, special agent Stanley Goodspeed (Nicholas Cage), a chemical weapons expert. Enter also a mysterious British agent named Patrick Mason (Sean Connery), who has apparently been held illegally by the American government for the last thirty years because he refuses to reveal the hiding place of some microfilm that contains the truth about the Kennedy assassination.

Pretty plausible so far, don't you think?

This microfilm also apparently contains other pieces of super-sensitive information vital to the security of the United States ... such as, for example, how they get that smooth, creamy caramel inside that rich milk chocolate ... Well, I actually don't quite remember the details, but it's important, believe me.

Wait, it just came back to me.

Mason apparently knows all about that UFO that is supposed to have crashed near Roswell, New Mexico, back in the fifties. Mason is also (coincidence!) the only man ever to have escaped from Alcatraz.

Isn't this great?

The FBI plan is to sneak a team of Navy Seals into Alcatraz and have Nicholas Cage's character defuse the missiles before the nutty General can launch them.

I will admit that the three excellent actors swimming in this silly plot almost make it interesting for a while. Of the three, Ed Harris has the biggest challenge: he must bring to life a character so cartoonish that Homer Simpson would not have seemed out of place. Interviewed after the release of *The Rock*, Harris candidly admitted that he had a very hard time keeping a straight face while shooting some of the scenes. Perhaps the producers should have gone all the way and hired Dan Castellaneta to dub Harris's voice. I can just picture our demented General on the phone yelling, "I can't come home *now*, Marge, we haven't even launched the missiles yet. I never have any fun!"

Nicholas Cage gives a solid performance as Stanley, the in-over-his-head intellectual who suddenly discovers that he has to get tough with the bad guys. As wretched as the script is, it actually gives him some genuinely funny lines. After one of the bad guys comes to a particularly brutal end, crushed beneath a huge ventilation unit, Stanley looks at Mason (Connery's character) and says, "That's just about the most awful thing I've ever seen." Later, when the corpse under the ventilation unit keeps twitching (as corpses often do in these movies) while Stanley is trying to defuse one of the missiles, Stanley looks over at Mason and asks him, "Isn't there anything you can do about that? It's very distracting." After staring at him icily for a moment, Mason says, "What do you want me to do, kill him again?"

Ha-ha.

Considering how inane most of the dialogue is in this movie, this witty exchange is the equivalent of a speech delivered by Gabriel Garcia Marquez to the Nobel Prize committee.

As far as the violence goes (and it goes quite far), this is a blatantly manipulative movie. The plan here is to make the bad guys so incredibly, cartoonishly nasty at the beginning that the audience will feel unashamed, in fact will be positively gleeful, when the time comes to dispatch them in increasingly brutal — even sadistic — fashion. *The Rock* is certainly not the first movie to employ this method, but it's a technique that I still find exploitative and morally reprehensible. If we are supposed to be the good guys, how can we be justified in cheering and applauding when our side uses methods every bit as sadistic as the ones employed by the enemy? I admit that this is an age-old question, and not one that is going to be answered in a film review, but it still merits some thought. That being said, if your idea of fun at the movies is watching bad guys get savagely impaled on fence posts, you will have a great old time with this one.

As I was leaving the theatre, I overheard one young man comment to his friend, "Well, that could have been worse." As I drove back home, I thought hard about this. I racked my brain. Could *The Rock* really have been worse? I was still pondering the idea when I went to bed. During the night, I was assaulted by nightmares of being held captive on Alcatraz by Ed Harris and director Michael Bay, locked in a cell with a giant thousand-pound ventilation unit dangling precariously over my head while Bay screamed insults at me and forced me to watch the director's cut of *The Rock*, all four hours of it. I awoke at dawn in a cold, clammy sweat. Later, struggling to brush my teeth, my hands still shaking from the memory, I unequivocally concluded that the young man at the theatre had been right: *The Rock* could have been worse.

39

Seducing Doctor Lewis

Over the past twenty years, it seems that I've heard the word "renaissance" mentioned every time a film produced in Quebec has done exceptionally well. In the short to medium term, thanks to the commercial success of both *Seducing Doctor Lewis* and *The Barbarian Invasions*, it may well become a little easier for Quebec directors to finance their projects. I've often said that if the federal and provincial governments really wanted to promote culture and unity they would invest much more in film, and assist writers, directors, and producers to make movies with good stories *about Canadians.* Certainly every citizen of *La Belle Province* knows only too well that more than enough money has been thrown — and thrown away — at the wrong projects in the name of promoting national unity. To achieve true unity, a people must share their experiences. I can't believe that it's healthy for any cultural group to consume so many stories, whether on film or on television, that are hatched in another culture. Canadians watch American movies *all the time.* We gobble them up, slack-jawed, wide-eyed, and mesmerized. I have nothing against American movies — I grew up with them and I love them dearly — but the stories they tell are often at odds with Canadian mores, social values, and cultural identity. American films celebrate — as they were meant to — American social realities and political culture, and in many cases they do so exceptionally well. I don't want to sound jealous, but Americans are annoyingly good at exporting their culture, and wrapping it up in irresistible celluloid packaging. I don't blame American cinema for celebrating American culture, I only wish more encouragement were given in Canada to filmmakers intent on celebrating Canadian culture. I'm not commercially naïve either. I've been a film critic long enough to know that violence sells tickets, as does sex, and that if you combine the two — a profoundly unhealthy union in my mind — you generate box office. But you also pander to the lowest common social denominator.

Director Jean-François Pouliot's film *Seducing Doctor Lewis* (French title: *La Grande Séduction*) contains no violence, and almost no sex apart from some suggestive talk and innuendo, yet it has had spectacular box-office success in both Quebec and France. I don't know if it's premature to talk about a renaissance, but I do believe that *Seducing Doctor Lewis* embodies the new maturity of Quebec cinema. It represents a new genre in Quebec, the humanist comedy.

We've had comedies before in Quebec — the bedroom farce was a staple back in the sixties and seventies — and we've had films that were huge commercial successes, like the *Les Boys* series of hockey farces. Quebec has also produced some good children's movies, and God knows in the eighties and nineties there were more dark, existential, nihilistic dramas made in Quebec than you could shake a crucifix at. For decades it seemed that just about every other Quebec production expounded the idea that life was essentially rotten and miserable. While some of these *très noir* films were quite remarkable, I believe that a film culture is only truly grown up when it can liberate itself from overwhelming existential angst. I know that the winters here are interminable and that things were bleak beyond belief in the fifties, but we lived through it, so can we have some fun now?

Seducing Doctor Lewis is not straight comedy, far from it. It looks at some very serious issues, such as welfare and unemployment, but it does so with gentle irony and a mischievous twinkle in the eye.

Set in the small, fictitious Gaspé fishing village of Ste-Marie-la-Mauderne, the story begins in an atmosphere of social unrest. The men are humiliated by having to line up for welfare cheques, and have lost their self-esteem. It is profoundly discouraging for these proud fishermen to have to accept government handouts, and they are finding it harder and harder to get up in the morning. In fact, for some of them, it's hard not only to get up but also to accomplish other tasks. The whole village is down, literally, if you get my drift.

If this sounds bleak, the treatment is just the opposite. The tone of the film is a bit like a fable. The script does not underline the misery of the situation, but rather the humanity, dignity, and resilience of the people being tested. After years of criticizing the Catholic Church, it seems that some Quebec filmmakers have placed the emphasis back on the positive elements of Christianity — solidarity, courage, and plain underhanded deception. Let me explain. The mayor announces that an opportunity exists for the village to attract a large factory, which would solve the unemployment problem. But the factory owners are insisting that they will only set up shop if the village has a full-time doctor running a full-time medical practice. For the residents of Ste-Marie-la-Mauderne, the challenge is clear: attract a young doctor from the big city and convince him to move his practice to their little village.

Through some shady circumstances, a young, successful doctor from Montreal named Christopher Lewis (David Boutin) is persuaded to practise medicine in the village for a month. The villagers now have thirty days in which to persuade him to stay permanently; if they don't succeed, they lose the factory. To be sure that young Dr Lewis will want to stay, they must try to convince him that Ste-Marie-la-Mauderne is heaven on earth.

In order to do this they must find out what he likes, so as soon as he arrives and moves into a vacant house they begin spying on him. They tap his phone to find out as much about him as they can. Their tactic is simple: once they know what he really likes, they can arrange for "providence" to provide it. When for example they find out what he likes to eat, the local greasy spoon, which usually features pâté chinois and poutine, starts serving boeuf bourguignon. Used to eating well, the young doctor is suitably impressed. As the charade continues, the villagers discover that the young upper-class doctor loves the game of cricket, and they set about convincing him that the entire village is composed of cricket fanatics. They build a cricket field (a pitch, as it is called) and they make uniforms, and even though they don't exactly have the right equipment, they use hockey pads and baseball gear to make the village team look credible. They even hook up a satellite dish, so that cricket matches can be shown on the local tavern's television. None of these shenanigans addresses a major problem, however: the villagers do not know the rules of cricket, indeed do not possess Clue One about how a game of cricket should be conducted.

Well, who can blame them for not knowing the rules of cricket? As a baseball fan, I know that baseball and cricket are related somehow, but only as distant cousins. They are related in the same way as a hamburger is related to a hockey puck: they have a similar appearance, of course, but everyone knows that hockey pucks are much more nutritious.

The portrait of contemporary Quebec society that *Seducing Doctor Lewis* draws is close to caricature, but not so far removed from reality as to transform it into cartoon. The movie points out the chasm that exists between the amusements of the wealthy and the popular culture of the workers, but the script also makes the point that social chasms can be bridged. Indeed, many social issues are explored in ways both subtle and entertaining. *Seducing Doctor Lewis* reminded me of *Local Hero*, the landmark Scottish film, directed by Bill Forsyth. *Local Hero* was a watershed in Scottish cinema, demonstrating with outstanding box office results that it was possible to open up to new cinematic genres and attitudes while at the same time expanding your domestic audience.

Seducing Doctor Lewis and *Local Hero* share a common theme: underdogs must band together not only to survive, but to eventually triumph over the forces that would place economic interests above human ones.

40

Shaun of the Dead

These days, movie titles are a bit like band names; it seems as if all the really good ones are taken. In the past we had the Beatles, and the Moody Blues, and even Vanilla Fudge, but today we have Puddle of Mud and Suicidal Tendencies. Movies used to have great titles like *Children Shouldn't Play with Dead Things* or *Bring Me the Head of Alfredo Garcia*. We're talking titles that meant something, titles that were literate, titles that were packed with meaning. Now, in the age of attention deficit disorder, we often get one-word titles like *Cellular* or *Collateral*. And you can forget using roman numerals in titles in the twenty-first century, because nobody knows how to read them. We live in an age when many people would guess that *Henri IV* must be a hospital drama.

But now comes one of the great punny titles of all time, a *Dawn of the Dead* parody called *Shaun of the Dead*. *Shaun of the Dead* is directed by Edgar Wright. Back in 1991 he directed a parody of western movies called *A Fistful of Fingers*. If nothing else, the man has a flair for titles.

Shaun of the Dead was co-written by Wright and the star of the film, Simon Pegg. What they have concocted is an idiot-savant blend of completely over-the-top gore, inspired performances, and a dazzling assortment of great one-liners. This is a very funny, gooey movie that splashes about merrily in intestines and brains.

Director George Romero is the man who started it all with his classic zombie movie, *Night of the Living Dead*, in 1968. *Night* was shot in Pittsburgh and made for about a buck ninety-nine, but it was effective (that is, scary), and influenced a generation of filmmakers to produce such memorable films as *Daffy Duck's Night of the Living Duck*, *Scooby Doo's Night of the Living Doo*, *Night of the Living Date*, and of course the cult family drama *Night of the Leaving Dad*. Other titles that pop into my mind are *The Evil Dead, The Evil Dead 2*, and, inevitably, *Return of the Living Dead* (which, I believe, is about either the Canadian Senate or Baseball Commissioner Bud Selig, I can't quite remember which; either way, it's really scary).

Over the past twenty years, the zombie genre has been in decline. Each zombie movie seems to have been worse than the previous one. The decline really became pronounced in 1989 with the release of *Chopper Chicks in Zombietown*, which was one of Billy Bob Thornton's first movies. Just think, if he had stopped there, we never would have been treated to *Bad Santa*.

When a film genre like the horror movie or the western goes into decline, it becomes not unlike a zombie itself. It is a sure sign that a genre is in decline when a plague of similar, derivative low-budget movies begins to infect the local Cineplex. It's not a pretty sight: poorly written plots wandering around aimlessly, consuming the money of living filmgoers, feeding ignominiously at the box office trough without providing audiences with any real entertainment value. Then the declining genre returns from the dead as a parody of itself. Inevitably, inexorably, at the point when no one knows what to do with a genre and every producer feels that it has been milked for all it's worth, the focus turns to comedy, and new money is generated at the box office.

Perhaps the first example of a serious, successful genre degenerating into parody is *Abbott and Costello Meet Frankenstein* (1948), the result of Universal's having run out of monster ideas, and the post-war public's having become more sophisticated in its horror demands. Mel Brooks's *Young Frankenstein* (1974), a hilarious film that brilliantly and gleefully navigates comedic waters undreamed of in Bud and Lou's philosophy, continued along the same lines. More recently, *Scary Movie* proved that the "slasher" genre is, if not in decline, then at least ready to undergo metamorphosis. And then of course came *Scary Movie 2* and *Scary Movie 3*. Successful films are like peanuts, you can't stop after just one.

Genre movies will always exist, because audiences enjoy — no, make that *need* — the stories that these pictures tell. As author Joseph Campbell pointed out in *The Hero with a Thousand Faces* (1949), his study of popular mythology, humans have been telling the same stories over and over again for thousands of years. The names change, and the settings, but the essential elements remain, disguised but ever-present. The hero may wear a bronze helmet or a cowboy hat or a space suit, but he (or she) is always the same hero, attempting with varying degrees of success to solve the riddle of existence, to right the multitude of wrongs that afflict the world.

Genres run out of gas, and then they get parodied, and sometimes they are reborn.

With *Shaun of the Dead*, the zombie genre has reached its parody phase. Interestingly, in 2005 George Romero attempted to rejuvenate the genre, which he had almost single-handedly created, by directing a film called *Land of the Dead*. In an effort to give the zombies a new lease on life (sorry!), *Land of the Dead* had them evolving into more intelligent creatures, and running for elected office (well, not really, but I couldn't resist).

The hero of *Shaun of the Dead* is twenty-nine-year-old Shaun (Simon Pegg), a sales clerk in an electronics store. He's a nice guy, but he seems a bit of a zombie himself, staggering day after day through his dead-end job. His lovely girlfriend Liz is sick to death of spending every evening watching the boys drink beer at the local pub, the Winchester. She is also sick to death of having Shaun's best buddy Ed (Nick Frost) constantly hanging around, making rude remarks and generally acting like a porker. Ed is indeed a piece of work. He "shares" a flat with Shaun; that is, he shares the space, but he doesn't seem to share much of the rent. He doesn't actually appear to do anything except play video games and occasionally sell pot, although when a potential buyer calls him on his cell phone he invariably answers that he hasn't got any.

When Liz announces that she's had enough, Shaun gets depressed and winds up — guess where — in the Winchester drinking with Ed. They get plastered, and next day, suffering a wicked hangover, Shaun gets up and takes a short walk to the corner store to buy his usual morning soda. He's so hung over that he fails to notice that everyone else in the neighbourhood seems to be either dead or turned into a flesh-eating zombie. Later, back at the house, Ed and Shaun turn on the telly and hear reports that some strange disease is bringing the recently dead back to life, and that they crave human flesh.

To give you an example of the humour here, when Ed and Shaun discover two zombies in their backyard, and they've just heard that to kill one you have to destroy its brain or cut off its head, they decide to defend themselves using Shaun's record collection. This makes sense, in a zombie movie kind of way. I mean if you fling an LP at a zombie, you might decapitate it. (Any rock musician will tell you that cymbals are much more dangerous than vinyl records.)

As two bloodthirsty zombies lurch slowly forward, our heroes bend over a milk crate filled with Shaun's collection of vinyl records. Shaun hastily decides which ones they can fling at the zombies and which ones he wants to keep. As the zombies approach, Ed pulls out the records one at a time. Shaun says, "No, no! That's an original pressing of 'Blue Monday' by New Order, not *that* one!" To which Ed responds, "Well, what about Sade?" They look at each other and yell "Okay!" and fling Sade at the zombie … woosh! And the LP bounces harmlessly off the growling creature. Simon Pegg and Nick Frost perform this inspired silliness with expert comic timing. By the way, our heroes quickly discover that a cricket bat is much more effective.

The violence and silliness escalate until the climactic scene, which finds our heroes and a few friends holed up in the Winchester (where else?) surrounded by hordes of zombies. There seems no way out. But all is not lost …

A word to the squeamish: the movie goes completely over the top with blood and guts. I would have cut out perhaps ten minutes (and several feet of intestines), but I may be becoming too sensitive in my old age.

41

The Snow Walker

It's true confessions time.

I almost passed on *The Snow Walker*, because of its title. The press screening was held in March, and, as usual, I was sick to death of snow by then. I'm not a "Winter Wonderland" kind of person. Winter for me consists mainly of toughing it out until spring. By March, even the word "snow" is enough to spark feelings of hostility, so I was thinking, "Oh, no! a movie set in the Arctic! yuck! ... I don't think I'm up to this."

Speaking of Canadians and their intimate relationship with winter, I read some statistics recently that I thought were pretty surprising, if not downright weird. Imagine this: 15.5 percent of Canadian women and 11 percent of Canadian men say that they have had sex in the snow.

I'm not sure what to make of that.

I could believe maybe in a chair lift, or even on a zamboni, but in the *snow*?

While Statistics Canada has performed a wonderful service in bringing this to light, I think we need more specific information. The survey should have asked the respondents the particulars of their activities, such as whether these events took place in a tent in the snow, or on snowshoes (that would be a challenge!), or in a snowbank behind the arena. I for one would like to know more. I'll bet that these statistics would come as a bit of a shock to our American cousins, most of whom are convinced that it's just a big frozen bore up here in the land of parkas and poutine.

Poor Americans. They have no idea what we're really up to, eh?

Unlike most of his compatriots, American actor-director Charles Martin Smith knows more than a thing or two about Canada: he portrayed the naturalist in the superb film adaptation of Farley Mowat's *Never Cry Wolf* in 1983. One of his most memorable screen incarnations was as "Toad," the short, nerdy guy with the thick glasses who winds up with the ditzy blonde, in George Lucas's now classic *American Graffiti* (1973). He also portrayed Ray Bob, the bass player, in *The Buddy Holly Story* (1978), and a Federal agent in Brian De Palma's *The Untouchables* (1987).

As a director, Smith was responsible for *Air Bud* (1997), a mildly entertaining Disney movie about an athletic pooch. He also directed one of the worst bombs of 1992, *Boris and Natasha*, a bizarre, excruciatingly unfunny movie featuring Dave Thomas (of *SCTV* fame) as Boris Badanov and Sally Kellerman as Natasha Fatale. You haven't really paid your dues as a moviegoer until you've had to sit through *Boris and Natasha*. Of course it's a well-known fact that every director, no matter how brilliant, has at least one turkey in his closet.

Okay, except Orson Welles. But every *other* director has made at least one very bad movie.

The Snow Walker is based on a Farley Mowat short story called "Walk Well My Brother." It is in fact a very short story, which placed Charles Martin Smith in the unusual position of having to flesh out his source material. Usually, a person adapting a literary work faces the opposite problem, and the delicate decisions concern what to cut out rather than what to add. To fill out his screenplay, Smith borrowed elements from other Mowat stories. *The Snow Walker* is set in the high Arctic — although it was shot in and around Rankin Inlet and Churchill, Manitoba — and it perfectly captures the spirit and style of Farley Mowat. CMS — my fingers are cramping up from calling him Charles Martin Smith — should at the very least be considered an honorary Canadian for doing this, or maybe he should be awarded a special Governor General's Award.

The year is 1953, and our hero is Charlie Halliday (Barry Pepper). Charlie, a hotshot bush pilot, is employed by a small northern airline that flies single-engine Otters out of Yellowknife. It transports supplies, but it will also take along tourists and hunters and anybody else who wants to go up north. In his early thirties, Charlie is a popular, good-looking bon vivant who has a girl in every town. Charlie is a good guy, but, like a lot of other white people, he doesn't have much knowledge of or deep respect for Inuit culture. He's not outwardly racist or mean-spirited, just ignorant.

His perspective is about to change.

One day as he's delivering supplies to a remote outpost, he meets up with three Inuit, a young woman in her late teens or early twenties and two men. The young woman is sick; she coughs constantly. The men speak very little English, but they manage to communicate to Charlie that they want him to fly the young woman to a hospital in Yellowknife. At first he refuses. Charlie is very much a "What's in it for me?" kind of guy. After the men offer him two large walrus tusks, which are worth quite a lot of money, Charlie agrees to take the woman. On the way to Yellowknife the plane has a mechanical failure, and crash-lands in the middle of nowhere. Charlie and the young woman are now engaged in a struggle for survival. The only bit of luck on their side is that the weather is not too harsh, at least for now.

The Snow Walker is a captivating story of survival in the immensity of the Canadian North. Without any hope of rescue from the outside — Charlie was not following his flight plan at the time of the crash, so it is extremely unlikely that anyone will locate them — these two strangers from very different worlds are forced to rely exclusively on each other. It soon becomes obvious that Charlie is totally unprepared, and unable to fend for himself in this environment. Traditional roles are quickly reversed, as the strong young white man from a technologically advanced culture becomes dependent for his life on a frail young Inuit woman. If these two characters were interacting in a white, urban environment, Charlie would be in control. But this is her world, a world that Charlie flies over every day but that is alien to him, and his white technology is useless: the plane is a wreck, its radio beyond repair.

Desperate to find help, Charlie decides to walk to a camp he believes to be about one hundred miles away. He heads out one morning, leaving the woman, whose name, he has learned, is Kanaalaq, in the shelter and relative safety of their downed plane. After a few days of walking, all of the vestiges of his white culture begin to fail him: his inadequate clothes are soaked from the constant rain, his wet matches won't light and he doesn't know how to start a fire from scratch, and the rifle he carries becomes nothing more than a dead weight, because there isn't really anything to shoot at. When he does take aim at something, he has no hope of hitting his target; Charlie couldn't hit a moose if he was sitting on it. Shivering, exhausted, and hungry, he is soon knocking on heaven's door. He is saved *in extremis* by Kanaalaq, who has gone out after him and has managed to find him. She nurses him back to health, and takes control of their situation by using her knowledge of traditional ways — knowledge Charlie can only marvel at — to feed, clothe, and shelter them.

Aside from the stark but spectacularly beautiful environment and the perfectly understated performances of the actors, what makes *The Snow Walker* such a fascinating film is the way the story stands the cultural power structure on its head, working against our early expectations so as to neatly shift the balance in favour of the young woman Kanaalaq. By saving Charlie's life, she instils in him a new, profound respect not only for herself, but also for her culture. But as Kanaalaq grows weaker by the day, increasingly racked by coughing and fever, Charlie must face the dire truth: if they do not reach an outpost soon, she will die. Can he save her, and himself?

While shooting *The Snow Walker*, the crew endured many hardships, including wind chills that sometimes plummeted to minus 45 degrees Celsius. At one point, near Churchill, the cast and crew were charged by polar bears and forced to run for the safety of their trucks. After that incident, guards armed with tranquilizer guns were posted around the set. In the spring the set was invaded by mosquitoes, and if you think the black flies are bad up at the cottage, you should try making a movie while gigantic swarms of mosquitoes fill the air, getting in your eyes, your nose, your mouth. In an interview, CMS recounts how shooting was interrupted one day because the cameraman could no longer see the actors through the clouds of mosquitoes. The little pests covered everything, sometimes making the actors look as if they were wearing coats made of some strange, buzzing, moving fur. Pay special attention to the scene in which Charlie runs around screaming in frustration at the mosquitoes swarming around and nibbling on him. Pepper wasn't acting.

The crew also lugged a huge crane around the wilderness to help them find camera positions high enough that they could capture the beauty of the landscape. The result is a beautiful film, but the viewer gains much more from *The Snow Walker* than an aesthetically satisfying experience. The script uses dialogue sparingly and to great effect, and the actors' use of gesture, facial expression, and body language combine with Smith's enlightened choice of shots to reveal with subtle intelligence the complex relationship that develops between the two characters. *The Snow Walker* is clothed in the accoutrements of the survival/adventure film, but the true goal of Charlie and Kanaalaq's journey is soon revealed to be not only salvation in the physical sense, but, more importantly, self-discovery through spiritual transformation, perhaps the only journey that truly matters in the end.

The Snow Walker is certainly an anomaly: a Canadian production directed by an American and starring one of the very few Canadian-born actors (Pepper) ever to portray an American icon: he was baseball great Roger Maris in Billy Crystal's film *61**, which aired on HBO in 2001. In *The Snow Walker*, Pepper gives an excellent, believable performance, and the chemistry he shares with first-time actor Annabella Piugattuk, who is perfect as Kanaalaq, is outstanding.

This is the kind of thoughtful, moving, low-key film that is often produced in Canada, only to be received with general indifference at the box office, and then quickly relegated to the bottom of a video store shelf. In this case, the situation is made even sadder by the fact that *The Snow Walker* is a nuanced, supremely satisfying exploration of both the interplay between traditional and technological cultures and the complexities of human interdependence.

42

Star Trek IX: Insurrection

My nephew, who is very bright but who is also unfortunately one of those mixed-up people who believes that Elvis really is dead, pointed out to me recently that there is a curse hanging over the odd-numbered *Star Trek* movies, that in fact numbers 1, 3, 5, and 7 are considered by trekkers to be inferior products. The Bambino notwithstanding, I don't really believe in curses, but I would agree that the odd-numbered *Star Trek V: The Final Frontier* should have been aborted. This was a script that seemed to have been hatched at 3:00 a.m. by several screenwriters on a Saurian brandy binge.

The main weakness of *The Final Frontier* was director William Shatner. Never a great actor, Shatner has nevertheless been known to turn in a convincing performance when guided by a strong director. Under the direction of Leonard Nimoy in *Star Trek IV: The Voyage Home* (an *even-numbered* movie), Shatner was quite good. Unfortunately for Shatner — and for everyone who had to watch — his performance in *V* was wooden and self-conscious. In his defence, I will say that there are very few actors who can direct themselves successfully.

Directing yourself is a little like trying to shag your own fly balls. Woody Allen has done it brilliantly, ditto Orson Welles. That's pretty rarefied company. Jonathan Frakes (Riker) took on the challenge in number *IX*.

Remember the Prime Directive?

> As the right of each sentient species to live in accordance with its normal cultural evolution is considered sacred, no Star Fleet personnel may interfere with the healthy development of alien life and culture. Such interference includes the introduction of superior knowledge, strength, or technology to a world whose society is incapable of handling such advantages wisely. Star Fleet personnel may not violate this Prime Directive, even to save their lives and/or their ship unless they are acting to right an earlier violation or an accidental contamination of said culture. This directive takes precedence over any and all other considerations, and carries with it the highest moral obligation.

This is a great piece of moralistic legislation, but having watched the original *Star Trek* television series, I am firmly convinced that no one on the *Enterprise* ever actually paid any attention to it. Oh, they quoted it a lot (especially Spock), but they always managed to circumvent it rather neatly by the time push came to shove. Of course if they hadn't, the episodes would have been about fifteen minutes long.

This time around, the *Next Generation* gang is involved in a study of a small planet that shows strange atmospheric anomalies. The planet is populated by only a few hundred people, and they seem to live in perfect peace and contentment, the way Alien populations so often do in these movies. Must be the atmosphere. Anyway, it turns out that the planet is a kind of Fountain of Youth. And if you've been keeping up on your science-fiction movie conventions, you'll know that Fountain of Youth-type planets are magnets for evil Aliens.

Enter the evil Aliens.

The evildoers, who call themselves the Sona — pretty catchy name if you're an eighties-type New Wave band — want to deport the population and use the planet's wonderful powers for themselves. One look at these guys and I immediately understood why they are obsessed with the planet's regenerative powers. They are a mess. They're not just wrinkled, they look as if they've been soaking in prune juice for about two hundred years. They are so wrinkled they should be hooked up to an Oil of Olay IV drip.

This gives F. Murray Abraham (a great actor) a chance to ham it up while looking as if he's wearing the world's most wrinkled nylon stocking over his face. His portrayal of the evil leader is delivered with great panache — and thank goodness for that, because most of the other actors often seem to be cruising on impulse power alone. This movie would be in real trouble without someone we really love to hate.

To make a long story short, Picard must rebel against Star Fleet's orders (and completely ignore the Prime Directive — are you shocked?) in order to save the planet's population from deportation or annihilation.

The special effects are pretty good, but not great. It seems that a lot of the effects had originally been done with computer animation, but the producers were unhappy, so they decided to scrap them and start over, using scale models. To my eyes, the models look like ... well ... plastic scale models, but what do I know? Maybe in the distant future everything will be made out of plastic and look exactly like this.

Wonderfully silly sci-fi clichés abound. My favourite effect occurs every time the *Enterprise* suffers damage in battle. Red lights flash, the camera tilts, and enormous jets of steam engulf the sets. Have you ever asked yourself where all this steam is coming from? Is the *Enterprise* steam-powered? Is that the secret of warp drive? Or are the bad guys simply targeting the hot water tanks?

The elements that made *Star Trek* unique were numerous. There was often a happy convergence of interesting characters, even more interesting interaction between them, good writing, and original stories and concepts. *Star Trek IX: Insurrection* is entertaining and it does have some fine humorous moments, but the sub-plot involving Data and a little boy who befriends him is a model of tired clichés about lack of emotion, human nature, and friendship. Worse, the little boy owns a pet Alien caterpillar-type creature with big, googly eyes. This little product tie-in is enough to blow out all of the Cuteness Sensors on the *Enterprise*. Are the producers planning to market the plush toy version at Wal-Mart? Will it be made in China by underpaid, exploited workers?

Writers Rick Berman and Michael Piller have decided to use Data (Brent Spiner) almost exclusively for comic relief. Spiner is a talented actor, and he does a good job with the material he is given, but this comical approach really cheapens the character and eliminates much of the complexity that has made the android so interesting in the past.

By the way, did you know that Klingons undergo the equivalent of puberty? This was news to me too, but after having seen Mr Whorf's face ravaged by the Klingon equivalent of acne, I am a believer. While this may be one of the all-time silliest plot devices ever concocted by a *Star Trek* screenwriter, it is actually pulled off pretty well, although the potentially embarrassing (but amusing!) questions raised by the idea of Klingon puberty are never posed, let alone answered. Having gone through this phase of life with my own pre-teen, I was concerned that Mr Whorf was going to start talking back to Picard and refusing to clean up his room.

To my great dismay, every time the characters start to have some real human interaction or philosophical conversations — as when Picard is smitten with a beautiful woman, who, he learns, is actually three hundred years old — a sudden plot twist brings the engaging proceedings to a dead stop. For example, a potentially hot scene between Riker and Troi in the bathtub goes quickly down the drain when an emergency call comes in from Star Fleet. Too bad.

Don't get me wrong, this is still an enjoyable film. The acting is generally solid, and Jonathan Frakes does a fine job on both sides of the camera. But the script obstinately refuses to boldly go anywhere we haven't been before. *Star Trek* as I knew it has almost ceased to exist. It has become close in spirit to all other mainstream science-fiction franchises. The special effects-driven script is filled with predictable plot devices, and the emphasis is entirely on action. This is unfortunate, because the mythology of this series is much richer than anything big-budget Hollywood is willing to explore.

Inevitably, as studios invest astronomical amounts of money on films, a process of homogenization occurs that tends to downplay the more original and artistic aspects of stories in favour of pre-tested "sure-fire" approaches.

Science fiction used to be about possibilities, speculation, surprises. The Unknown.

It's appropriate, I think, that the *Enterprise* crew discovers the Fountain of Youth in *Star Trek IX*. The whole science-fiction genre is desperately in need of rejuvenation.

43

Star Wars: Episode III — Revenge of the Sith

Loyal fans of *Star Wars* don't care a Wookie's growl about my opinion of *Episode III – Revenge of the Sith*. Flock to it the fans will, and marvel at the splashy special effects they will, but by bad dialogue and poor performances assaulted they will be.

No one mangles English syntax as amusingly as Yoda, except maybe Jean Chrétien, and we don't have him to kick around any more, do we? Yoda is featured prominently in *Episode III – Revenge of the Sith*, and he *is* a lot of fun to watch. But not all of the actors in this last instalment are up to the little green one's standard. By the way, I seem to recall that in *Episodes V* and *VI*, Yoda was more of a bluish-green, whereas now he is greener — not quite Kermit green, but close. Perhaps his change of colour can be explained by the fact that he's younger in this episode. In *Episode III* he's only 875 years old, after all. Maybe when he hits 900, instead of going grey he'll go blue.

Star Wars is an extraordinary cultural — and financial — phenomenon. It has generated some $3.5 billion in profits since the first release in 1977. An entire generation has grown up on this stuff. You could even say that *Star Wars* has had a profound effect on American defence policy. It was after all part of the inspiration for Ronald Reagan's so-called Star Wars Missile Defense scheme.

And "scheme" was a good word for it.

In the twenty-first century, Reagan's chimera has been replaced by that ultimate defence industry cash cow, the Missile Defense Shield. The name has changed, but the bottom line remains the same: this is a major money moo-moo for defence contractors. And the technology involved *still* doesn't work.

With *Episode III*, after years of speculation, we finally arrive at the resolution of the ultimate question posed by *Star Wars*: what makes a good person, a kind person, go over to the dark side? I'm not referring to Belinda Stronach crossing over to the Liberals, but rather Anikin Skywalker's transformation into Darth Vader.

The ongoing plot of *Star Wars* has been getting more and more convoluted since George Lucas decided to go backwards and shoot *Episode I*. *Episode III* tells the story of how the democratic Republic becomes the Evil Empire.

Damn Yankees.

As the movie opens, the Republic is at war with the Sith. The Republican head of state is Chancellor Palpatine. He is using the war as an excuse to clamp down on basic freedoms, and he has assumed emergency powers. He is increasingly engaged in a power struggle with the Jedi Council. The Council is a kind of United Nations, only with major firepower at its disposal. What the Jedi don't know is that Chancellor Palpatine is really a Sith Lord, and a master of the dark side. His plan is to influence the still young and impressionable Anakin and to lure him to the dark side.

Anakin (Hayden Christianson) is secretly married to Padmé (Natalie Portman), the queen of Naboo, an important diplomat. Their marriage is secret because Jedi aren't supposed to marry or even to have deep romantic attachments. Why is this? you ask. Because you can't be married and expect to be out every night being a Jedi with the boys — bowling every Wednesday is bad enough.

The point is that by marrying Padmé, Anakin has already betrayed his Jedi oath.

I need to say a word or two here about the story's internal logic, or rather lack of it. How is it possible for Anakin, who is in constant contact with Yoda and other Jedi masters, to have managed to shield his feelings for Padmé and keep his relationship secret? It seems, frankly, impossible. Remember now that Yoda is an 875-year-old Jedi master — he may be short and green, but he is every teenager's worst nightmare. When you come home at two in the morning and Yoda is waiting up for you and he looks you in the eyes, you don't get away with, "Oh, I was just over at Freddy's." So it seems impossible to me that this relationship could have been kept a secret from Yoda. Early on in the movie it becomes clear that Obi-Wan Kenobi (Ewan McGregor) *does* sense that there is something going on between Anakin and Padmé, yet, illogically, he doesn't confront Anakin about it. In other words, the plot conveniently ignores the fact that this relationship should have been detected (and ended) by the master Jedis. This contrivance exists because it is vitally important that the relationship be kept a secret in order for the plot to advance in the way that Lucas wishes it to, indeed in the way that *Episode IV* dictates that it must.

When Padmé reveals to Anakin that she is pregnant, he is surprised. Well, the news had a jarring effect on me too. You would think that a society that has light sabres and clones would have foolproof birth control! As if being secretly married weren't bad enough for a Jedi. But this plot event has to happen, because Lucas has written himself into a black hole from which there is no escape: he is obligated —

after the fact — to explain certain events that occurred in *Episodes IV, V,* and *VI*.

After the announcement of Padmé's pregnancy, Anakin starts having nightmare visions of her dying in childbirth. It is his growing anxiety that begins to turn him toward the dark side. I hate to be a spoilsport, but this plot device also seemed rather clunky and unconvincing. Given the incredibly advanced state of medicine in this galaxy, Padmé's dying in childbirth is about as likely as Yoda's dying of mad cow disease.

Nevertheless, these nightmares obsess Anakin, who is still haunted by his own mother's death. But instead of confiding in his master Obi-Wan (as I believe he would if this were happening in a more plausible galaxy), Anakin gets even chummier with Chancellor Palpatine, who begins to hint to him that the dark side can offer immortality (read: save Padmé). There we have it: Anakin is ultimately drawn to the dark side to protect his wife and their unborn children.

Most of the acting in *Episode III* seems like an afterthought. Because of the special effects-heavy script, the actors had to play out almost all of their scenes in a studio in front of a blue screen. Almost everything that is seen on screen is computer-generated. The movie was in post-production for eighteen months, and the cost of putting in the effects and matching everything up and inserting the actors was 150 million dollars.

Acting? The most important thing for Lucas it is not.

That being said, Ewan McGregor does well at channelling Alec Guinness. He's got the impeccably trimmed beard and the proper British accent and he at least tries to stay in character. Most of the other characters sound as if they're speaking in twenty-first-century American English, which is annoying and ultimately distracting. At one point, while dangling from a rope, Anakin yells to Obi-Won, "We've got a situation here!"

No kidding. And the situation is bad writing.

Hayden Christensen does not have the charisma to carry his role convincingly. He is a rather flat, dull Anakin, not the larger-than-life fireball we would believe could become the evil Lord Vader. The tender scenes between Christensen and Natalie Portmam are also flat; there is little chemistry between the two. In the love scenes, the actors don't seem to have been directed so much as pushed off the dock. Portman in particular flounders. Her performance weaves between unconvincing earnestness and sniffle-heavy histrionics, a kind of Gidget-in-space. In defence of the two actors, they are dragged to the bottom by the gooey and awkward *Young Romance* dialogue they have to spout. Only in a galaxy far, far away could people actually talk like this.

Simply put, George Lucas writes cartoonish dialogue. There's nothing wrong with cartoonish dialogue if you're writing for cartoons, but these are flesh and blood actors, and they deserve better. Some of you will now be thinking, "So what? *Star Wars* is a cartoon, and the quality and believability of the dialogue is about as important as the kind of flea powder Chewbacca uses." You may be right, but almost every time one of the characters opened his or her mouth in *Episode III* I found myself hoping that it was only to take a deep breath, not spout more inane dialogue.

Samuel L. Jackson as Jedi knight Mace Windu doesn't seem to have any deep convictions about which speech pattern or accent he should adopt. I had the feeling that at any moment he could be ordering a "Royal with cheese." Much more believable is Christopher Lee as Count Dooku. He's suitably dark and menacing, but he is sent packing after only a brief time on screen. Ian McDiarmid as the evil Chancellor Palpatine is quite good, however. Suitably menacing, he delivers his lines with intensity and panache, and seems to be having a terrific time.

While George Lucas doesn't write very convincing dialogue, at least the names he comes up with for his characters are original and entertaining. For example, the Chancellor's evil alter ego is named "Darth Sidious."

Hello?

I can imagine someone knocking at his door and asking, "Are you in, Sidious?"

Mace Windu is another weird name. On the one hand you have "mace," which is sprayed in an attacker's face to neutralize him, and you have the word "windu," which suggests "Windex," also something that you do not want in your face. Perhaps this is Lucas's idea of a sly joke: Samuel L. Jackson is known for portraying characters unafraid of "getting in your face."

Or maybe the character names are just generated by some kind of anagram program.

For example, Jimmy Smith's character is named Bail Organa, which is an anagram of "Arabian Log." This may explain the wooden performance. We won't explore what the word "Sith" might be an anagram of.

One thing about *Episode III* that *is* clever is Lucas's use of the story to make some apropos, if slightly oblique, references to the state of his own real-life republic. In the climactic scene between the now evil Anakin and Obi-Wan Kenobi, Anakin declares, "If you aren't with us, you are the enemy," which I can only interpret as a reference to George Dubya's now infamous "If you're not with us you're with the terrorists" post-9/11 comment. Obi-Wan responds that only the Sith speak in absolutes.

Wrong, Obi-Wan. A lot of Republicans do also.

If you think I'm stretching it, consider that the plot focuses on how a democracy is hijacked, and how people are manipulated into committing foul acts by being made to think that they are protecting their loved ones.

Sound familiar?

As I'm fond of saying, movies are not created in a vacuum. Science-fiction has long been an excellent vehicle for disguised political and social commentary. I've actually heard that there have already been some calls in American conservative circles to boycott *Episode III*. To add fuel to the controversy, it has been reported that Yoda is considering seeking the Democratic nomination in 2008, although the rules governing the age requirement would have to be modified. The little green guy for president? Why not? If Ahnold can be governator of California, anything is possible.

I sense a disturbance in the Force.

44

The Sum of All Fears

I have always been extremely suspicious of people who use two first names. You often can't trust them. Think about it: John Wilkes Booth, Lee Harvey Oswald, Kenesaw Mountain Landis, Maharishi Mahesh Yogi — the list goes on.

Phil Alden Robinson wrote and directed *Field of Dreams*, a baseball movie that many people (myself not included) consider the best baseball movie of all time. He gets points in my book for even making a baseball movie, but actually I hated *Field of Dreams* when I first saw it. I thought it was corny beyond redemption, and I'm not referring to the crops in the field. Funny thing, however, I saw it again years later, when I was quite a bit older and had a son of my own, and you know what? I *still* thought it was corny beyond redemption.

I don't seem to be mellowing in my critical old age.

I spend an inordinate amount of time at the movies, and the hours I spend are, quite simply, gone forever. Given the fact that nothing is more precious than time — as Artie Shaw once said, time is all we've got — I think that film studios should offer a kind of Movie Insurance, which would be similar to Flight Insurance. It would work something like this: you get to the multiplex and there's a little machine; you plunk in a dollar, and you get an insurance policy that states that if the movie is bad or boring and you've wasted two hours of your life, the studio will pay you a reasonable amount in compensation. In my case, let's see ... two hours of my life, that should be worth ... oh ... say $35,000.

I even have a name for this form of insurance. It would be called "Affleck." Think of that duck quacking "Affleck" and you get the idea.

Perhaps I'm still bitter about *Pearl Harbor.* Mr Affleck owes me for that one. And while we're at it, Kevin Costner can never adequately compensate me for *The Postman*, although if he's willing to leave a gym bag full of small unmarked bills behind the bus depot, I'll consider never mentioning it again.

In *The Sum of All Fears* Morgan Freeman plays the grizzled, reliable, wise old CIA agent who also happens to be the president's best friend. Freeman does his usual fine job. James Cromwell, another fine actor, portrays the president. Cromwell has carved a career playing authority figures, usually not very sympathetic ones. You may recall him as the despicable NASA project manager in *Space Cowboys*, or as the warden in *The Green Mile*.

I've never actually read any Tom Clancy novels, but I know that the character Ben Affleck portrays in *The Sum of All Fears* has been portrayed previously by Harrison Ford. This is the same character — Jack Ryan — who appears in *Patriot Games*, *Clear and Present Danger*, and *The Hunt for Red October*.

I don't know if Clancy is a great writer, but he's got really good titles.

In truth, I have a certain amount of respect for Ben Affleck — he is after all a die-hard Red Sox fan. He was quite good several years ago in an independent film that I liked called *Chasing Amy*, released just before he hit it real big with *Good Will Hunting*. Unfortunately, once he tasted success he immediately went for the blockbuster roles, becoming involved in several big budget stinkers, including *Armageddon* and *Pearl Harbor*. But his record is not all bad: he was very well cast in *Shakespeare in Love* and delivered a solid performance.

Here, Affleck's Jack Ryan is a young CIA operative who is an expert on the Russians. He comes to the attention of the president because he is also an expert on Russian President Nemerov. At first, with several teenagers enthusiastically chatting and crunching on their popcorn right behind me, I kept hearing Nemerov as "Nimrod." I started to imagine that the character's name really was Nimrod, and that this was actually a sly reference to the traditional founder of the Babylonian monarchy. Later I realized, no, it was just the popcorn.

After all that, it's a wonder that I managed to stay with the plot.

Young Jack Ryan eventually winds up uncovering the truth about a nefarious plot masterminded by a neo-Nazi named Dressler, well played by a fine actor named Alan Bates. Remember Jennings in *Gosford Park*? Unfortunately, these "mad Nazi" roles don't give an actor a lot of room to stretch, unless you're Laurence Olivier — but these days, who is?

Dressler wants to touch off a war between the Americans and the Russians so that he can proceed to muscle in and take over.

These stories don't always stand up to close scrutiny, do they? I mean, imagine a major nuclear conflagration between the superpowers; not much left to take over, is there?

I knew there was something really wrong with this Dressler guy early on in the movie when he declared during a speech that "a great poet once said 'Meet the new boss, same as the old boss.'" Excuse me, but the "great poet" is Pete Townshend, and the quotation is from a Who song called "Won't Get Fooled Again." Now, don't let me be misunderstood, I think that Pete Townshend is a great songwriter, but I hardly think that neo-Nazis consider him a conveniently quotable "great poet." Townshend has always seemed to me an enlightened bloke, not at all suitable as a source of neo-Nazi *Quotenfodder*.

This is a plot you've seen a million times, the kind that used to come with assembly instructions in boxes of Crackerjacks: world comes to brink of nuclear war, young hero saves world, young hero gets girl in the end, blah, blah, blah.

As far as special effects go, I found the scenes of Baltimore sustaining an atomic blast unconvincing — although it's not supposed to be much of a nuclear blast, because the script tells us that it is just a little (!) A-bomb, and it only manages to take out the baseball stadium and a few dozen hot dog vendors across the street. Heck, Sammy Sosa on steroids could cause more damage with a violent sneeze.

By the way, if there is a message I would like to give to Americans in general it is this: never elect a president who says "nukelar." If you don't know who to vote for, just line up the candidates and ask them to say "nuclear disarmament," and if one of them sounds like he's saying "nukelar disarmament," *don't vote for that guy!*

The Sum of all Fears is not Ben Affleck's finest hour. Often a bland actor, he has a lifeless acting style. I read somewhere that Affleck played Little League baseball with his friend Matt Damon. Having coached Little League — and having watched Affleck several times on screen — I suspect that Affleck was the kind of little leaguer whom coaches often yell at to "Look alive out there!" I'll bet that some of his directors have been tempted to do likewise.

45

Sweet and Lowdown

The release of a new Woody Allen movie used to be an automatic cause for celebration at my house. The sheer number of films he has directed — thirty-eight in the last forty years — is impressive enough, but even more impressive is the level of quality he has maintained. Of course, even Ted Williams struck out occasionally, and it is grossly unfair for movie critics (or anyone else) to expect a *Manhattan* or an *Annie Hall* every time out.

Woody Allen movies come in different flavours: hopelessly pessimistic, cautiously pessimistic, cautiously optimistic, and "To hell with the whole human mess, let's have a good time." When he is at his most severe, when he sees human existence as an endless series of flat tires in the rain, when he seems to be channelling Bergman and Kafka, as in *Interiors* and *Shadows and Fog*, he loses me. While those two films may have been fun for him to make, they were certainly no fun to watch. When he contemplates existence without quite so much angst, however, mixing his ingredients like a master philosopher-chef, finding salvation in love of family, as he does in *Crimes and Misdemeanors* and *Hannah and Her Sisters*, the results are wonderful, astonishing. I use the term "salvation" cautiously here. The salvation you get in a Woody Allen movie is pretty battered and pockmarked, but he does on occasion allow his characters some measure of joy — even contentment.

When Allen decides to really have some fun, the results are at the very least entertaining, and often superb. As prolific as he is, Allen has made few flat comedies. When he's on his game, as he was with *Manhattan Murder Mystery* and *Broadway Danny Rose*, his gift for comical and absurd situations combines with his finely tuned ear for witty dialogue in a comedic alchemy of rare inspiration and humanity.

In an alternate universe, Woody Allen would be spending his nights playing clarinet in a Dixieland jazz band. It's no secret that Allen loves old-time jazz, and that he has played gigs in New York clubs for decades. In the mid-nineties he was invited to tour Europe with his combo. The tour was the subject of a hugely entertaining Barbara Kopple documentary released in 1997 called *Wild Man Blues*.

I left the theatre after seeing *Wild Man Blues* with two strong impressions: first, Allen has a profound and genuine love for traditional jazz; second, he is at best a mediocre clarinetist. Of course, if he had spent as much time over the past forty years practising the clarinet as he has making movies, he would undoubtedly be a much better musician. Music doles out its rewards pretty much in direct relationship to the time one devotes to it. Despite the immense allure of instant gratification — especially in this era of sensational Become-a-Star-*Now*! television programs like *Canadian Idol* and, in Quebec, *Star Académie* — there are no real shortcuts to excellence in music. I'm talking not about fame or celebrity, which are as easy to come by as they are fleeting, but rather about the excellence that emerges when even a modestly talented musician truly devotes his or her time to refining the craft of music. The next time you hear a jazz musician who is saying something, moving you, touching you with the music, think about this: what you're hearing is hard work and dedication, respect for the tradition of music-making, countless hours of practice and of paying dues.

A teacher once told me, "The music fairy will not leave a golden pair of magic drumsticks under your pillow."

Sweet and Lowdown is Allen's tribute to jazz, and a celebration of the musicians who make the wondrous sounds. Allen being Allen, he prefers to litter the road of admiration with a few well-placed banana peels. *Sweet and Lowdown* is first and foremost a comedy, but it is also a multi-layered creation, a *mélange-savant* of hilarity and pathos. For all of its improbable characters and silly situations, it is also a cautionary tale, its hero a tragic victim of his own ego, a man who realizes, too late, that he has foolishly and irrevocably placed his music above the only woman who ever loved him.

Sweet and Lowdown is not a remake, but it shares its title with a mediocre musical released in 1944, which featured Benny Goodman as himself. One screening is sufficient to understand why Goodman never had a film career; even portraying himself, he's pretty awful. But Goodman was a great clarinet player — many jazz lovers feel he was the best of them all — and he remains Woody Allen's hero.

When we first meet guitarist Emmet Ray (Sean Penn), he is a thoroughly unreliable scoundrel. He shows up for his gigs either late, or drunk, or both — when he shows up at all. He is not above exploiting women for money. He doesn't hesitate for a second to lie to get his way. But there is another side to Emmet, an alter ego musical magician, a wonderful guitarist who can pluck shimmering clusters of notes out of thin air and transport his listeners on waves of dizzying joy or profound melancholy. As he loves to repeat to anyone who will listen, he is an artist. To any woman who gets too close, who becomes too "serious," he delivers his prepared speech: "I can't get attached to one person, you know? I can't let anyone get to close to me. I reveal my emotions in my music. I'm an artist." After this speech, one of his girlfriends responds, "If you could let out your feelings more, if you weren't afraid to reveal yourself, your music might be better."

By Emmet's own admission, he is the world's "second-greatest guitar player." As he often says, "There's this Gypsy in France, his name is Django. He's the best." What Emmet cannot see is that Django is the best because he isn't afraid to mine the depths of his emotions when he plays, he isn't afraid to suffer in public. Art involves revelation. In order to create something meaningful, the artist must reveal some hidden, protected facet of his emotional life, something deeply felt. Underneath Emmet's bravado and ego-thumping hides a frightened man, always holding back, never daring to be emotionally naked before a woman, let alone before an audience.

Woody's *Sweet and Lowdown* (I've spent enough time watching his movies that I feel I should be allowed to call him Woody) is a "mockumentary" rather than a conventional fiction film. Various real-life jazz critics and connoisseurs, such as Nat Hentoff, Daniel Okrent (wearing a ridiculous fake moustache and goatee and billed as "A.J. Pickman"), and even Allen himself, appear as talking heads, interrupting the narrative from time to time to comment on Emmet Ray's music and to share sometimes differing accounts of his various exploits. From them we learn that Ray emerged from the Chicago scene of the thirties, that his recorded output was modest but brilliant, that he disappeared without a trace just before the Second World War, and that when, in 1935, he met his idol Django Reinhardt for the first and only time, he was so overwhelmed that he fell to the floor in a dead faint.

Emmet Ray as imagined by Woody Allen in *Sweet and Lowdown* is an unlikely and eccentric human being, but Sean Penn's performance brings believability to the character's every quirk and contradiction. At various times insufferable, vulnerable, supremely confident, and insecure, Emmet Ray is one of Penn's most perfectly realized screen incarnations. I'm tempted to say that Penn hits exactly the right note in every scene, and I'm referring not only to his dramatic performance and his knack for physical comedy, but also to his impeccable miming of jazz guitar playing. I have seen too many unconvincing, even embarrassing examples of actors pretending to play instruments. Penn does a superb job. In reality, the guitar parts are played with impeccable taste and virtuosity by Howard Alden. His playing significantly enriches repeated viewings of this film.

Penn's performance alone would be enough to carry *Sweet and Lowdown*, but we are also treated to Samantha Morton's tour de force as Emmet's mute — but not deaf — girlfriend Hattie. Using only facial expressions and body language, Morton brilliantly conveys every nuance of the vulnerability, love, trust, and disappointment that Hattie experiences, and the look of absolute beatitude that comes over her face when Emmet plays her favourite song, "I'm Forever Blowing Bubbles," speaks more eloquently about the transcendent power of music than mere dialogue ever could.

We realize that, despite his often callous behaviour, Emmet does feel real affection, if not love, for Hattie, but that a profound flaw in his emotional make-up will not allow him to admit it. Inevitably, he leaves her one night while she is asleep, without a word of warning. Now free and living high, Emmet hooks up with Blanche (Uma Thurman), a rich socialite who sees him primarily as amusing source material for a book she is writing on the "jazz life." She quickly dazzles him with her sex appeal and easy sophistication, and he does something he thought he would never do: he gets married. It doesn't take long, however, before things get bumpy, and a bored Blanche begins an affair with a local gangster in the employ of a rich club owner who is one of Emmet's biggest fans. After confronting Blanche, Emmet realizes his terrible mistake and runs back to Hattie, only to discover that she too is married — but happily, and to someone else.

Masquerading at first as a spry musical comedy, *Sweet and Lowdown* slowly reveals its darker, cautionary intent, its hero ultimately shattered by the realization that he has thrown away a relationship infinitely more precious than celebrity or riches could ever be. The scene in which Penn's character smashes his beloved guitar against a tree while repeating over and over in anguished tones, "I made a mistake! I made a mistake!" is almost shocking in its emotional nakedness, and one of the most powerful images to be found in any Woody Allen film.

Sweet and Lowdown has been dismissed by some as "minor" Woody Allen, but its comical disguise masks a profoundly moving and thoughtful film, as subtle and swinging as the music it celebrates.

46

Swimming Pool

It seems nowadays that in order to be considered truly hip, a movie critic has to occasionally declare a movie to be "postmodernist." The use of the term postmodernist gives the review a slightly mysterious air of "deeper meaning"; it fills the reader, or listener, with sugarplum visions of wonderful cinematic secrets about to be revealed by the philosopher-critic.

But what the heck does it really mean, jellybean?

One of the brightest postmodernist thinkers is a Frenchman named Jean-François Lyotard. If his name conjures up images in your mind of a middle-aged university prof in black tights, that's your problem, not mine. In essence, what Lyotard says is that postmodernism is about incredulity. A movie produced by a postmodernist filmmaker is not governed by pre-established rules, and therefore the film cannot be evaluated according to a determined judgment.

Do you suddenly feel as if your snorkel has sprung a leak in the murky waters of aesthetic discourse?

Want to come up for air?

Quite simply, in a postmodernist movie, interpretation is everything. "Reality" is defined as what the world means to each of us individually. In a postmodernist movie, the script can subversively — and often with great irony — topple the house of cards of our traditional expectations of narrative form. Postmodernist artists often amuse themselves by standing the audience members on their heads and laughing while all the loose change falls out of their pockets — metaphorically speaking of course. Some critics are extremely skeptical of postmodern art in general, and feel that much of it represents a kind of "fleecing" of the audience. This is overly harsh criticism, I think, but it's important to remember that some artists out there seem to have taken off without a flight plan. However, this is not the case with François Ozon, the director of *Swimming Pool*, a finely constructed, wonderfully engaging postmodernist psychological thriller.

In *Swimming Pool*, veteran international actress Charlotte Rampling portrays British mystery novelist Sarah Morton. Her character is based on a mix of literary types. When he was casting this part, Ozon looked at the photographs of a number of mystery writers, including Patricia Highsmith, P.D. James, and Ruth Rendell. Amusingly, Ozon was quoted as saying that he found something quite masculine about these female mystery writers, and that they also gave him the impression that life had stopped in the 1970s. This explains Sarah's short hair and her colourful polyester double-knit wardrobe.

When we first meet the best-selling crime author, she is obviously stressed. On her way to a meeting with John, her long-time publisher (Charles Dance), Sarah stops at a bar for a few quick drinks. During the tense meeting that follows, we immediately suspect that at one time John was her lover. It becomes obvious that things are a bit strained between them, and that she is more than a bit jealous of the attention he is lavishing on a new, much younger writer. Poor Sarah seems to be having one of those terrible episodes of uncertainty and discouragement that can only happen to authors who have sold fifty million books. I guess we can all imagine how it is:

you have all this success and all this money, and people just love your work, but you are riddled with self-doubt.

Well, maybe it's not really that easy to imagine, but it certainly seems to describe Sarah's mindset. After she voices her concern to John that her writing has degenerated into "dime store crap," he offers her the use of his villa in France, so that she can, in his words, "rest up and get a fresh perspective, maybe start a new book."

Sarah accepts. The villa, in the Luberon region, turns out to be lovely, and it is located within walking distance of a picturesque little town. It is off-season, although the weather is gorgeous, and, except for the elderly caretaker Marcel, who comes around occasionally to do some chores, Sarah is all by herself. Feeling energized by the idyllic, peaceful setting, she sits down at her laptop and begins to work on a few ideas. After a few uneventful days pass, her retreat is suddenly shattered in the middle of the night by the arrival of a beautiful young woman who introduces herself as John's daughter Julie. Sarah is not only astonished — she had no idea that her publisher had a daughter — but also extremely annoyed, because she will now have to share her space with this stranger. Ludivine Sagnier, who portrays Julie, is the type of actress that film producers used to describe, in the old politically incorrect, sexist days of French cinema, as a "bombshell." Physically, Sagnier is cut from a cloth similar to Brigitte Bardot, but, of course, times being what they are, she is thinner than Bardot, and even more *gamine*.

It's not very long before Julie has turned the mystery writer's quiet retreat into a kind of "love shack." Idle by day, Julie seems to be training by night for the French Olympic debauchery team. Every night, just as Sarah, in her sensible jammies, is getting ready to retire, Julie returns to the villa accompanied by a different, usually intoxicated man she has picked up in a village café. Invariably, Julie and her conquest then engage in extremely enthusiastic sex. After a few nights of this, Sarah is reduced to going to bed with earplugs firmly in place. Needless to say, the relationship between Sarah and Julie quickly degenerates into recriminations, accusations, and icy glares.

But there is more going on here than we think. In truth, despite all her outward signs of annoyance, Sarah is secretly fascinated by this wild child. One day while Julie is out, Sarah steals her diary and starts to read, fishing for inspiration for her new book. Is Sarah perhaps concocting a plot about a female mystery writer who becomes sexually involved with a much younger, freewheeling woman with whom she shares an idyllic French villa?

The title *Swimming Pool* refers to the villa's in-ground pool, in which Julie, almost always nude, or at least topless, loves to swim. Outwardly feigning indifference to Julie's exhibitions, Sarah seems to be secretly enjoying the view. Might it be that Sarah is developing a physical attraction to Julie?

Enter a young, good-looking waiter named Franck (Jean-Marie Lamour), who serves lunch to Sarah every day in a small village café. It soon appears that Sarah is developing a strong interest in the younger man, and the dramatic possibilities are multiplied when Julie returns to the villa one night with Franck in tow. Will the reluctant housemates perhaps become bitter rivals?

Working with acclaimed author Emmanuèle Bernheim, Ozon has concocted an irresistibly enigmatic script. Like an inspired master chef, he perfectly balances all of the suspenseful ingredients, and serves up the gradually thickening intrigue with great style. Thanks to Yorick Le Saux's exceptional cinematography, *Swimming Pool* is also an erotically charged visual experience. His luminous images of Julie — crystal blue water sparkling on perfect, silken skin — entice and fascinate us. As Sarah is increasingly tempted by Julie's glistening form, Le Saux's lens becomes an active participant in the seduction of both Sarah and, vicariously, the viewer.

I began this review by touching on postmodernism. My second viewing of *Swimming Pool* confirmed the influence of David Lynch — a postmodernist master — on François Ozon's style and method.

Consider the following elements: an accumulation of unlikely plot twists; exciting "clues" that ultimately lead to dead-ends; the surprising introduction of unusual characters (Ozon's seemingly arbitrary inclusion of a dwarf is perhaps the most obvious, and amusing, example of his Lynchian sensibilities); the protagonist's growing confusion about her own feelings and motivations; the increasingly surreal, dreamlike quality of the narrative.

These elements all combine in subtle ways to create a film that, although it masquerades as a thriller, is in reality a postmodernist exploration of the creative process itself.

Swimming Pool reminded me of Charlie Kaufman's *Adaptation*. In the former, we are presented with a mystery writer struggling to find inspiration, a character pulled into a series of increasingly risqué situations, which may or may not be real. In the latter, the protagonist is a writer struggling to adapt a work of non-fiction for the screen who is pulled into a series of increasingly outlandish, and surreal, situations. In both films, the characters are pulled into a universe possibly of their own creation, in which subjective perception and objective reality at first merely bump into each other, then intersect, and eventually collide.

The real mystery that lies at the bottom of *Swimming Pool* cannot be elucidated solely by carefully weighing the elements of the plot, because most of the apparent clues are only red herrings thrown at us for dramatic effect. To effectively pierce the mystery of *Swimming Pool*, the viewer has to consider the substance of Sarah's work in progress, what she is actually writing. Does her writing merely echo, or somehow generate, the events that unfold at the villa?

47

3,000 Miles to Graceland

In the distant future, when people want to describe something as really exciting, perhaps they'll say, "That's so Elvis! So totally Elvis!" Or maybe when they want to say that something or someone is garish and tacky, they'll say, "That's beyond awful, it's ... it's ... Graceland!" Elvis certainly was, among other things, excessive. After all, who else could have eaten a half-dozen fried banana and peanut butter sandwiches at 3:00 a.m. while watching a re-run of *Viva Las Vegas*?

For better or worse, Elvis has attained a cult status that almost defies explanation. And he's sighted almost every day, pumping gas in Arizona or flipping burgers in Kanata.

Do you realize that "Elvis" is an anagram of "Lives"? Scary, isn't it?

As someone pointed out to me recently, it's also an anagram of "Levis" — and he did split a pair or two before he left the building, didn't he?

Elvis, or rather the popular idea of Elvis, is at the heart of this film. In the popular imagination, Elvis has come to personify both the best possibilities and the worst excesses of American culture. Elvis was a great rock 'n' roll singer; he was "the king." He changed the world. But in later years he also became a weird, eccentric parody of himself, a bloated, tragic figure trapped in his own stardom, crumbling under his own weight. In the future, this late-period Elvis might replace the bogeyman. Parents could threaten, "Don't stay up too late, little Johnny, or the Elvis will get you, and you know what he does to little kids who won't sleep: he takes them to Graceland and stuffs them full of fried banana sandwiches until they bust their Levis!"

Early on in *3000 Miles to Graceland*, five bad guys in full Elvis costume (you know, the sideburns and the white studded jumpsuit) decide to visit Las Vegas during Elvis Week, when a large portion of the population will also be dressed up to look like Elvis. By the way, we understand immediately that they are bad guys because they wear dark glasses and chain-smoke. The "Elvis Gang" is planning to blend in with the crowds and rob a casino. Surprise, surprise! — things will go very wrong very quickly, and the movie will turn into a seemingly endless festival of shootouts, double-crosses, more shootouts, car chases, yet more shootouts, and explosions.

Director Lichtenstein has previously helmed numerous music videos. This may explain the silly camera angles, the incessant loud music, and the underdeveloped characters. As for the excessive number of bloody shootouts, they can perhaps be explained by Lichtenstein's experience directing rap music videos, although this is only speculation on my part. I stopped paying attention to music videos around 1986.

Whatever its shortcomings, however, *3000 Miles to Graceland* is technically insnovative. It is in fact the first feature film to make use of the new FPTS (Female Posterior Tracking System) technology. This system allows the camera to focus immediately on the derrière of any female character entering or leaving a scene. While delivering surprising results, not to mention making Courteney Cox look terrific in tight jeans, it also gets pretty redundant after the twelfth time it's used; by then even the most single-minded guys in the audience may have concluded that enough is enough. I won't even speculate on the ramifications of using FPTS technology in combination with Imax, because that is still in the experimental stages.

In one of the early scenes, Mike (Kurt Russell) drives up to a dilapidated gas station somewhere in the Nevada desert. He's cool, he looks like Elvis, and he's driving a bright red 1959 Cadillac convertible. While he's looking around for service, a young boy about ten years old steals his chrome-plated valve caps. Our hero Mike chases after the kid and comes face to face with the kid's mom, Cybil (Courteney Cox). At this point Mike forgets all about his valve caps, and before you can hum a few bars of "Let Me Be Your Teddy Bear," things get hot and steamy between the two. We also discover that Mike is recently out of jail and headed for Las Vegas.

Enter the "evil Elvis," Murph (Kevin Costner). Murph is the leader of the gang preparing to knock over the casino. Costner is convincing as Psycho-Elvis. He looks dangerous. He looks maniacal. He looks as if he's just been reading reviews of *Waterworld*. When David Arquette's character makes a joke about the real Elvis, Murph almost bites his head off. I felt at this point that Arquette should be sporting a sign around his neck reading "expendable crewmember."

Soon, the robbery of the casino gets very messy, with about five hundred rounds of ammunition being fired in all directions, with predictable results, and the Elvis Gang is picked off the roof by helicopter, barely escaping with the money. The boys wind up in a crummy motel arguing over how to divide the money. The gang is soon lighter by a few Elvises.

The film then becomes a chase movie, with Costner's Psycho-Elvis in hot pursuit of Mike, Cybill, and Cybill's young son, Jesse. When the director doesn't know what the heck to do next — which is most of the time — he breaks out the heavy artillery and shoots up the scenery. Costner, now channelling Rambo and Yosemite Sam and having a particularly good time, blows things up *real good*.

Between hails of bullets, there are some laughable attempts to develop some kind of relationship between the young boy Jesse and Russell's character Mike, but the whole thing wobbles in that never-never land that can only really exist in five-minute music videos. In this script, push-up bras and bulletproof vests are considered character development.

After being assaulted for two hours by this noisy nonsense, I was so numb that I didn't even flinch when, in the final ten minutes, the script floated the mother of all silly plot twists: we discover that either Costner's character or Russell's character might actually be the illegitimate son of Elvis himself. By that time, my brain had left the building.

48

Vampires

John Carpenter's *Vampires* explores a genre that some would say has been explored — and exploited — to the point of lifelessness. Still, if anyone could inject new life into it, I would bet my money on Carpenter, a talented director with a flair for the horror/science-fiction genre, as he demonstrated in *The Fog* and *The Thing*. To my dismay, he doesn't quite seem to know what to do with the material this time around. Oh, he bats it around with gusto, and he sets it ablaze, and he commits enough mayhem that he almost makes you think he's got a solid handle on the proceedings, but the end result is very messy indeed.

I believe that the vampire movie continues to thrive as a genre because it offers endless possibilities for showing scantily clad (or unclad) females.

I'm kidding. There's more to it than that.

There may even be something to the psychoanalytical babble that interprets the vampire myth as a fantastic manifestation of arrested development. After all, vampires, like children, get their gratification orally. Children haven't yet discovered the purpose of certain organs, and vampires are essentially dead from the neck down. All I know is that when I was a kid, vampires held a profound fascination for me. I wouldn't quite say that they were "heroes," at least not in the way that Superman and Bugs Bunny were, and I did recognize that they were "evil," but Dracula was an object of envy. After all, he got to stay out all night, and turn into a bat or a wolf, and he wore that cool cape, and he just seemed to having a really good time. For a nine-year-old, the idea of staying up all night running around all over town was incredibly exciting.

Now that I'm much older, the idea of being undead still fascinates. Let's face it, as we get older the concept of immortality — in any form — has appeal, even if it involves spending the daylight hours in the dark, in a coffin, in a damp dungeon.

In the old Saturday matinee days, vampires lived in majestic, albeit rundown, castles. They had class, too. They were almost always aristocratic, erudite gentlemen with European accents. And as much as I admired Dracula, I found that the master vampire slayer, Van Helsing, as portrayed by the suave and sophisticated Peter Cushing, was someone I could look up to. He was noble, courageous, wise, and pure. I felt an almost personal connection with him, because when he fought the vampires he used a lot of objects that I saw and touched in my own everyday life as a Catholic: crucifixes, holy water, and even ... yuck! ... garlic. After seeing this mess of a movie, I miss Peter Cushing terribly.

In *Vampires*, James Woods portrays Jack Crow, the leader of a team of vampire slayers. Woods is good at playing these tough-as-nails, no-nonsense types. And he looks great in black leather and dark glasses. But then, who doesn't? His team of slayers look like roadies for a heavy-metal band. And you can forget about quaint trappings of religion like crucifixes; these slayers use shiny chromium-plated state-of-the-art high-velocity equipment that looks as if it must have cost a fortune. We are soon informed that money is no object, because this is a Vatican-funded project. This revelation brought snickers of disbelief from some audience members at the advance screening. I chuckled also, but for different reasons. I know from my Catholic upbringing that the true source of the Vatican's incredible wealth is Bingo. In my childhood parish, one Thursday Bingo Night in the church basement would have brought in enough to keep Woods and his boys in hi-tech anti-vampire weaponry for a year.

As the story begins, Woods and his motley crew are running around California and New Mexico searching for "nests" of vampires. Their objective is simple. As one of the crew states emphatically, "We are going to find those bloodsuckers and *kick their butts!*" We are treated to a strong, suspenseful scene early on when Crow and his boys descend on what looks like an abandoned house in the middle of nowhere. When they move in, things get very nasty. Crisp editing and excellent special effects make this scene one of the highlights of the movie, at least for the first five minutes. Unfortunately, however, Carpenter goes off the deep end with graphic, brutal violence.

The character of the master slayer, Jack Crow, is light-years removed from that of Dr Van Helsing. Crow is a semi-psychotic, sadistic macho who will do anything to kill vampires. Anything! *Understand?*

Early on, the script informs us that Crow's profound, maniacal hatred of vampires comes from the fact that vampires killed his parents when he was a child. (Don't laugh. According to certain tabloids I've read, this occurs more often than the mainstream media is willing to report.) After his parents' murder, we are told, Crow was raised by the Catholic Church, and trained by priests to be a vampire slayer.

After the opening scene, in which several vampires are messily dispatched, the slayers unwind by partying to the max in a sleazy motel in the company of a bevy of hookers. By the way, in this revised version of the vampire myth, the undead can be active during daylight hours, as long as they are not exposed to sunlight. To kill a vampire, a group of slayers has only to drag one of them kicking and screaming into the sun, where the poor thing immediately explodes in flames like a gasoline-filled corn dog on a campfire. This is actually a very cool special effect. In fact the special effects generally are very good. But they are no substitute for a good script.

But back to our victory party in the motel: combining sleaze with brutality, the script introduces the Big Kahuna of vampires, the 600-year-old Valek, a party-pooper who proceeds to massacre everyone in sight. Members of the slayer crew are decapitated, cut in half, and disembowelled, all in disgustingly graphic detail, the camera lingering on every atrocity like a kid transfixed by a display in a toy store. Crow and his sidekick Montoya (Daniel Baldwin) manage to escape to fight (or slay) another day. Also escaping death is one of the hookers, Katrina (Sheryl Lee), who has been bitten by Valek during the massacre — in a pretty intimate place, by the way — and becomes absolutely crucial to the abysmal, cliché-ridden plot when Crow and Montoya discover that she now has a psychic connection to Valek that may help to lead our heroes to him and to victory, or, alternatively, may lead them to their doom.

If this sounds bad, believe me, it's worse if you have to watch it unfold.

Character development is out of the question here. Performances run the gamut from passable (Woods) to good (Baldwin) to laughable (Lee), and the dialogue is vintage comic book issue. There is also a nasty streak of misogyny running through *Vampires*: female characters are killed — or at the very least slapped around — a lot in this film. Priests, too, get slapped around and killed, with decapitation being the most popular method used to send the holy fathers off to the great Bingo Night in the sky. The puerile script allows Woods's character to comment incessantly on a certain physiological manifestation of male arousal. This might be funny once, but it practically becomes a leitmotif. I'm sorry to report that during the screening I attended, these jokes were hugely popular with many male audience members (sorry!).

Vampires contains many of the worst elements of contemporary Hollywood horror films: it is loud, poorly written, and brutally graphic. In other words it is trashy, and a colossal waste of time.

I miss Peter Cushing *so much*.

Information age? Welcome to the *dis*information age.

49

Vertical Limit

For those of you unfamiliar with mountain climbing — or with the French language — allow me to explain that a "crevasse" is a deep chasm in a glacier. If you're a mountaineer climbing K2 — the main activity depicted in this movie — you don't want to fall into a crevasse from which you may never escape. If you're a screenwriter, on the other hand, you don't want to fall into a crevasse of ludicrous plot twists, illogical behaviour, and events that spectacularly defy the laws of physics, unless you're writing a Roadrunner and Coyote cartoon. *Vertical Limit* is truly mind-boggling nonsense. But it almost works — kind of like a '69 Buick I used to own.

Opening scene: a Utah desert. Five climbers are scaling a gigantic vertical wall of rock. One is Annie (Robin Tunney). Another is her brother Peter (Chris O'Donnell). The lowest climber is their father. There are two other climbers up near the top, but I immediately suspected that these were the expendable members of the expedition. You can't fool me. I cut my critical teeth on the original *Star Trek* television series. I know an expendable crewmember when I see one. The group is climbing slowly. It's a beautiful day, and everything is going wonderfully. The two siblings and Dad begin to sing "Take It to the Limit," by the Eagles. I've always wondered what songs people sing as they cling to a rock face three hundred feet above the desert floor. Now I know.

All of a sudden the two expendables lose their grip and fall. Suddenly, it's showtime! Annie is hanging onto the rock face, and Peter and Dad are dangling below her. Peter has a knife. Dad tells them, "Save yourselves! Cut the rope, Peter. Cut me loose, there's too much weight! Save yourselves! CUT THE ROPE, PETER!" At the same time, Annie is screaming, "Don't do it, Peter!"

Peter cuts the rope.

In the next shot, the camera is at ground level, and Dad's body falls into the frame with a thud. Unfortunately, this way of framing the shot makes the scene look comical. There are many good ways to shoot this moment, but director Martin Campbell chose one that would be appropriate for a Roadrunner cartoon. Fixed shot: body falls into frame and comes to a crunching stop on ground. This approach makes the tragic event appear silly. I burst out laughing, and got some really dirty looks from the couple next to me.

After the tragedy, Peter gives up climbing and becomes a nature photographer. Meanwhile, his sister Annie is hired by billionaire Elliot Vaughn (Bill Paxton) to help him set a new speed record for the ascent of K2.

Have you noticed that there are no millionaires in films any more? Millionaires are boring. Now you have to be a *billionaire*.

Annie's brother Peter just happens to be hanging around the K2 base camp, and we soon realize that all has not been well between brother and sister since Dad's unintentionally comical death. Well, in two shakes of a lama's tail, Annie and the billionaire (wasn't that a sitcom in the seventies?) and another expendable character wind up in a crevasse.

Are you surprised?

Brother Peter decides to lead the rescue team. Enter Montgomery Wick (Scott Glenn), a really crusty mountain climber who lost his wife four years earlier in a climbing tragedy during an expedition also led by dastardly billionaire Elliott Vaughn. His wife's body was never found. Wick has since converted to Buddhism and has spent the last four years running around K2 looking for his wife's body. I don't want to give anything away here, of course, but his wife's body may or may not be frozen in an upright position, and may or may not be stumbled upon by the rescue team at a crucial point in the plot.

Also along for the rescue mission are a couple of Aussie daredevils, as well as a Pakistani climber. I was concerned about this character right from the beginning, because all of his equipment was stamped "not to be returned."

Time for my action movie plot checklist:

Three people trapped in a crevasse at 26,000 feet.
Check.
A helicopter that can't fly above 21,000 feet.
Check.
A rescue team racing toward the crevasse while carrying tubes of incredibly volatile nitro-glycerine that they are going to use to blow the crevasse open.
Check.
This very special type of nitro-glycerine can sometimes explode if you no more than look at it, but it can also withstand rough treatment if carried by an important (read: non-expendable) team member.
Check.
Back at the crevasse, our survivors are slowly dying from lack of water, and their lungs are beginning to fill with fluid.

Check.

Back in the theatre, the audience is slowly going into a coma from lack of a believable script.

Check.

It's remarkably easy to tell the sick people from the healthy ones in this movie: the sick ones cough. A lot. The healthy ones merely wheeze. And there is lots of wheezing going on, because we are above 21,000 feet and no one is using oxygen.

Why?

Because oxygen masks would hide their faces, and why would you, as a producer, agree to spend a crevasse full of money on recognizable Hollywood actors like Chris O'Donnell if you couldn't show their faces and the audience couldn't tell them apart? You could get an unknown for a tenth of the price!

The consequence of having the characters go without oxygen masks is that everybody gets to talk in short, gasping bursts.

The trapped climbers carry cell phones, but they are generally unable to communicate with the rescue team because of heavy static. This sets the scene for another implausible twist: the transmission will occasionally become crystal clear, but only when one of the trapped characters has a deep, private confession to make to one of the rescue team members.

The ending is mind-numbing.

Imagine this: *Cut*: from exhausted rescuers dangling above the crevasse *to*: base camp. All of a sudden, everyone is safe. This remains one of the most profound mysteries in the history of Hollywood movies. How have the rescuers managed to haul Annie out of the crevasse and then carry her down 5,000 feet? And in a storm? It is so mysterious, in fact, that even screenwriter Robert King couldn't figure it out; he just left it out completely. I was reminded of a phrase that I often heard in my Catholic household when I was a child: "Don't worry about that, son; it's a mystery."

50

The X-Files

From the moment it was first announced that a film version of *The X-Files* was in production rumours flew, and fans speculated in hushed tones — sometimes during semi-clandestine midnight meetings in parking garages — about the possible storyline of the film. What was this going to be about? The plot of *The X-Files* was one of the most closely guarded secrets in Hollywood history. Demonstrating great marketing savvy, *X-Files* creator Chris Carter managed to guard the secret while at the same time stoking the already enormous advance buzz by actually circulating false information and phony plot twists on the Internet.

Information age? Welcome to the *dis*information age.

The press screening I attended was held at ten o'clock on a Monday morning and had many of the security trappings of a G-8 summit. Members of the press were searched — although I'm relieved to report not strip-searched — to ensure that none of them had planned to commit some such insidious act as trying to record scenes from the movie on a cell phone (which I don't own, by the way).

I was amused by all of this hoopla, but largely unimpressed. Actually, I have never watched even a single episode of this program. Twenty-four hours before I attended the screening, I couldn't tell a Scully from a scullery.

That being said, you don't really have to know anything about the TV show to enjoy the film version, but you will undoubtedly get more out of it if you've been paying attention to the small screen.

The X-Files (the movie) was budgeted at $70 million, and directed by Rob Bowman, who directed about twenty-five episodes of the television series. Anyone who has spent that much time directing television programs certainly knows a thing or two about sinister conspiracies. And at the heart of this story lies (of course) a very dark conspiracy indeed.

Aliens are insidiously trying to re-colonize the earth by unleashing some weird kind of plague. They are being aided in this nefarious scheme by some shadowy figures who belong to a sinister organization headed up by Conrad Strughold (Armin Mueller-Stahl doing a first-rate ex-Nazi impersonation). The plague being unleashed on the (mostly) unsuspecting human population is pretty repulsive; it's a kind of oozing oil that creeps up your legs and makes its way very quickly into your brain. The victims go gaga and their eyes become clouded over with black sludge, not unlike the look many people get when they watch Question Period on the parliamentary channel.

So, when the black sludge seeps into your brain, who you gonna call?

Agents Mulder and Scully are Earth's only defence against this Alien gook.

The bad guys in the series don't actually have names, so the fans have given them cute little nicknames like "Marlborough Man" — or is that "cigarette-smoking man"? or "cancer man"? Anyway, this dude is bad news, obviously a very nasty *Grand Fromage*, and also the only one who smokes cigarettes in the movie. This is an interesting (if obvious) use of nineties sensibilities to convey character, because even a neophyte can figure out that anyone smoking a cigarette is a bad guy.

There's also a bad guy called "Oxford-educated British accent man," or "well-manicured man," or something. This is another foul personage you wouldn't invite to your Little League fundraiser. Other characters are more ambiguous. For example, Assistant Director Skinner, Mulder and Scully's boss, seems to be on their side, but who knows if he isn't a clone just waiting to lead them into a trap?

This Alien plague doesn't just kill you, it is actually genetically engineered to transform its human victim into a host, allowing an evil and snarly Alien entity to gestate. What do you think of them crabapples? Remember poor Kane in *Alien*? Holy stomach popper, Batman!

To make things more interesting, some of the bad guys, who are now terrified of the Aliens because they have finally realized the true implications of what's going on, have started to develop a vaccine against the plague. Do they have one yet? ... Don't ask me, I'm not telling ...

At this point, some of you may be growing impatient with all of this Alien plague nonsense; you're wondering if I'm ever going to discuss the really *important* plot question of this movie: do Scully and Mulder become romantically involved?

Never mind "romantically involved"! This is a conspiracy, remember? As Oliver Stone would say, "Everyone's involved." But I'm a critic, not a blabbermouth. Do you think I'm going to reveal that Mulder actually tries to kiss Scully, only to have this potentially tender moment ruined by a genetically transformed killer bee (!), which has been hiding in Scully's jacket (!!) waiting until this much-anticipated cinematic moment before stinging her, thereby possibly plunging her into an experience *worse than near death*? You didn't hear that from me. And if you ever tell anyone I said that, I'll deny it and I'll tell everyone that you have a big purple Barney suit hidden in your closet.

Remember David Caruso from *NYPD Blue*? He tried to parlay a successful television career into a successful movie career and didn't do very well. Small screen charisma doesn't necessarily translate into big screen charisma. In this case, however, the transition is successful. David Duchovny and Gillian Anderson are very good. They have a great tongue-in-cheek relationship (this may or may not be a sly reference to that kiss that may or may not actually take place). The chemistry between them is good. The supporting cast is fine, and includes one of my favorite actors, Martin Landau, portraying a character I will call "Jack-in-the-box man." You have seen this character in several films. Think of Donald Sutherland's character in *JFK*: a shadowy character pops up out of nowhere to clue our heroes in on what's actually going on and to suggest possible areas of inquiry.

In a movie like this, it is crucial to keep things moving along at a brisk clip. If you give the audience too much time to think, the suspension of disbelief that is *de rigueur* if any of this is to be truly enjoyed may collapse entirely. As it stands, this stuff is right out of Tabloidland, but it still manages to be convincing. And besides, who can say with any certainty that this stuff is just nonsense? Who among us can claim to really know what goes on behind the well-guarded doors of those secretive, obscure government agencies?

Appendix

	DIRECTION	WRITING	CINEMATOGRAPHY
The Adventures of Rocky and Bullwinkle *USA/Germany, 2000; 88 min.*	Des McAnuff	Jay Ward (television series), Kenneth Lonergan (screenplay)	Thomas E. Ackerman
Armageddon *USA, 1998; 150 min.*	Michael Bay	Robert Roy Pool (story), Jonathan Hensleigh, J.J. Abrams (screenplay)	John Schwartzman
The Beach *USA/UK, 2000; 119 min.*	Danny Boyle	Alex Garland (novel), John Hodge (screenplay)	Darius Khondji
The Big Lebowski *USA, 1998; 117 min.*	Joel Coen	Joel Coen, Ethan Coen	Roger Deakins
The Bone Collector *USA, 1999; 118 min.*	Phillip Noyce	Jeffery Deaver (novel), Jeremy Iacone (screenplay)	Dean Semler
Boogie Nights *USA, 1997; 156 min.*	Paul Thomas Anderson	Paul Thomas Anderson	Robert Elswit
Capote *USA, 2005; 98 min.*	Bennett Miller	Gerald Clarke (biography), Dan Futterman (screenplay)	Adam Kimmel
Casino *USA, 1995; 178 min.*	Martin Scorsese	Nicholas Pileggi (novel), Nicholas Pileggi, Martin Scorsese (screenplay)	Robert Richardson
Cellular *USA, 2004; 94 min.*	David R. Ellis	Larry Cohen (story), Chris Morgan (screenplay)	Gary Capo
Chicken Run *UK, 2000; 84 min.*	Nick Park, Peter Lord	Nick Park, Peter Lord, Randy Cartwright (story), Karey Kirkpatrick (screenplay)	Tristan Oliver, Frank Passingham

RODUCTION DESIGN	FILM EDITING	ORIGINAL MUSIC	CAST
avin Bocquet	Dennis Virkler	Larry Dominello, Mark Mothersbaugh, Carlos Rodriguez	Jason Alexander, Rene Russo, Randy Quaid, Robert De Niro, the voice of June Foray
lichael White	Mark Goldblatt, Chris Lebenzon, Glen Scantlebury	Jack Blades, Harry Gregson-Williams, Trevor Rabin	Bruce Willis, Billy Bob Thornton, Ben Affleck, Liv Tyler, Steve Buscemi
ndrew McAlpine	Masahiro Hirakubo	Angelo Badalamenti	Leonardo DiCaprio, Tilda Swinton, Virginie Ledoyen, Robert Carlyle
ick Heinrichs	Roderick Jaynes, Tricia Cooke	Carter Burwell	Jeff Bridges, John Goodman, Julianne Moore, Steve Buscemi, John Turturro, Tara Reid
igel Phelps	William Hoy	Craig Armstrong	Denzel Washington, Angelina Jolie, Queen Latifah, Michael Rooker
ob Ziembicki	Dylan Tichenor	Michael Penn	Burt Reynolds, Mark Wahlberg, Julianne Moore, Don Cheadle, John C. Reilly, William H. Macy, Heather Graham, Nina Hartley
ss Gonchor	Christopher Tellefsen	Mychael Danna	Philip Seymour Hoffman, Catherine Keener, Chris Cooper, Clifton Collins Jr.
ante Ferretti	Thelma Schoonmaker	N/A	Robert De Niro, Sharon Stone, Joe Pesci, James Woods, Frank Vincent
aymes Hinkle	Eric A. Sears	Garrett Dutton, John Ottman	Kim Basinger, Noah Emmerich, Chris Evans, William H. Macy
hil Lewis	Robert Francis, Tamsin Parry, Mark Solomon	Harry Gregson-Williams	The voices of Mel Gibson, Miranda Richardson, Julia Sawalha, Jane Horrocks, Imelda Staunton

	DIRECTION	WRITING	CINEMATOGRAPHY
Childstar *Canada, 2004; 98 min.*	Don McKellar	Michael Goldbach, Don McKellar	André Turpin
City of God *Brazil/France/USA,* *2002; 130 min.*	Fernando Meirelles, Katia Lund	Paulo Lins (novel), Braulio Mantovani (screenplay)	César Charlone
Confessions of **a Dangerous Mind** *USA/Canada/Germany,* *2002; 113 min.*	George Clooney	Chuck Barris (autobiography), Charlie Kaufman (screenplay)	Newton Thomas Sigel
The Day After **Tomorrow** *USA, 2004; 124 min.*	Roland Emmerich	Roland Emmerich, Jeffrey Nachmanoff	Ueli Steiger
Dogtown and Z-Boys *USA, 2001; 91 min.*	Stacy Peralta	Stacy Peralta, Craig Stecyk	Peter Pilafian
Downfall *Germany/Italy/Austria,* *2004; 156 min.*	Oliver Hirschbiegel	Joachim Fest, Traudl Junge, Melissa Muller (sources),	Rainer Klausmann
Eyes Wide Shut *USA/UK, 1999; 159 min.*	Stanley Kubrick	Arthur Schnitzler (novel), Stanley Kubrick, Frederic Raphael (screenplay)	Larry Smith, Stanley Kubrick
Fahrenheit 9/11 *USA, 2004; 122 min.*	Michael Moore	Michael Moore	Andrew Black, Mike Desjarlais
Far from Heaven *France/USA, 2002;* *107 min.*	Todd Haynes	Todd Haynes	Edward Lachman
The Fog *Canada/USA, 2005;* *100 min.*	Rupert Wainwright	John Carpenter, Debra Hill (1980 screenplay), Cooper Layne (adaptation)	Nathan Hope, Ian Seabrook (underwater)

RODUCTION DESIGN	FILM EDITING	ORIGINAL MUSIC	CAST
ohn Dondertman	Reginald Harkema	Christopher Dedrick	Don McKellar, Mark Rendall, Jennifer Jason Leigh, Alan Thicke
Tulé Peak	Daniel Rezende	Ed Cortês, Antonio Pinto	Alexandre Rodrigues, Leandro Firmino, Phellipe Haagensen
ames D. Bissell	Stephen Mirrione	Alex Wurman, Peter Thomas	Sam Rockwell, Michelle Sweeney, Drew Barrymore, George Clooney
Barry Chusid	David Brenner	Harald Kloser, Thomas Wanker	Dennis Quaid, Jake Gyllenhaal, Ian Holm, Kenneth Welsh
Craig Stecyk	Paul Crowder	Paul Crowder, Terry Wilson	Sean Penn (narrator), Jay Adams, Tony Alva, Steve Caballero, Tony Hawk
Bernd Lepel	Hans Funck	Stephan Zacharias	Bruno Ganz, Alexandra Maria Lara, Corinna Harfouch, Heino Ferch
Leslie Tomkins, Roy Walker	Nigel Galt	Jocelyn Pook	Tom Cruise, Nicole Kidman, Sydney Pollack, Leelee Sobieski
Dina Varano	Kurt Engfehr, T. Woody Richman, Chris Seward	Jeff Gibbs, Bob Golden	Michael Moore, George W. Bush, Donald Rumsfeld, Paul Wolfowitz, Osama bin Laden
Mark Friedberg	James Lyons	Elmer Bernstein, Max Lichtenstein	Dennis Quaid, Julianne Moore, Dennis Haysbert, Patricia Clarkson
Michael Diner, Graeme Murray	Dennis Virkler	Graeme Revell	Tom Welling, Maggie Grace, Selma Blair, Kenneth Welsh, Adrian Hough

	DIRECTION	WRITING	CINEMATOGRAPHY
The Game *USA, 1997; 128 min.*	David Fincher	John D. Brancato, Michael Ferris	Harris Savides
Godzilla *USA, 1998; 140 min.*	Roland Emmerich	Ted Elliott, Terry Rossio, Dean Devlin, Roland Emmerich	Ueli Steiger
Grace of My Heart *USA, 1996; 116 min.*	Allison Anders	Allison Anders	Jean-Yves Escoffier
The Hitchhiker's Guide to the Galaxy *USA/UK, 2005; 109 min.*	Garth Jennings	Douglas Adams (novel), Douglas Adams, Karey Kirkpatrick (screenplay)	Igor Jadue-Lillo
House of Wax *Australia/USA, 2005; 113 min.*	Jaume Collet-Serra	Charles Belden (source), Chad Hayes, Carrey Hayes (screenplay)	Stephen F. Windon
I Am Sam *USA, 2001; 132 min.*	Jessie Nelson	Jessie Nelson, Christine Johnson	Elliot Davis
Jurassic Park III *USA, 2001; 92 min.*	Joe Johnston	Michael Crichton (novel), Peter Buchman, Alexander Payne, Jim Taylor (screenplay)	Shelly Johnson
Kinsey *USA/Germany, 2004; 118 min.*	Bill Condon	Bill Condon	Frederick Elmes
The Lord of the Rings: The Return of the King *USA/New Zealand/ Germany, 2003; 201 min.*	Peter Jackson	J.R.R. Tolkien (source), Peter Jackson, Fran Walsh, Philippa Boyens (screenplay)	Andrew Lesnie

RODUCTION DESIGN	FILM EDITING	ORIGINAL MUSIC	CAST
effrey Beecroft	James Haygood	Howard Shore	Michael Douglas, Sean Penn, Deborah Kara Unger, Armin Mueller-Stahl
Oliver Scholl	Peter Amundson, David Siegel	Billie Joe Armstrong, David Arnold	Matthew Broderick, Jean Reno, Maria Pitillo, Hank Azaria
François Séguin	James Kwei, Harvey Rosenstock, Thelma Schoonmaker	Larry Klein, Burt Bacharach, Elvis Costello, Joni Mitchell	Illeana Douglas, John Turturro, Matt Dillon, Eric Stoltz, Bridget Fonda
oel Collins	Jerry Chater (titles), Niven Howie	Bernie Leadon, Joby Talbot	Martin Freeman, Zooey Deschanel, Stephen Fry, Mos Def, Warwick Davis (Marvin the robot)
Graham "Grace" Walker	Joel Negron	John Ottman	Elisha Cuthbert, Paris Hilton, Chad Michael Murray, Brian Van Holt
Aaron Osborne	Richard Chew	John Powell	Sean Penn, Dakota Fanning, Michelle Pfeiffer, Dianne Wiest, Laura Dern
Ed Verreaux	Robert Dalva	John Williams, Don Davis	Sam Neill, William H. Macy, Téa Leoni, Laura Dern
Richard Sherman	Virginia Katz	Carter Burwell	Liam Neeson, Laura Linney, Chris O'Donnell, Peter Sarsgaard, Timothy Hutton
Grant Major	Jamie Selkirk	Howard Shore, Annie Lennox	Elijah Wood, Sean Astin, Viggo Mortensen, Ian McKellen, Orlando Bloom, Cate Blanchett, Liv Tyler, Ian Holm, Andy Serkis (voice of Gollum)

	DIRECTION	WRITING	CINEMATOGRAPHY
Lost in Space USA/UK, 1998; 130 min.	Stephen Hopkins	Irwin Allen (TV series), Akiva Goldsman (screenplay)	Peter Levy
Lost in Translation USA/Japan, 2003; 102 min.	Sofia Coppola	Sofia Coppola	Lance Acord
Mission to Mars USA, 2000; 113 min.	Brian De Palma	Jim Thomas, John Thomas, Graham Yost	Stephen H. Burum
Mulholland Drive France/USA, 2001; 145 min.	David Lynch	David Lynch	Peter Deming
Open Range USA, 2003; 139 min.	Kevin Costner	Lauran Paine (novel), Craig Storper (screenplay)	James Muro
Open Water USA, 2003; 79 min.	Chris Kentis	Chris Kentis	Chris Kentis, Laura Lau
Pollock USA, 2000; 122 min.	Ed Harris	Steven Naifeh, Gregory White Smith (biography), Barbara Turner, Susan Emshwiller (screenplay)	Lisa Rinzler
Psycho USA, 1998; 105 min.	Gus Van Sant	Robert Bloch (novel), Joseph Stefano (from Psycho [1960])	Christopher Doyle
The Rock USA, 1996; 136 min.	Michael Bay	David Weisberg, Douglas Cook, Mark Rosner	John Schwartzman
Seducing Dr. Lewis Canada, 2003; 108 min.	Jean-François Pouliot	Ken Scott	Allen Smith
Shaun of the Dead UK/France, 2004; 99 min.	Edgar Wright	Simon Pegg, Edgar Wright	David M. Dunlap

PRODUCTION DESIGN	FILM EDITING	ORIGINAL MUSIC	CAST
Norman Garwood	Ray Lovejoy	Bruce Broughton	William Hurt, Heather Graham, Gary Oldman, Matt LeBlanc, Jack Johnson
K.K. Barrett, Anne Ross	Sarah Flack	Jean-Benoit Dunckle	Bill Murray, Akiko Takeshita, Scarlett Johansson
Ed Verreaux	Paul Hirsch	Ennio Morricone	Tim Robbins, Armin Mueller-Stahl, Don Cheadle, Gary Sinise
Jack Fisk	Mary Sweeney	Angelo Badalamenti	Naomi Watts, Laura Harring, Justin Theroux, Lee Grant, Billy Ray Cyrus
Gae S. Buckley	Michael J. Duthie, Miklos Wright	Michael Kamen, Julianna Raye	Kevin Costner, Robert Duvall, Annette Bening, Michael Gambon, James Russo
N/A	Chris Kentis	Graeme Revell, Nathan Barr	Blanchard Ryan, Daniel Travis
Mark Friedberg	Kathryn Himoff	Jeff Beal	Ed Harris, Marcia Gay Harden, Jennifer Connelly, John Heard, Val Kilmer
Tom Foden	Amy E. Duddleston	Bernard Herrman (from *Psycho* [1960]), Rob Zombie	Vince Vaughn, Anne Heche, Julianne Moore, Viggo Mortensen, William H.Macy
Michael White	Richard Francis-Bruce	James Newton Howard	Ed Harris, Sean Connery, Nicolas Cage, John Spencer, David Morse
Daniel Hamelin, Normand Sarazin	Dominique Fortin	Jean-Marie Benoît	David Boutin, Lucie Laurier, Pierre Collin, Donald Pilon, Raymond Bouchard
Marcus Rowland	Chris Dickens	Dan Mudford, Pete Woodhead	Simon Pegg, Kate Ashfield, Nick Frost, Lucy Davis, Bill Nighy

	DIRECTION	WRITING	CINEMATOGRAPHY
The Snow Walker *Canada, 2003; 103 min.*	Charles Martin Smith	Farley Mowat (short story), Charles Martin Smith (screenplay)	David Connell, Jon Joffin, Paul Sarossy
Star Trek: Insurrection *USA, 1998; 103 min.*	Jonathan Frakes	Gene Roddenberry (TV series), Rick Berman, Michael Piller (screenplay)	Matthew F. Leonetti
Star Wars: Episode III – Revenge of the Sith *USA, 2005; 140 min.*	George Lucas	George Lucas	David Tattersall
The Sum of All Fears *USA/Germany, 2002; 124 min.*	Phil Alden Robinson	Tom Clancy (novel), Paul Attanasio, Daniel Pyne (screenplay)	John Lindley
Sweet and Lowdown *USA, 1999; 95 min.*	Woody Allen	Woody Allen	Fei Zhao
Swimming Pool *France/UK, 2003; 102 min.*	François Ozon	Emmanuèle Bernheim, François Ozon (screenplay), Sionann O'Neil (sub-titles)	Yorick Le Saux
3,000 Miles to Graceland *USA, 2001; 125 min.*	Demian Lichtenstein	Richard Recco, Demian Lichenstein	David Franco
Vampires *USA, 1998; 108 min.*	John Carpenter	John Steakley (novel), Don Jakoby (screenplay)	Gary B. Kibbe
Vertical Limit *USA/Germany, 2000; 124 min.*	Martin Campbell	Robert King, Terry Hayes	David Tattersall
The X-Files *Canada/USA, 1998; 121 min.*	Rob Bowman	Chris Carter, Frank Spotnitz	Ward Russell

RODUCTION DESIGN	FILM EDITING	ORIGINAL MUSIC	CAST
Doug Byggdin	Alison Grace	Mychael Danna, Paul Intson	Barry Pepper, Annabella Piugattuk, James Cromwell
Herman Zimmerman	Peter E. Berger	Jerry Goldsmith	Jonathan Frakes, Patrick Stewart, Brent Spiner, F. Murray Abraham
Gavin Bocquet	Roger Barton, Ben Burtt	John Williams	Ewan McGregor, Natalie Portman, Hayden Christensen, Samuel L. Jackson
Jeannine Claudia Oppewall	Nicolas De Toth, Neil Travis	Jerry Goldsmith	Ben Affleck, Morgan Freeman, James Cromwell, Liev Schreiber
Santo Loquasto	Alisa Lepselter	Dick Hyman	Sean Penn, Samantha Morton, Uma Thurman, Woody Allen, Daniel Okrent
Wouter Zoon	Monica Coleman	Philippe Rombi	Charlotte Rampling, Ludivine Sagnier, Charles Dance, Jean-Marie Lamour
Robert de Vico	Michael J. Duthie, Miklos Wright	George S. Clinton	Kurt Russell, Kevin Costner, Courteney Cox, David Arquette
Thomas A. Walsh	Edward A. Warschilka	John Carpenter	James Woods, Daniel Baldwin, Sheryl Lee, Maximilian Schell
Jon Bunker	Thom Noble	James Newton Howard	Chris O'Donnell, Robin Tunney, Scott Glenn, Bill Paxton
Christopher Nowak	Stephen Mark	Mark Snow, Noel Gallagher	David Duchovny, Gillian Anderson, Martin Landau, Blythe Danner

RELATED TITLES

ALWAYS AN UPDRAFT
A WRITER REMEMBERS
Munroe Scott

Munroe Scott, one of Canada's most dedicated freelance writers, began as a staff writer with Crawley Films in the early 1950s. He is best known as the writer and director of CBC-TV series *The Tenth Decade*, *First Person Singular* (The Pearson Memoirs), and *One Canadian* (The Diefenbaker Memoirs).

1894131711 | HC | $ 34.95 | 6"x9" | 368 PAGES | PHOTOS

ON THE ROAD AGAIN ... AGAIN
Andrew Clyde Little, foreword by Wayne Rostad

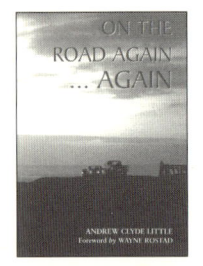

Seldom without his camera, Andrew Little loved to capture "ordinary Canadians doing extraordinary things." *On the Road Again ... Again* features Andrew Little's portraits of the remarkable Canadians he met while field producer for the TV show during its formative years.

1894131177 | PB | $ 24.95 | 6"x9" | 208 PAGES | PHOTOS

WALK-ONS & BIT-PARTS
Sara Lee Stadelman

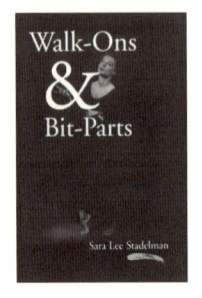

Actor and director Sara Lee Stadelman recollects a life on stage. From premiering on Broadway with Gregory Peck to founding The Bird Cage theatre, her memoir transcends the who-what-where. She explores the intimate moments along the way, recounts intense friendships (Frank Lloyd Wright, Thornton Wilder), and offers frank reminiscences of the human drama.

1894131096 | PB | $ 24.95 | 6"x9" | 208 PAGES | PHOTOS

WWW.PENUMBRAPRESS.CA

A THEATRE NEAR YOU
150 YEARS OF GOING TO THE SHOW IN OTTAWA-GATINEAU
Alain Miguelez

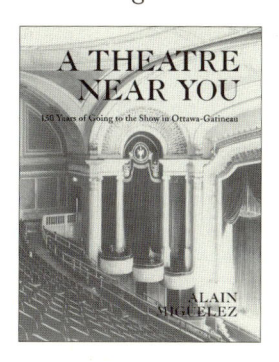

Ottawa cinephile and urban planner Alain Miguelez tells the story of each motion-picture theatre ever built, renovated, or demolished in the National Capital Region — from peep shows and nickelodeons to movie palaces and megaplexes. With passion and skill, Miguelez offers a profound, accessible look at this city's cultural and architectural heritage.

189413138X | HC | $45.00 | 8"x 10" | 376 PAGES | 315 VINTAGE B&W PHOTOS

MONTREAL MOVIE PALACES
GREAT THEATRES OF THE GOLDEN ERA 1884-1938
Dane Lanken

Dane Lanken spent twenty years studying Montreal's movie palaces, interviewing the people who were there, searching for rare and previously unpublished archival photographs, and commissioning new views — while the theatres still stood — from leading architectural photographers. The result is a comprehensive and richly illustrated social, artistic, architectural, and corporate history of an exuberant and little-known era in Montreal's history.

0921254482 | HC | $39.95 | 12"x 9" | 194 PAGES
180 PHOTOS BY BRIAN MERRETT AND JULIE GRETO

Movies Ate My Brain is set in Stempel Garamond and printed on Rolland Opaque Vellum, Natural. Cover stock is Cornwall Coated.

PENUMBRA PRESS
P.O. BOX 940, MANOTICK, ON K4M 1A8
TEL (613) 692-5590 • FAX (613) 692-5589
www.penumbrapress.ca